The Psychology of
Conflict and
Combat

The Psychology of Conflict and Combat

Ben Shalit

PRAEGER

New York
Westport, Connecticut
London

Library of Congress Cataloging-in-Publication Data

Shalit, Ben.
    The psychology of conflict and combat / Ben Shalit.
      p.   cm.
    Bibliography: p.
    Includes index.
    ISBN 0-275-92753-9 (alk. paper)
    1. Combat—Psychological aspects.   2. Conflict (Psychology)
  I. Title.
    U22.3.S43   1988
    355'.001'9—dc19
    87-23729

Library of Congress Catalog Card Number: 87-23729

ISBN: 0-275-92753-9

First published in 1988

Praeger Publishers, One Madison Avenue, New York, NY 10010
A division of Greenwood Press, Inc.

Printed in the United States of America

The paper used in this book complies with the Permanent Paper Standard
issued by the National Information Standards Organization (Z39.48-1984).

10 9 8 7 6 5 4 3 2 1

This book is dedicated to the memory of General Haim Laskov who inspired and supported me both in my work in Israel and in the years that followed.

Contents

Tables and Figures

The Psychology of
Conflict and
Combat

1

Introduction

BACKGROUND

The glow of the lights of Haifa and Mount Carmel were just fading over the horizon. The night was as dark as a moonless cloudy night at sea can be, and the muffled sounds of the MTB (Motor Torpedo Boat) engines were hardly sufficient to break the monotony of the swooshing sounds of waves. The figures on the dark deck were lost—their outlines diffusing in the grayness—and only the larger dark shadow of the rubber boat gave some outline that the eye could fasten to and trace with some comforting assurance.

I was a psychologist—just released on the world from the university and standing now in the lee of the bridge, feeling rather confused and exhilarated. I was doing my national service as a psychologist in the Israeli Navy, and had convinced the various levels of command (thus, incidentally, myself also) that one cannot possibly serve as a psychologist in the military without sharing the world of experience of those one is supposed to work with. So here I was, on board one of three MTBs going north on an active mission. We were supposed to land commando troops and their boats, wait while they carried out their tasks, and then collect them and return to base.

If all went well, this would be a simple (if tense) operation, involving—on my part—hours of waiting in a boat that was tossed about just a few meters west of the enemy shore. If all did not go well . . .

It was curious—and quite a bit unsettling—to realize how much I really wanted things to happen—in fact, to go wrong. Not because I wanted to see any of my friends in danger, not because I had any feelings or desire to hurt the enemy, but simply so as to experience the tension of action—the thrill of the challenge and danger. This bears no relation to not being afraid, for I was scared stiff and could well visualize the possible disastrous outcomes; but, regardless of all that—I wanted action.

The tension was mounting. We were waiting for a signal from the commando group ashore to draw nearer and evacuate them. I was now next to the captain on bridge. The continuous hiss of the open channel wireless was at the center of our attention, for just three short interruptions of that hiss—with no word said—would be our signal to creep inshore to the rendezvous point. Time was getting short, the captain was restless, and the operation's commander could not even pretend to be the calm figure that he had always admired in war films (especially with a psychologist standing there watching).

Suddenly, it all blew up. Shooting on shore . . . violent outbursts . . . lights streaking in all directions . . . and signal lights. . . . Our boat lurched forward; we raced into the enemy harbor and immediately became the focal point for a barrage that, whatever its objective danger, looked as if it would finish us off in no time. I was paralyzed: My eyes were fixed on the tracers seemingly heading specially and only at me; I was unable to think, and unable to do—but what was there for me to do?

The pressure on me was mounting to what I felt must be the breaking point; the boat swung in, firing from all its weapons; the noise and light were hammering at me so that it seemed I must collapse, for there was nothing I could do—when a sudden transition occurred.

Looking back—in retrospect—I can describe and understand what happened. At the time, it felt as if a weight had suddenly lifted, and as if I were suddenly released from bonds. I could breath again; I could control my fate again. In fact, I had not moved, although my muscles must have relaxed. Nothing had changed: The firing and screaming of bullets and commands went on, but now I was observing.

At last, I had something to do—in fact, I was doing what I had set out to do in the first place—to study how others react. Now the pressure was off me; now the situation—as far as I was concerned—was clear, and so was my response to it.

On my right was mounted a heavy machine gun. The gunner (normally the cook) was firing away with what I can only describe as a beatific smile on his face. He was exhilarated by the squeezing of the trigger, the hammering of the gun, and the flight of his tracers rushing out into the dark shore. It struck me then (and was confirmed by him and many others later) that squeezing the trigger—releasing a hail of bullets—gives enormous pleasure and satisfaction. These are the pleasures of combat, not in terms of the intellectual planning—of the tactical and strategic chess game—but of the primal aggression, the release, and the orgasmic discharge.

Being shot at is no pleasure, but being able to shoot seems to give most people a feeling of great satisfaction and release. This is partly a response to the release of tension; but, to a great extent, it also seems to be satisfying in its own right, having nothing to do with the consequences of the act. It is not the pleasure of killing the enemy; indeed, in Israel, hate toward the enemy rarely plays a role in motivation for combat. Wars are often irrational; the arguments for having a war are often irrelevant or meaningless for the ordinary soldier ("not for us to reason why, but for us to shoot and die"). Nevertheless, hundreds of thousands of people have gone to war and died—being motivated by what?

On the very personal level, I had to ask myself why I had chosen to expose myself to unnecessary dangers: What made me, like so many others, find thrill in combat—whether as a direct participator or a vicarious observer? What makes us seek combat, when rationally it is often unnecessary; and how do we manage to function in conditions under which, logically, we should not function? Not only do we manage to function well under such conditions, but often even enjoy it.

It was a traumatic introduction into the psychology of combat—one that raised many questions on motivation, the ability to cope, the meaning of courage, and the function of leadership. It took many years of direct and indirect participation in such experiences to be able to clarify the questions involved—and then some more, to outline a few possible answers. But never again did I experience such a shock of realization that combat—for combat's sake—can be a strong motivation and source of pleasure and that a man must know his function or role in any situation in order to be able to cope with it.

This is a book about combat. Whether we like it or not—and without needing a better laboratory proof than human history—combat is an integral part of human behavior. There is a need to study it, understand it, and comprehend its dynamics and manifestation; but one must first accept it as an integral part of human behavior. Such behavior might well be modified, contained, assimilated, and directed; nevertheless, it will remain a basic human characteristic. To study it in a completely detached academic (or even clinical) way—without allowing for the nonquantifiable and unformulaic aspects—is to dehumanize it. This would not only make such studies inaccurate; it might well make their outcome misleading and dangerous.

Several investigations have shown that the further a person is from the consequences of his decisions or acts, the more extreme and often callous those acts become. It seems to me that much the same rule applies to one's analysis and evaluation of the behavior of others. The more detached, clinical, and withdrawn one is about such evaluations, the more one might be willing to reach conclusions and advocate methods that—although they appear neat and efficient—involve coercion and loss of respect for the human spirit.

I do not pretend to know (or even guess) what the "human spirit" is; and in the context of this book, it is not a relevant question. It may well be viewed here as a black box in which some process of interaction and integration between personal and environmental inputs occurs, according to rules that we cannot (or cannot yet) describe. But one must not discount this element—for, by discounting it, one falsifies the nature of human behavior. Since we cannot define it and we must not discount it, the best we can do is to fill in with our own feelings and perceptions as human beings. No doubt, this introduces a strong noise factor into any analysis, and renders any description and model less than perfect and objective—and yet it gives such a system or analysis a greater veracity than one from which this subjective element has been exorcised.

Thus, when writing this book, I did not attempt to remove the personal element from it. In fact, I believe that if I have succeeded in attaining any clarity and offering any coherent explanation for some aspects of combat, it is precisely because of my involvement in combat situations.

However, one must constantly retain awareness of this involvement. It is essential to be aware of the explicit subjective contribution to the interpretations and discussions; and so, whenever possible, I have attempted to point these out.

Some of what is reported must be seen in the context of the current Israeli-Arab conflict. This book is in no way an attempt to take sides on the issue, or to analyze the impact of geopolitical factors on the psychological behavior. But, being an officer in one of the armies in that conflict—with all the implications of being on a particular side in certain campaigns—must have shaped my perception of events. No doubt, things would have been seen and felt differently had I been an officer in the other army. I can only hope that the essential elements of human behavior and attitude toward combat would have been described similarly by me, even were I starting from the other point of view. It is my hope that the model derived in one emotional setting (and later tested a little in another setting) relates to essential features of behavior—so that it will prove valid even when applied in other—greatly dissimilar—contexts.

But not only is this book based on my experiences as an Israeli, it is also heavily affected by my life in Sweden. Coming from the highly active, aggressive and turbulent environment of Israel to live in Sweden proved to be going from one extreme to the other. Sweden has not had war for about 190 years; it is a basically homogeneous country with a strong sense of social responsibility, order, and stability. The contrast between the two countries—both good and bad (subjectively perceived, of course)—helped to highlight many points in the different aspects of human conflict behavior. Because of this, I shall often contrast findings and impressions of the two countries, when they serve to illustrate points.

THE SCOPE AND STRUCTURE OF THE BOOK

This book is about the psychological factors that enable and lead men to engage in combat. In the United States, *Standard Dictionary* defines "combat" as "to fight, to resist, to do battle"; while the British *Chambers Dictionary* defines it as "to contest, to oppose, to debate." Both definitions indicate the essence of combat to be conflict and striving against—whether in a purely physical context or in a more intellectual setting.

There is another way one may differentiate combat: differentiation in accordance with the nature of the interaction between the combatants or combatting forces. In fact, combat does not have to take place between men alone, it is often described as occurring between man and his environment—fighting the forces of nature or even blind fate. In combat against the stormy seas, one is required to pit skill, courage, knowledge, and judgment against elements that are essentially unpredictable and do not obey rules of behavior set by men. Most important of all—in all combat against nature, we can respond, avoid, or adapt, but can never affect and shape our protagonist's behavior. Combat between men is a match between two sides that are (theoretically, at least) equally capable of understanding, predicting, and affecting each other's behavior.

Combat against nature—much like gambling—involves a risk situation in which we cannot change the odds; we can only decide how big a risk we are willing to take. In combat against men, we aspire to reach complete control of the other's behavior, to act with absolute certainty or—at least—to actively reduce the odds against us. It is when the gambler feels that he can be absolutely certain—or the soldier feels that he can gamble—that the most diastrous results often occur.

This book will focus on combat between men—the deliberate aggressive behavior of man to man. Some such behavior may involve naked violence, hostility, and fear—even if theoretically governed by so-called civilized rules of war. Other behavior involves ritualized disputes and patterns of negotiations, without evoking any physical threat. Yet they all have in common the deliberate behavior aimed at "getting the better of" (a much more dramatic version of S. Potter's "one-upmanship") the opponent—whether by actual annihilation or by dictating and coercing the other's behavior. The opponent has a precisely similar aim; and the ideal outcome for either side—total success—would, necessarily, be at the expense of the other.

The most dramatic examples of combat behavior are found in the military setting; but, even if we think of combat in physical terms only, it is not restricted to the military. Men seek legitimate combat with men in the police and prison service, and under many other less organized and certainly less respectable establishments. Daily industrial strife and even family life are often a setting for combat. These versions may at times be less dramatic, but they inevitably obey the same psychological rules as those that govern the more explicit, physically oriented combat of war.

An attempt will be made to explore and explain the factors that build up in a person or a group to make them willing and able to engage in combat. Further, an attempt will be made to explain how such factors can be influenced so as to make people more capable of combat. It seems to be an inescapable fact that combat of some kind is an essential part of the psychological and social structure of mankind. Even Isaiah—in his famous vision of the peaceful days to come (Isa. 11:6) in which the lion will cease combat with the lamb—prophesies that men will go on warring as usual (Isa. 11:14): "and the Philistines you will cast into the sea." However, one does not necessarily have to follow the bloodthirsty biblical prescriptions. Combat may be essential, but this does not mean that it requires the horrors of war—of megatons and megadeath. Understanding the mechanisms of combat might well allow us to fulfill the psychological needs and to allow the benefits derived from human challenge, conflict, fear, courage, and victory, without the excess that is often associated with it today.

Before one is ready to engage in conflict, one must have answered (at least unconsciously) three basic questions:

1. "What is it all about?" That is, is the perceived situation sufficiently clear that it can be understood and thus acted on?
2. "Does this concern me?" That is, even if I understand, do I consider this relevant for me at this point in time?
3. "Can I do something about it?" That is, even if I understand and consider it relevant, do I have the potential to cope with it—and thus fight for it?

These are questions that have no objective answer. The individual must appraise the situation; make his judgment on the basis of all his past experiences, knowledge and expectations; and come to some conclusion. This is the process by which objective reality is translated into the subjective reality of the individual, and forms the basis for all his behavior.

This book is focused on the process of appraisal—the way we perceive ourselves and our relationship to the environment. Naturally, emphasis will be placed on the relationship between the process of perception and appraisal, and combat behavior.

Chapter 2 discusses and illustrates the idea that truth (like beauty) is in the eye of the beholder. One cannot talk of reality—even in regard to a battle—other than through the eyes of those appraising it. It is only after mapping this appraisal that one can understand the behavior of an individual or group in a given situation.

In Chapter 3 I present a model covering all aspects of behavior that determine the fighting potential of an individual or group. As stated above, this model is based on the appraisal process that, stage by stage, deals with the perceived environment—as well as on the internal perceptions leading to the final perception that, together with the objective parameters of the situation, determines the actual combat performance. This is a theoretical and often speculative chapter, but is aimed at offering a coherent structure on the basis of which some known findings and observations can be integrated.

It is not sufficient to appraise a situation as one that you understand, consider relevant, and feel you can handle. You must also have the need, drive, or desire to do so. Individuals with identical appraisals of a situation might differ in their combat readiness, because of this difference in the underlying willingness to get involved or committed to conflict. This underlying drive is often expressed as aggression, and Chapters 4 and 5 are dedicated to this concept. Chapter 4 briefly summarizes some of the literature and offers a model for classifying aggression. Chapter 5 goes into the origins of aggression and its evaluation. This chapter is not an essential part of this book. It is offered as background and interesting speculation. However, the reader may skip over it without affecting his or her understanding of the rest of the book.

Chapter 6 is dedicated to an explanation of what an enemy is: different ways that environment can be perceived and evaluated as "an enemy" and the effect that such an evaluation can have on behavior (that is, what or whom will the aggressive drive be directed at?).

Chapter 7 is concerned with the nature of courage—both in the eye of the beholder (that is, the social norms of heroism and medal awards), and in terms of the hero (that is, the motivations and perceptions behind heroic acts). In a way, this chapter addresses the question "Does this concern me?" for it describes the emotional involvement or committal that an individual has to a situation and that leads him to unusual or heroic acts.

Chaper 8, which discusses discipline, is an adjunct to the chapter on courage. While courage is seen as involving behavior that is unconventional and unusual, discipline confines behavior to predetermined and fixed routines. The effects of discipline—both punitive and directive—on combat efficiency is discussed and mapped. Obedience and its consequences—as well as formal and informal discipline in relationship to combat motivation—is taken up. This chapter deals with the question "What is it all about?" for it describes the framework for behavior—the norms and laws that create the structure and "make sense" of a situation.

Chapter 9 takes up some problems of assessing the psychological combat potential. It presents the results of an investigation made during the 1973 Yom Kippur War—which used conventional means as well as newly developed behavioral checklists. The chapter also presents an instrument for mapping the perception of any situation, along with some of its applications in military and nonmilitary settings.

Chapter 10 focuses on some psychological problems associated with the 1982 Lebanon War. The aim of this chapter is to analyze these problems from the point of view of the perceptual model outlined in Chapter 3.

As mentioned above, this has not been an attempt to write a strictly scientific book. My primary aim has been to stimulate, challenge, and convey ideas. I hope the reader will be able to accept the switch from formal to associative—from strictly factual to speculative. The "nothing but" syndrome was described by Jung (1959) as that "which superficially lends an air of scientific contribution, but in the long run explains nothing." My aim has been to describe more than to explain; but if a description is to be valid, it must lead to explanations—because of our basic need to make sense. Thus, if the reader finds this book as much a challenge to read as I found it a challenge to write, I shall be amply rewarded.

SUGGESTION FOR READING PLAN

I have aimed my writing at those who are concerned with conflict and combat in their daily life—soldiers, police, and social agents, as well as the academic who is interested in this aspect of human behavior. Thus, the book is a mixture of the abstract theoretical and the concrete practical. Chapters 3, 4, and 5 are the more theoretical: The reader who would like to go directly to the more concrete part could delay reading them until he has read the rest of the book. Then, hopefully, he will go back to these chapters and find the conceptual basis for what he has already read.

2

The Perception of Conflict and Combat

PERCEPTION OF BATTLE IS IN THE EYE OF THE BEHOLDER

"What are you here for?" I was often asked this question by soldiers and officers of the units I visited in the field. Answering—as any psychologist worth his salt would answer—"What do *you* think I am here for?" produced most frequently, "To help us overcome fear, to function better." (Of course, there were always some soldiers who thought I was the best pipeline for psychiatric discharge, but I do not wish to discuss them in the context of this book.) My initial assumption was that the soldiers would be most concerned with their combat ability; but I soon discovered that, as often as not, they were concerned with their ability to cope with more mundane issues.

There are enough peacetime problems—from physical stresses to military police, from loneliness to boredom—that are difficult to handle. Even during a war, only a relatively small portion of the time is spent in actual combat with the enemy—and less so during routine military service where real war and active engagements are comparatively rare, if not totally absent. For different persons in the same situation, there might well be different problems to cope with. Obviously, the platoon commander has different problems—and thus, a different perception of the problems of his platoon—than the private in the same platoon. But it is equally likely that two privates in the same platoon at the same time will have different perceptions of their problems within the platoon. One might have difficulty in tackling the physical demands and the constant physical pressure, and can just manage to keep up with the training; the other finds the physical demands very easy and not strainful, but finds the problems of social relationship—integration within the group—very difficult and most stressful.

Both would possibly like help in coping with their problems, but the kind of help and the type of coping that each needs help with are vastly different. As Magnusson and Ekehammar (1976) have shown, different individuals can interpret identical situations in different ways. Even the same situation, depending on the context within which it is perceived, can be perceived differently by the same individual at different times.

This is possibly the most critical foundation for the thought behind this book, and will be referred to again and again. We cannot discuss any situation—whether it is the face-to-face battle or the afternoon rest in camp—in objective terms. One may be able to describe the physical parameters of the situation: the speed of the tanks, the noise in decibels of the bomb, or the number of casualties in the platoon. However, each of these is likely to be differently perceived, and thus differently interpreted and differently reacted to by each individual who is exposed to the conditions. Truth is in the eye of the beholder—as are falsehoods. Or, to make it more explicit, "one man's meat is another man's poison." It is therefore critical to have a picture of how each individual perceives a situation, because *each person will* have a problem in coping with those aspects that are the most critical for him.

After a battle, I often asked soldiers what they found to be the most frightening or stressful aspect factor. The answer that I expected (based on readings of war literature, Hollywood films, and the scientific literature) was "loss of life"—or, even more so, "possible injury and abandonment in the field": See, for example, Stouffer et al., *The American Soldier* (1949): "From the standpoint of the individual soldier it is primarily the danger of death or injury which makes the combat situation so harassing an experience." But surprisingly enough, this proved to be rated as the most critical factor by only part of the population investigated.

Table 2.1 presents a list of the most frightening aspects of battle, as rated by veteran Israeli soldiers (privates and NCOs) and officers (lieutenants, captains, and majors; platoon and company commanders)—all with battle experience. It is clear that there is a great diversity of perception on what makes for the most frightening aspect of battle. These data give a picture of soldiers and officers in one infantry brigade. It is not necessarily—and, in fact, very unlikely to be—identical with a picture given by, for example, soldiers and officers in an armored unit. Nor is this picture necessarily the one that would have been given by the same brigade after further experience or after a different kind of experience. A factor such as "letting comrades down" might vary in importance with the sense of cohesion of the unit; while "being abandoned" or "being captured" might increase in importance following some unfortunate experiences in battle, or a change in perception of the enemy. For example, fear of being captured by the Syrians was greater than of being captured by the Egyptians; thus, this factor might have rated differently in the Sinai or Golan fronts.

Table 2.1
Factors Listed as "The Most Frightening Aspect of Battle" by Veteran Israeli Platoon
and Company Soldiers and Officers

	Officers & Senior NCO N = 69		Other Ranks N = 468	
	N	%	N	%
Letting dependents down	29	42.0	2	0.5
Letting comrades down	1	1.4	189	40.4
Loss of limb, injury	10	14.5	124	26.6
Death	7	10.1	97	20.7
Letting the unit down	5	7.2	19	4.1
Being captured	2	2.9	15	3.2
Being abandoned	1	1.4	13	2.8
Letting the country down	3	4.3	5	1.1
Showing fear	5	7.2	1	.03
Making wrong decisions	4	5.8	—	—
Being a coward	1	1.4	—	—
Letting my family down	—	—	3	.08
Being incompetent	1	1.4	—	—

Source: Israeli Defense Force (IDF), Unit of Military Psychology, unpublished report, 1974.

However, two points do emerge as probably relevant and applicable to many circumstances: (1) the relative unimportance of the fear of bodily harm and death (24 percent for officers and 47.2 percent for other ranks), and (2) the great emphasis on letting others down—for officers, the "others" being their charges (42 percent); and for the other ranks, this being their peers (40.4 percent). If one looks at the total "letting down" factors, 55 percent of the officers rate them as most critical, while 46 percent of the other ranks rate them similarly.

The same question (on "the most frightening aspect of battle") was asked of 113 Swedish UN troops, who had but a theoretical concept of battle. For these troops, perception of the danger of death or injury played a larger role (57 percent for men and 47 percent for officers)—but, nonetheless, not an overwhelming role. "Letting the side down" accounted for most of the other factors (34 percent for men letting peers down and 48 percent for officers letting their charges down). Again, this same question was administered to 217 Swedish UN soldiers and officers after their return from duty in Lebanon, during which they had some contact with active hostility. The list they generated was much shorter; it contained five factors, as shown in Table 2.2.

Table 2.2

Factors Listed as "The Most Frightening Factor in Battle" by
Swedish UN Soldiers (N = 217; in percent)

	Officers	Men
Letting comrades down	—	45
Letting dependents down	52	—
Death and injury	41	53
Making wrong decisions	5	
Being a coward	1	2

Source: National Defense Research Institute, Stockholm, unpublished research report, 1980.

The two Swedish samples are not perfectly matched, but both involved similar infantry units serving in the UN troops. On an administrative basis, part of these troops were chosen to serve in Lebanon, while the rest stayed behind in the Sinai. It would appear that exposure to battle and physical danger did not increase fear of death and injury, but decreased it—approaching the style of perception given by the Israeli soldiers. One explanation to this change in perception is that "the devil you know is better than one you do not know." One's picture of battle and its dangers are modified in the light of experience and successful survival. That is, the appraisal of the situation has changed and physical danger is perceived as less threatening or likely, while social dangers become more threatening or relevant.

Similar questions were asked of Israeli soldiers under many other conditions and in a variety of units. Responses were obtained from tank crews during their refueling pauses between battles in the Sinai, from attack divers in the rubber boats after returning from a mission, from submariners in the submarine on the way home after surviving a very unpleasant depth-charge attack in the Mediterranean, and from infantry soldiers returning after a successful assault on an enemy-held hill in the Golan. This also includes responses from missile operators on board a missile boat, and from gunners far away from the front. Obviously, these soldiers faced different battles. Some were directly exposed to the enemy and experienced a face-to-face battle; others never saw the enemy, but slid in and out of his territory under cover of night and water; while still others relied on their technical skills in manipulating controls in accordance with electronic information—for whom the enemy was but a light spot on the screen or verbal commands in their earphones. Some of the soldiers had a chance to hit directly back at the enemy, and actually kill him; others had a chance to place the charge that would go off—hopefully—long after their return to base; while others—like the submariners—had no opportunity to hit back at all, and could just hope for the best and rely on electronic and mechanical aids—as well as the enemy's mistakes—to allow them to escape.

Each of these battles had objectively different characters; each was also perceived differently by those who partook in them. If the soldier who considered the most frightening outcome to be physical injury were placed in the infantry or tank units, he might well have experienced this battle as extremely stressful. The same soldier might have felt much less stressed in the sterile and peaceful missile-control room. A soldier sitting in the hold of the submarine resting at the bottom of the sea outside Alexandria—being unable to move or talk so as not to make a noise that could be detected by the sonar equipment of the Egyptian destroyer searching overhead—such a soldier, being scared stiff, might well be more ashamed to show his fear or even the spreading wetness on his pants to the comrades in the hold with him, than of a possible injury. For a soldier more sensitive to social relations than to possible injury, such a situation would be much more stressful than the same situation to a soldier worried mostly about his bodily health. Even more dramatic differences are likely to be found between situations in which a soldier is not exposed to any physical danger—such as the ground–air controller, but whose wrong decisions would be immediately spotted and judged by his fellow operators. Were such an operator most sensitive to his social relationships, this situation would be more stressful than direct battle; while, for a soldier who is most scared of physical injury, conditions at the control center would not be so stressful.

It is perhaps not surprising that Levav, Greenfeld and Baruch (1979) report that the type of unit and the type of task imposed on it determined the rate of psychiatric casualties during the Yom Kippur War—as in similar reports by Noy, Nardi, and Salomon (1986) following the 1982 Lebanon War. Clearly, some people have a poorer coping and adjusting potential than others; and, at the extreme ends, we find those who cannot cope under any circumstances, as well as situations so extreme that nobody can cope with them. But in the middle range, we can expect that the appraisal by an individual of a given situation at a given time will determine his ability to cope with it or the fight in it.

THE CRITICAL FACTOR

What is the most frightening factor in battle may vary from individual to individual and from time to time; but, whichever is that factor in a given situation, success in dealing with it determines the limits of success in dealing with the whole situation. Like the strength of a chain, which is determined by the strength of its weakest link, so success in handling the perceived critical factor determines success in coping with the total environment.

A person who cannot handle the factor that he is most frightened by cannot cope with the situation by handling other factors. As the critical factor is successfully handled or is removed by other means, the next factor in the hierarchy becomes the critical factor—and so on, down the line.

Naturally, the factors may change their order of criticalness with circumstances, and several factors might be perceived to be equally important. A soldier entrenched in a position surrounded by the enemy might well consider his physical safety—escape from the sniper or falling shells—as the most critical issue, to the exclusion of all others. But if this situation goes on for days and the soldier runs out of water, eventually the need for food and water will become the most critical issue—so much so, that the soldier will ignore the physical dangers and try to sally out in order to obtain water. Priorities change, and with them changes the perception of the situation.

Different priorities are perceived by different soldiers according to their personal disposition, the information available to them, as well as according to the formal or informal roles they have within the organization. This was noted above in the difference between the perceptions of the officers and the men. The more similar the priorities of the group, the more effective will be their action. Such action may be positive—in accordance with the needs of the battle—or negative—as when there is mass desertion because of panic resulting from a similar perception by all in the group on the hopelessness of the situation. But in either case, if the situation is similarly perceived—if all members of the group give the same priority to the same critical factor—this group will act most effectively. The role of a leader—whether the platoon commander or the head of state—is to create this similar perception and similar priorities for all members of the group. One might even argue that a definition of a group— differentiating it from a gathering of people—is that members of a group have a similar perception of the situation.

The command may also try to impose a change in priorities—for example, by ordering a position taken or maintained at all costs. The command requires the factor of keeping the position to be ranked first, even above keeping alive. The success of such re-ranking is one of the critical attributes of a leader, and—as often as not—depends on his ability to convince others that he has similarly re-ranked his own priorities.

COPING

It may appear that the above discussion confused the terms "critical factor," "the most frightening aspect," and "coping," as well as "readiness to fight." The link between these terms is the concept of perception and appraisal. "Coping behavior," "adaptive behavior," "adjustment"—all these terms describe an individual's attempt to handle the perceived demands that he has to face. There are many ways to tackle a problem—provided a problem is perceived to exist—but they must all be aimed at the problem's removal. Coping can only be considered successful if the individual perceives that the problem has ceased to exist. The individual may have a false picture of his success—in which case the problem does persist—but, at the point in time when the problem is felt to be solved, coping is *felt* to be successful, regardless of the rude awakening that might later follow.

Perception of the closing of the gap between the undesired situation and the state of the individual—perception of fit between the individual and his environment—leads to the feeling of successful coping. When there is an imbalance, a poor fit, or incongruence—that is, a perception by the individual that the state of affairs is not as he would like them to be—an attempt at coping or adjusting follows.

In an environment that contains many factors, there could be a perception of many incongruences—a need for closing the gap on many issues: tiredness, hunger, fear, and so on—but the critical factor in each environment will receive the priority. Coping—attaining congruence—will be attempted first toward the factor that appears most important—and, in combat, most threatening.

Conflicts in general and military conflicts specifically are likely to involve a state of disharmony; but, unless the situation is perceived as a conflict situation, it will not lead to adjusting or coping behavior. Soldiers have to be convinced of the need to fight—whether on an abstract ideological level ("for king and country") or as the very basic, individual, and physical survival need. Only when the situation is so appraised will there be an attempt to cope—to restore the equilibrium. It is not sufficient to be aware of the need to cope or fight; one must also appraise one's ability and chances for handling the situation. Unless one appraises that there is some chance for success in coping, no coping behavior will take place. As stable equilibrium can be perceived in a situation that is totally satisfactory (contentment) or one that is totally hopeless (apathy), neither perception will lead to action. Only a perception of incongruence—of imbalance—will lead to adjustive behavior.

Thus, I shall view combat potential in terms of coping—which, in turn, can be analyzed by looking at the congruence of perception between the appraisal of environmental demands and the potential the individual feels he has for handling these demands.

The essential background or trigger to all coping is the person's "awareness" or "feeling" that an existing state must be altered. I have put "awareness" and "feeling" in quotation marks because the detection of incongruence—the disparity between the existing state and the desired or optimal state—does not have to be conscious. The body invaded by harmful bacteria copes with the situation by utilizing biochemical defenses and deploying white blood cells, without the person becoming aware of this (so long as this coping is not too stressful; we become aware of it in the case of fever, shivering, and so on). But even if we are unaware of this coping process, it goes on; and the organism attempts to cope with the factors that disturb its balance. When we are placed in extreme environments—cold or hot—the body has to cope with them. Biological mechanisms such as shivering or perspiration will be triggered in order to keep the blood's temperature within the very limited range that must be maintained for proper functioning of the organism. This homeostatic process—the process aimed at maintaining stability—is the basis of all body functions, whether maintaining the acid/base balance, the blood temperature level, or the muscular balance when walking. For the body, coping means to keep a stable equilibrium at all costs, whether or not we are aware of this process. When conditions frighten us or are perceived as unpleasant or stressful, we attempt to restore the balance—to remove the offending factor, affect it, or withdraw from it. We try to maintain homeostasis—to return to equilibrium in the emotional, social, or psychological domains—thus to return to a state we found satisfying, or at least less disturbing. Any change in our circumstances—psychological, social, or physical—or any threat to the existence of conditions perceived to be desired will trigger a homeostatic process in an attempt to redress the balance.

Thus, a perception (conscious or unconscious) of a state of imbalance or incongruity between the organism and its environment (internal or external) will trigger a coping process. Needs such as food, sleep, or sex will trigger a coping mechanism because of the incongruence between the state of satiation and the feeling of hunger. Feelings such as fear, insecurity, or need for love will also trigger coping mechanisms that try to close the gap and reduce the incongruence between the present feeling and that of security or love. Some incongruities are easily banished; coping with them offers no problem, as would be the case if I felt the need to drink water just now. But the same need—requiring in principle, the same coping act—might be much more difficult to deal with in the desert, with no water available. Coping that is easily done requires little physical or mental energy. But coping that is difficult—whether because of scarcity of resources (water in the desert), lack of skills (inability to start a car), or inhibitions (approaching an attractive girl)—involves the investment of much physical or mental energy and generates much stress. This is not the framework for a discussion of stress (the number of definitions for which can be approximated by the number of psychologists); but, to clarify the issue or at least help to explain my viewpoint—stress is taken to be the energy that has to be invested into returning the equilibrium—that is, the easier the homeostatic process, the less stress is involved.

While the need for water is an objective, biologically determined factor (although experiencing thirst is not), the need for security—for example—

is completely subjective. We have seen that the same situation may well be appraised differently by different people; thus, security may also have a different stress potential for each of them. Even if the situation is appraised similarly (as a "threat to security")—for one, coping by gaining feelings of security about the situation may be easy; for another, the same type of coping may be much more difficult—thus generating much more stress.

Thus stress—like truth—is in the eye of the beholder; and one man's stress may be the other man's—if not pleasure—at least nonstress. As Lazarus and Cohen (1977) stated; "Many environmental events that are stressful for one individual may be neutral or even positive for some persons and negative for others. It would appear that the impact of the environmental stressor depends on how a person appraises its significance and how much control he or she has over such noxious conditions."

According to these authors, coping is a continuous ongoing process aimed at mastering new situations, which can potentially be threatening, frustrating, challenging, or gratifying. Failure to master such situations—or even appraisal that the demands of the external environment exceed the person's resources for managing them—will result in stress.

There are many different ways of coping. One may attack or deny, reject or repress, rationalize or transfer. The literature is abundant with descriptions of such strategies for coping. A very rough but efficient description—or mapping—of all possible strategies can be made. There are three basic strategies with which any situation can be handled: (1) One can *act on* the situation; (2) one can *abstain* from action; or (3) one can *withdraw* from the situation. There are three basic aims for any action on the situation: (1) One may want to *change* the situation; (2) one may want to *maintain* the situation; or (3) one may want to *adapt to* the situation. Thus, a person has nine basic coping strategies available for any perceived situation—which we can express as a mapping sentence:

A PERSON (X) CAN RESPOND TO ANY SITUATION AT TIME (T)

	Mode		*Aim*
	acting		change
By	abstaining	in order to	maintain it
	withdrawing		adapt

People develop coping styles as much as they develop perceptual styles. They show a disposition to utilize one particular form of coping, at least with regards to a specific kind of situation. Although, theoretically, all nine basic coping strategies are available to an individual (or a group), as a result of past learning—and even, possibly, some innate disposition—one of these strategies will tend to be used preferentially. Lazarus, Averill and Option

(1974) explain these differences in terms of a difference in threshold for different coping styles. People differ in their hierarchies of preferences for the different ways of tackling a threat or a challenge; they differ in the choice of behavior deployed for the restoring of equilibrium between themselves and their environment.

Since coping is clearly related to the perceived situation we have to look at the way this perception takes place. The next chapter is devoted to the perceptual process and its relation to behavior.

3

A Model for Conflict and Combat Behavior

In the previous chapter, I discussed the importance of appraisal in determining the style and efficacy of coping. Not surprisingly, the model presented below is structured around the central theme of appraisal.

In order to react and cope with a situation, it is essential to have a mental picture of the situation. Such a mental picture is attained by a process of perception. The perceptual process requires several stages through which stimuli are transposed to perception, on the basis of which a response is formed. Since the appraisal process is based on the individual's past experience, learning, biological factors, as well as expectations and fears, different individuals will perceive a similar situation in different ways. Thus, the same objective situation can be perceived as threatening to one and as positive or neutral to another. In order to be able to understand and affect behavior of a person in a given situation, we must understand the person's perception of the situation, rather than the situation's objective nature.

Perception is an active process, during which the stimulating signal—the external or internal signal that triggers the perceptual process—is evaluated from different aspects and levels. This is a sequential process that can be described as a Markov chain—each stage in the process sets the limit to the effectiveness of the following stage.

"The process of cognitive appraisal represents a judgement of the significance of an event or a flow of events for the personal wellbeing," according to Lazarus and Launier (1978). Coping—the ultimate result of the appraisal process—follows a three-stage appraisal process (Lazarus 1966):

1. Primary appraisal—in which the individual decides whether a situation is benign (harmless or irrelevant) or meaningful (noxious or attractive), that is, he decides whether it requires a response or not.

2. Secondary appraisal—in which the individual decides the range of coping responses available to him in dealing with the situation
3. Reappraisal—in which the individual looks at the outcome of his previous coping or adaptive behavior

This is the basic model for appraisal on which I shall build a more elaborate model, which aims to clarify the sequential stages of processing a biologically registered signal and transforming it to a behavioral response.

APPRAISAL AS A PROCESS

According to Lazarus as expanded by Folkman (1984), ambiguity of information is considered part of the situational factors. One has to differentiate between ambiguity, which is lack of clarity about the meaning of a situation, and uncertainty, which is mental confusion of the individual about the situation. These aspects are independent of one another; thus, an individual may be confused about the meaning of objectively good information. The author argues that a state of ambiguity per se is not necessarily detrimental to the coping process. While ambiguity may indeed hinder some coping—especially that involving nonemotional situations—other environments are best handled when they are perceived as more ambiguous. However, as noted by Lazarus (1976), "The more ambiguous are the stimulus cues, the more important are the general belief systems in determining the appraisal process." It seems that, when there is a perceived lack of objective information, it is supplemented by subjective information in order to attain a coherent picture. The greater the demands or the potential stress in the situation, the greater is the need to reduce its ambiguity—either by obtaining more data or by "filling in" with subjective data based on past experience, expectations, wishful thinking, and so forth. Individuals differ in their tolerance of ambiguity—that is, they differ in their acceptance of a level of information as the basis for appraisal. One can compare individuals according to the amount of information (about any given situation) that they will consider sufficient for classifying the information and responding to it, but each individual will require sufficient data (objective and/or subjective) to be able to arrive at an appraisal of the situation.

Unless such data is available—unless some coherent perception of the situation can be made—no further appraisal can take place. It seems to me that perceived situational ambiguity combined with uncertainty as to its meaning cannot be viewed as part of the objective situational factors, but is an essential and autonomous product of the appraisal process.

Ambiguity and uncertainty—or rather no ambiguity and no uncertainty—combine to form coherence. The attainment of this coherence is the first step in the process of appraisal. Unless the individual knows where he is (what situation he is in), he cannot determine whether the situation is noxious or benign (primary appraisal), and thus neither can he cope with it (secondary appraisal).

I propose to use the term *structure appraisal* or *orientation appraisal* to describe this initial appraisal stage. Meeting a traffic situation that cannot be analyzed, the initial onslaught of battle, or the impact of diffuse radio communication—all require the attainment of coherence, structure or orientation, before any further processing can occur. The extreme stress and disorientation involved in total sensory deprivation is probably not so much due to the potential threat of the situation, as to the threat of being unable to classify the situation in any way. The most critical environment-interaction issue for any person—involving the biggest stress potential—is the inability to clarify what the environment is. This is the basic hurdle that one has to overcome, in daily life as well as in more extreme situations. Normally, this is a very short-term process, but conditions such as the fog of battle or any diffuse threat may impose a state of confusion and incoherence for a longer period.

It does not matter whether this stage of the appraisal process is managed by "wrong" appraisal: Any coherent perception—objectively right or wrong—can form the basis for further appraisal and reappraisal, which will eventually lead to a more objectively correct evaluation. Thus, one can view the incoherence of a perceived situation as the universal and primary stress factor. Perhaps this is the state described by Durkheim (1897) as "anomie"—lack of clarity; rootlessness; and personal disorientation. It could even be argued that drives such as "intrinsic motivation" (Deci 1975)—described as "behavior aimed at decreasing incongruity"—as well as "curiosity drive" (Berlyne 1971)—aimed at seeking information and understanding nature—are drives expressed in the structure or orientation phase of appraisal.

To emphasize the roles of Lazarus's primary appraisal and secondary appraisal in the coping process, and to emphasize the fact that the "primary" appraisal is actually not the first—but the second—stage of the appraisal process, I propose to use different terms for these stages: Primary appraisal I shall refer to as *motivation* or *valence appraisal* (the value of the situation, or its valence). Secondary appraisal I shall refer to as *coping appraisal* or *control appraisal* (the goodness of fit or congruence between the perceived abilities and facilities and the perceived demands).

Magnusson (1981) differentiates situations into "situation types" and "momentary situations." He argues that one can expect cross-situational stability in the appraisal style to the former category of situations; no such stability can be expected toward momentary situations. These involve unique responses and appraisal, which cannot be generalized nor even given normative assessment. Thus, while one can differentiate between individuals' tolerance of ambiguity, this differentiation is only valid when appraising situation types and not momentary situations. Similarly, an analysis of all the appraisal process phases should be based on the relatively stable situation types.

Lazarus's model does not allow for such differentiation. Even if the appraisal process can account for such variations, there is no explicit short-term appraisal subsystem included or a system for evaluating a limited specific but temporary situation. The secondary appraisal, which assesses the coping performance, is a relatively fixed characteristic for the individual in all circumstances. However, one can imagine an individual who in general appraises and copes with a situation in a given way (for example, feels he can race to the bus stop in the last minute), but on a specific occasion adapts a different strategy (for example, he sprains his ankle and has to walk slowly). This individual primary appraisal (the danger of being late) and secondary appraisal ("I can manage in a given time") have not changed, but a temporary—possibly last-minute—change in appraisal has occurred. The point is that this does not involve a change in the basic values appraisal, but only a delay or a temporary suspension of the previous appraisal. Clearly, such appraisal might—if persistent—lead to a change in the value coping appraisal; but, initially, it is best an appraisal of the here and now.

This last phase of appraisal will be referred to as *status appraisal*. It occurs after the coping appraisal but before action is taken—thus also before the *reappraisal* stage, which is aimed at evaluating the outcome of the adaptive response.

Structure Appraisal

The structure appraisal is characterized by *cognition*—that is—the clarity and differentiation with which we can perceive and analyze the incoming signal and treat its information. Our appraisal of this information offers us a basis for further evaluation. Unless we can perceive at least some degree of information in a situation, we cannot possibly relate to it. Total chaos, or total ambiguity prevents us from any response. This was discussed in detail above.

Motivation Appraisal

Once we have some cognitive information about the nature of the stimulus, we must also appraise its relevance to us. We can appraise a stimulus as positive or negative—attractive or repulsive—and on this basis consider how to respond to it. However, if we appraise this stimulus or situation as completely irrelevant to us—as lacking all meaning for us—we

Figure 3.1
Schematic Presentation of the Process of Appraisal

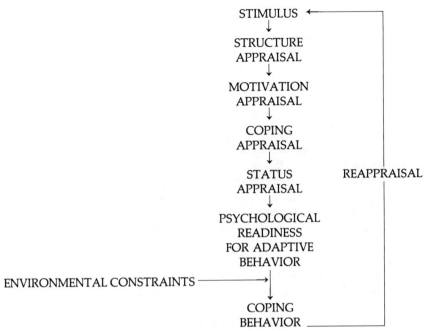

Source: Author.

shall ignore it and thus cease to process it. This is the motivational or *affective* phase: Unless we decide whether we care, we cannot decide whether we should do.

This is the appraisal stage that determines whether a situation is perceived as noxious or benign, whether it requires an adaptive response, or whether it can be ignored. As previously stated, adaptive behavior is required when a state of imbalance or incongruence is perceived to exist (or threatens to occur) between an individual and his environment. An environment that presents a challenge (by the very disturbance of equilibrium) becomes a protagonist or an enemy. In Chapter 6, I will enlarge on the concept of "enemy"—a concept that, in a military setting, is often very self-evident. But an enemy does not necessarily have to be the opposing troops; it can be the stormy seas, overwhelming tiredness, or even the sergeant major. Valence appraisal leads to one conclusion: There is—or there is not—"an enemy" involved in the situation. If the outcome of this stage of appraisal is that there is no protagonist or challenge involved in the situation, the appraisal process stops—that is, the situation is discounted or ignored as being of no relevance, and requiring no adaptive behavior. Leaders of nations or groups spend much effort in convincing their people that an enemy exists, because without this perception they cannot expect their followers to engage in the necessary combat behavior. Hence, we have Roosevelt's efforts to convince Americans of Germany's danger, the Russians' presentation of the capitalistic countries, and the motivation behind all the religion-inspired wars. Hence, also, the emphasis that the platoon leader places on convincing his soldiers that noise is "the enemy" during a night patrol, or that dirt is a real enemy in relation to weapons maintenance. Unless the dirt or the noise are directly perceived as the actual element to be fought—the element that threatens to upset the equilibrium—the soldiers will not be willing to give these issues the full attention and concern necessary for effective combat performance. Much emphasis is placed on the ideological orientation of soldiers—in convincing them that the cause of their war is just. But, as will be shown later, this is not essential, and often irrelevant to combat motivation. For the opposing troops to be perceived as "enemy," the soldier does not require a general ideological background. All that is needed is for the opposing troops to be seen as upsetting the soldier's personal equilibrium, either by direct threat to himself or to his peers. The more immediate and relevant the threat is perceived to be, the more likely it is to be appraised as negative.

It is therefore highly critical that the leader show the soldier the reason for all his actions—that he explain how they are aimed to restore or maintain a critical balance. A functional explanation is necessary, in order to facilitate the valence appraisal stage. Forcing a soldier to carry out actions that are not perceived as contributing to his welfare in terms of coping with a perceived challenge are likely to be counterproductive. An imposed action or discipline that does not make sense will in itself be perceived as "an enemy," rather than as a positive or helpful guideline. This will lead to behavior aimed at coping with the enemy—leading to breach of discipline and all the well-established ways soldiers have of avoiding what they consider stupid or unnecessary. In Chapter 8, I will take up the issue of discipline, but the main point can be emphasized here: For discipline to be effective, it must be functional. It must be perceived by the soldier to contribute to his ability to cope with a perceived enemy—to handle a potential challenge in his environment. It is only once the situation has been appraised as involving a potential threat or challenge that the next stage of appraisal is reached.

Coping Appraisal

Once we have established the structure or frame of reference of the situation and its relevance to us, the third phase follows—the *instrumental*; the active response. We must appraise the situation in such a way that we perceive a possible response to it—that we can do something about it. This does not mean that we must perceive a possible positive solution; it can also mean a perception of the need to escape and avoid. But we must perceive some possibility of reaction to the stimuli. Unless there is such an assessment we cannot assume that the perception process is complete: Unless we decide whether we can do, we cannot decide to do.

This stage of appraisal is aimed at establishing how well we can cope with the perceived enemy. Clearly, such appraisal involves the assessment of both enemy and self, it is an appraisal of relative potentials, rather than one of absolute quantities or qualities. What will make us decide whether we can cope with a given situation is that we appraise our abilities and facilities to exceed that of the enemy—regardless of what these qualities or quantities really are. During the previous stage of appraisal, it was of no consequence to which domain it related—whether the threat was perceived as physical, social, or psychological was but a secondary issue, because the primary issue was that a threat existed; at the coping stage of appraisal, the actual content comes into closer scrutiny.

Beaumont and Snyder (1980) list factors the perception of which—when incongruent with expected perception—reduce combat effectiveness:

1. Culture shock
2. Comradeship—fitting into the group
3. Macro and micro systems—the discipline and rules of the organization and group
4. Inertia—maintaining and breaking off action
5. Keystone people—the perception and expectation from authority
6. Weapons—"refusal to accept information (about their quality etc.) which does not match expectations"

One could summarize the above, and say that coping appraisal requires congruence in four domains:

1. Psychological—attitudes, perception, motivations
2. Social—identifications, grouping, norms
3. Instrumental—means, skills, facilities
4. Physical—health, conditions, time

Appraisal in these domains will look at both the cognitive (knowledge, skills facilities) and the affective (attitudes, feelings, qualities) aspects. The result of such appraisal can be positive—"we can handle"—or negative—"we cannot handle." This conclusion is separate and independent for the cognitive and affective areas. We might appraise our skills to be sufficient for dealing with the enemy's skills, but our motivation for combat to be less than his. A positive appraisal of the affective aspect gives us the feeling of confidence. We develop the feeling of confidence when we feel that our affective resources are sufficient to deal with the problems—when we feel that "we are on top of the situation." Such a feeling can develop even if we assess our facilities to be less than the enemy's, because we feel that we can overcome all challenges. This is the feeling of optimism and confidence (which might indeed be false) that enables us to take up a struggle and persist in the face of overwhelming odds.

A positive appraisal of the cognitive side gives us the feeling of handling capacity. On the basis of an appraisal of our relative skills, facilities, and so forth, we conclude that we can cope with the situation (always assuming that we want to do so).

A negative appraisal can be changed into a positive appraisal by two strategies: We can increase our motivation and involvement, and/or increase our skills and facilities; or we can decrease our perception (whether or not on objective bases) of the enemy's motivation, skills, and so on.

Much psychological propaganda is aimed at decreasing the perception of the enemy's qualities, so as to produce a positive outcome of this stage of appraisal. The obvious danger of such a technique is that reality might upset the perception, and then decisions made on its basis will lead to disastrous results. Similarly dire consequences could follow an overappraisal of one's own potential, and military history is abundant with evidence of such mistakes.

Status Appraisal

Unless we decide how to react here and now, we shall not react at all. At this point of the appraisal process, the individual has established his readiness to cope by conflict with a specific enemy in a specific situation. However, this appraisal is still on a general conceptual level, and is not necessarily tied to an exact time and place. For example, the platoon leader and his platoon are quite willing—and have assessed themselves as quite able—to attack an enemy position. But at this specific instant, a technical problem with their communication equipment or a fault in their machine gun, delays the attack by a few minutes, until the hitch is overcome. Thus, the final appraisal—the here-and-now appraisal—must be made immediately prior to undertaking action. This is the status appraisal, which can be viewed as a rapid reappraisal of the coping appraisal; but it occurs after committal to action has already taken place. Its effect is only in delaying, not in evaluating.

However, if such a delaying function extends too long, it might lead to new coping appraisal, because the situation might be perceived to have changed. Thus, once committal has been made, there is much pressure to carry out action as soon as possible, without further delay. Because of the pressure of committal on carrying out the action in spite of possible changes in the situation, emphasis is often placed on the "check and recheck" procedure—the status appraisal—which will prevent hasty response based on the coping appraisal only.

As stated previously, the first three stages are dependent and sequential. Some structure is essential for some motivation, and at least some motivation is essential for a feeling of coping potential. These are the psychological prerequisites for coping, but they offer no guarantee for successful coping. Further psychological processing is required before the original perception can be translated into a response. This is an elaboration on the three basic steps described above. Finally, successful coping depends on the combination of adequate psychological perception potential as well as adequate resources such as skills, equipment, available time, and so forth.

THE SEQUENTIAL APPRAISAL MODEL

The discussion up to this point focused on the process of appraisal by looking at what makes for the *perception* of a situation. Three levels of this appraisal were discussed. They can be generically labeled as three modalities:

1. Cognitive-appraisal of the structure; differentiation and categorization of the elements in the situation
2. Affective-appraisal of the emotional value of the situation
3. Instrumental-appraisal of the acts and responses possible in the situation

However, between the appraisal of a situation and the response to it, other psychological phases are required. Much in the same way that physiological arousal—be it adrenaline secretion, muscle tension increase, or heart rate change—is a prerequisite for a coping response, so is it necessary to have psychological arousal or *mobilization*. This mobilization occurs on the same three modalities: cognitive, affective, and instrumental.

Lastly, after mobilization it is necessary to apply the psychological potential in order to realize it. This last phase—again pertaining to the three modalities—will be referred to as *realization*.

We thus obtain a 3 × 3 table—3 levels × 3 phases. In mapping terms, this can be summarized as:

Modality	*Phase*
m1 Cognitive	p1 Appraisal
m2 Affective	p2 Mobilization
m3 Instrumental	p3 Realization

Nine possible profiles are generated.

As we previously stated, perception is viewed as a sequential process, as a Markov chain, or—in mapping terms—as a simplex. The appraisal process will thus follow the sequence:

m1p1	Cognitive appraisal	AWARENESS
m1p2	Affective appraisal	CONCERN
m1p3	Instrumental appraisal	CONTROL
m2p1	Cognitive mobilization	UNDERSTANDING
m2p2	Affective mobilization	INVOLVEMENT
m2p3	Instrumental mobilization	READINESS
m3p1	Cognitive realization	SKILLS
m3p2	Affective realization	COMMITTAL
m3p3	Instrumental realization	ADJUSTMENT (COPING)

The process is called the Sequential Appraisal Model (SAM). Each of the above steps can be illustrated by a question: The beholder going through the process has to "answer" a sequence of questions. Only if he can answer successfully does the process continue. These questions are summarized in Figure 3.2. Each stage is illustrated by the "perceptual question" that the process poses, which has to be cleared before proceeding to the next step.

The SAM process does not look at "why"; it is only concerned with "how"—how signals that have been registered by the individual are processed and appraised; and how this appraisal affects the final output or response. Naturally, the response—once made—becomes part of the appraised situation, and thus leads to reappraisal in a continuous looplike process. A process broken at any one stage might also lead to reappraisal.

Figure 3.2
The Nine Stages of the Sequential Appraisal Model (SAM)

Process Modalities	Process Phases		
	Appraisal	*Mobilization*	*Realization*
COGNITIVE	[1]IS it?	[4]Do I UNDERSTAND?	[7]HOW shall I do?
AFFECTIVE	[2]Does it CONCERN me?	[5]Do I WANT?	[8]Shall I COMMIT myself?
INSTRUMENTAL	[3]Can I AFFECT it?	[6]Am I READY?	[9]DO!

Source: Author.

This process can be imagined as a spiral with three loops—a loop for each phase, with the three modalities present in each loop. This loop can be represented by a tube, while each modality is represented by a faucet. Water running down the tube is psychological potential, which could drive a turbine at the tube's opening. Each stage or faucet can be open or shut. If it is open, water runs out, and less is available to drive the turbine. The best utilization of the available potential is when all perception stages are most effective—that is, all faucets are watertight.

The application of the SAM model for analyzing a combat situation might be perceived as follows:

A platoon leader who leads his platoon on a combat patrol hears a rustle in the bushes, and the perception of the situation is as follows:

APPRAISAL

1. Cognitive   Was the noise a rustle of bushes, or was there no sound at all?

2. Affective   Could that rustle be of relevance—that is, does it signal something threatening?

3. Instrumental   If it is threatening, is there something I can do about it? Must I know more?

MOBILIZATION

4. Cognitive   What can be done—attack, escape, ignore?

5. Affective   Do I want to do; am I interested? I may not want to react because I feel unsure of myself, and do not want to make a fool of myself. Can I depend on others to follow?

6. Instrumental   Am I ready to act—to give an order that I know can be carried out?

REALIZATION

7. Cognitive   How do I set about acting—by signal, verbal order, or opening fire myself (depending on stage 4 conclusions)?

8. Affective   Now that I shall act, commit myself.

9. Instrumental   Act.

Stages 1–3 (appraisal phase) focuses on the platoon leader's own interaction with the situation, with little involvement of others. Stages 4–6 (mobilization phase) involve the matching or goodness-of-fit between the perceived potential and perceived demands. In stage 4 (cognitive), resources such as firepower and level of training are matched with the possible threat—that is, the enemy strength. Accordingly, attack or escape strategies will be reached. In stage 5 (affective), emotional resources are matched with perceived threats: Can the leader feel that his men will follow him and obey orders; can he feel that he will keep his lead? Stage 6 (instrumental) reflects the synthesis of stages 4 and 5. He is ready to act if a coping strategy has been made clear and he has a feeling that the soldiers will follow; the leader then has a high morale.

Stages 7 and 8 (realization phase) focus on the execution of strategies. Stage 7 (cognitive) demands a detailed planning of the action—for example, jump to the side and open fire. Stage 8 (affective) is the actual formulation and acceptance of the order, with the last-minute check; while stage 9 is the actual order.

In more general terms the role of each step in the sequence leading to action can be summarized as in Figure 3.3. A similar analysis can be made for the perception process on a group level, as in Figure 3.4. Group's status (3) is the group's appraisal of being accepted as competent for their task. Roles in the group (4) is the clarity of each member's task. Role conflicts (5) reflects the group's willingness to act together. Coordination (6) reflects the group's ability to act as one unit.

According to the model, *any* total break in the sequence will lead to coping failure. A decrease in the effectiveness in any stage will lead to a proportional decrease in all subsequent stages.

A study (Shalit et al. 1986) was carried out on soldiers who were in a plane on the way to their first parachute jump. The soldiers were asked to fill in a questionnaire—called the Wheel (see Chapter 9)—designed for mapping the perception of the first three stages of any situation, as well as ten other questions—two per stage. Those ten questions are presented in Figure 3.5.

The soldiers were then assessed by experts on their jump effectiveness. A five-point scale was used. Scores 1 and 2 were treated as "poor jump"; while 3–5, as "good jump". The scoring of the questions was made by categorizing scores below the mean on each question as "not cleared" (NC), and a score

Figure 3.3
The Role of the SAM Stages in the Perceptual Process Leading to Action

¹RULES FOR RECOGNITION	⁴RULES FOR PROBLEM SOLVING	⁷SKILL'S APPICATION
²APPRAISAL OF RELEVANCE	⁵FEELING OF IMPORTANCE	⁸INVOLVEMENT IN TASK
³DEVELOPMENT OF SELF-CONFIDENCE	⁶DEVELOPMENT OF KNOWLEDGE	⁹LEAD TO ACTION

Source: Author.

Figure 3.4
The Role of the SAM Stages in the Group Members' Perceptual Process Leading to Action

¹INFORMATION'S EFFECTIVENESS	⁴ROLES IN THE GROUP	⁷GROUP'S ACTION PLAN
²INFORMATION'S TRUSTWORTHINESS	⁵ROLE CONFLICT RESOLUTION	⁸GROUP'S COHESIVENESS
³GROUP'S STATUS	⁶GROUP'S COORDINATION	⁹CONTROL OVER ACTION

Source: Author.

Figure 3.5
Questions for Assessing SAM Stages 4–8 in the Appraisal of an Imminent Parachute Jump

Question	Response Poles	SAM Stage
1. Do you feel that there is something more that you would like to *know* about the jump?	nothing/much	4
2. Have you *understood* what you should do?	all/nothing	—
3. How much do you *want* to jump?	much/little	5
4. How much does jumping *attract* you?	much/little	
5. Are you mentally *prepared* for the jump?	very/not at all	6
6. Are you mentally *ready* for the jump?	very/not at all	
7. Do you feel that you can *cope* with the situation?	totally/not at all	7
8. Do you know how to *handle* the situation?	totally/not at all	—
9. Would you like to *continue* with parachute jumping?	definitely/not at all	8
10. How important is it for you *to jump neatly?*	very/not at all	—

Source: Author.

above the mean, as "cleared" (C). Any profile containing an NC score was treated as an NC profile. A profile analysis was carried out. The results are shown in Table 3.1.

Table 3.1
Cross Tabulation of the Jump Effectiveness
and Perception Criteria

	Jump Effectiveness		
Perception	*poor*	*good*	N
Not cleared	38	4	42
Cleared	42	22	64
Total	80	26	106

$x^2 = 8.46$; $p < 0.01$

Source: Shalit et al. (1986).

While only 9.5 percent of those who did not have a "perfect" sequential process jumped well, 34.4 percent with "good" perception jumped well. Clearly "good" appraisal is no guarantee for a good jump, but it is a prerequisite for it. That about two-thirds with "good" appraisal failed to jump well might depend on environmental constraints, such as physical conditions and level of training.

The limitation of this study is that we cannot estimate the relative importance of each stage. However, other assessments (taken up in Chapter 9) show that the earlier the break in appraisal occurs, the stronger the negative affect on coping.

A break in the process means that a certain question could not be answered. Since coherence or making sense of any situation is essential, this means that the explanation or excuse for failure will be found in the preceding stage. Thus—for example—if we feel we cannot cope with a situation (stage 3), our explanation will be that "we do not want to" (stage 2); or, if we feel we do not want to (2), we might react: "what the hell is it all about" (1). Lazarus (1983) points out that denial can, in fact, be a positive coping strategy: "If I cannot, it does not concern me." The reappraisal of the situation restores the psychological equilibrium—regardless of the objective demands of the situation.

FAILURE TO COPE

Figure 3.6 presents some typical symptoms of failure in each of the SAM stages. The stages of the process are not of any fixed duration. Such a process can be very slow—at any rate, the time for each stage easily measurable. But it can also be so rapid as to appear instantaneous. At times, one can describe each stage directly or by means of introspection and hindsight; at other times,

Figure 3.6
Examples of Symptoms That Might Arise from Process Failures in Each of the SAM Stages

[1]LONG REACTION TIME	[4]POOR PROBLEM ANALYSIS	[7]CLUMSY PERFORMANCE
[2]IGNORE SITUATION	[5]POOR MOTIVATION POOR COHESIVENESS	[8]POOR FIGHTING SPIRIT
[3]APATHY	[6]POOR DECISION MAKING	[9]REFUSAL TO ACT

Source: Author.

the whole process is unconscious and not analyzable. At the present state of knowledge, the available data does not allow a more precise description. By mapping the perceptual process, we do not gain insight into the etiology of the behavior, but we can understand the potential of an individual (or a group) for coping with a given situation. Thus, within the limits of the predisposing parameters, one can increase the coping capacity within any given situation, by modifying the perceptual process.

The most common failure to cope in the field of battle is the neuro-psychiatric dysfunction often described as "battle fatigue," "shell shock" or combat stress reaction. This can be expected to affect up to 25 percent of combatants (Siegel et al. 1979). (But see the discussion in Chapter 10.) The most typical syndrome of the dysfunction is withdrawal from the situation: The soldier ceases to react to his surroundings and, in fact, shows no ability to perform any coping or adaptive behavior. The onset of this syndrome rarely follows the first exposure to battle, but develops after continuous exposure to combat and with a frequency that increases relative to the duration and intensity of exposure. It was usually assumed that several days of exposure are required before the threshold of this symptom is reached. Experience in the 1973 war has shown that, under the extreme conditions of the initial Egyptian surprise attack battle fatigue occasionally sets in after only a few hours: The total amount of exposure to stress determines the point of failure to cope. Intense stress over a short period has a similar effect to milder stress over a more extended period. The most common explanation of this syndrome is the inability of the soldier to handle the situation: The environmental demands made on him exceed his ability to cope; and, as a defense, he ceases to relate to them altogether. Thus, this cannot be viewed as a case of failure of appraisal, for the situation had been appraised as "threatening" and "impossible to handle." Appraisal has already gone through the valence and coping appraisal stages, as if the soldier had negatively answered the question "Can I do something about the situation?" On the other hand, failure of structure appraisal can account for the symptom of "freezing"—the inability to react when faced with a sudden threat. Such behavior is not classified as a neuropsychiatric symptom, because it is unlikely to last long enough to be brought to medical attention. The individual is likely to recover after a short while or—because the delay was too critical—be injured or killed. The initial reaction time determines whether a soldier will survive an ambush, whether a tank crew will detect and destroy the enemy's tank, or whether a hand grenade will be avoided or even returned. Cases of battle fatigue can be seen in soldiers who were exposed to heavy aerial attack by their own air force, who failed to identify them. These soldiers could not make sense of their situation; they failed to function, because they could not even clear the first appraisal stage. They coped with an attack of the same intensity by enemy forces with many fewer casualties.

One of the most critical functions of learning—indeed, overlearning—is to reduce the time required for structure appraisal. By acquiring knowledge of clues and cues that signify "a situation," appraisal is expedited. The less information we require to be able to categorize seemingly random data into some coherent structure, the quicker we can clear the stage of structure appraisal. Much as we can recognize familiar persons by a slight glimpse of their gait without need for detailed scrutinization of their face, an experienced soldier can recognize an ambush by a slight rustle of leaves or the sound of a breaking twig without need to see or hear the opening fire. But however detailed and effective the training is, any battle is likely to produce the unexpected and unfamiliar situation. It is in such circumstances that the role of the leader as the one who creates structure and coherence becomes critical. By giving orders, and by guiding and channeling information—however sparse—the leader must lay the basis for making sense out of the initially chaotic situation.

It is impossible to predict what the appropriate speed of structure appraisal for any given situation might be; but the more we know about the general perceptual clarity a soldier has of a type of situation, the better we can assess his ability to clear the appraisal stage.

MODIFIERS OF THE APPRAISAL PROCESS AND MORALE

The discussion above relates to the appraisal process on various levels, but not to the drive behind it. As previously mentioned, aggression is an important driving factor leading to combat behavior. This can be viewed as an affective factor. But another, cognitive factor must also be considered highly relevant: the coping strategies available to the individual—that is, responses known and acceptable to him.

The assertive or aggressive disposition of an individual—his need and motivation for behaving in an aggressive way—must play a big role in determining his willingness to engage in a conflict. The next chapter will be devoted to an analysis of aggression—whether acquired or innate—on the behavior of individuals and groups. At this point in the presentation, all I would like to say is that one can differentiate individuals and groups by their disposition toward aggressive behavior. Individuals who have a strong disposition toward aggression or assertion will develop an attitude that, in association with their feelings about themselves (confidence), will combine to form a disposition of readiness to engage in combat—which is often considered a morale factor.

Perception of confidence results from the feeling that one's affective potential can handle the situational demands—that one can overcome. This by itself does not mean that one is willing to take up a specific struggle and overcome a given challenge. It is only those with an aggressive potential (as will be explained and defined in the next chapter) who are going to translate the feeling of being able to overcome into the fighting spirit or morale. A discussion of various definitions of morale will be taken up in the following chapters, but they all have in common the view of morale as a willingness to fight—a willingness based on a feeling of doing the right thing, whether for oneself, one's country, or comrades. Ingraham (1984) describes military units who had high morale but a low willingness to engage in battle. According to my model, high morale is a result of a positive coping appraisal, leading to a feeling of confidence combined with a disposition for aggressive behavior. This does not necessarily mean that the behavior will be congruent with that desired by the authorities.

Although this definition is most applicable to the military area, the same could apply to all conflict and struggle behavior. A researcher willing to take up a research challenge, a team committed to irradication of disease, or a leader of a political campaign—all need both a positive appraisal of their abilities and an aggressive disposition to carry out the action.

Morale is often used as a global term describing a final psychological state or disposition. However, in the process terms used here, one would expect several morale values to be generated at the various stages.

Morale A is that disposition generated after the second valence stage (SAM stage 5). This will be reflected by a willingness to engage in battle or any task perceived to be relevant for the individual or his group. This is the aspect often measured by the type of question "How willing are you to fight (or jump, or whatever)?" Such questions often reflect very labile values—values that can change daily, depending on external factors. In Sweden, for example, the "willingness to defend my country" values are directly affected by external events, such as a suspected Soviet submarine in the Swedish archipelago. A better term for this morale index would be "mood." Mood can and will fluctuate easily. Even when the mood is right and soldiers are willing to go into action, this is no guarantee that they will continue to fight when circumstances become difficult.

Morale B is based on the final coping stage of appraisal (SAM stages 7 and 8). It is based on a combination of confidence and the feeling of coping potential. This morale type can be called "resilience." This is the morale factor that guarantees the continuation of action in spite of losses, fears, and uncertainty. This is the critical aspect that must be developed before the onset of battle. It requires adequate perception to cope; it is insufficient to be only motivated.

It is essential to assess the mood-type morale and the resilience-type morale separately. Assessing only one level can lead to serious misjudgment of the combat potential. Ingraham's (1984) findings can be explained in terms of high mood and low resilience.

THE COPING STRATEGIES

As discussed in the previous chapter, different individuals adopt different coping strategies toward the same situation or toward themselves in a given situation. This seems to depend on the availability or accessibility of different strategies for an individual interacting with a particular environment. Thus, one person will react to physical threat more readily by attack, while the other will withdraw. Clearly, in a combat situation, the ready availability of an "acting to change" strategy will be more congruent with combat effectiveness than a "withdrawing to adapt" strategy (see Chapter 2). This is not to say that the latter strategy would not be the optimal military strategy, under some circumstances. But this is to say that a person disposed to handling his "enemies" by the "action to change" strategy is more likely to generally seek active confrontation.

A person who arrived at an appraisal of "high handling capacity" and who has, at the same time, a preference for an "acting to change" coping strategy will show a stronger confrontation style than another who may have a similar appraisal of his handling capacity, but who prefers to cope by withdrawal. The confrontation style can be viewed as the cognitive equivalent of morale. It is the measure of the availability of fighting behavior, while high handling capacity appraisal measures the willingness for engagement in such behavior.

The sum total of the perception process leads to the attack behavior—that is, the psychological equipment deployable (if so motivated) in a particular conflict situation.

COMBAT PERFORMANCE

The end result of the perceptual process—the combat potential—is an indicator of the state of mind—or psychological state of readiness—of the individual. It determines the maximum performance that can be expected of him; but it cannot indicate his ultimate performance, which must depend on the objective constraints that play a part in any given situation. It is not within the domain of this book to discuss the impact of these factors on ultimate performance; but, for the sake of clarity, a very brief summary of the factors will be made.

Facilities

1. Weapons deployed by both sides—their capacity, efficiency, quantities, and so forth
2. Geographical constraints—territory, weather, visibility, and light and temperature conditions
3. Temporal constraints—time available for decision making, action, and correction of mistakes
4. Intelligence—knowledge of own and enemy disposition and potentials; efficiency of communications and data processing
5. Physiological factors—health, physical condition, and tiredness (the objective effects of fatigue on cognitive and physical performance)

Social Factors

1. Leadership—the effectiveness of the leader; his ability to reach decisions, communicate and clarify his commands, coordinate within and without the unit, and so on. This does not include trust in the leader—an aspect that has an effect on the appraisal process. It is not sufficient for the leader to evoke trust—for, unless his actions are competent, combat effectiveness will decrease.
2. Peers—the ability to function as a team, the knowledge of each other's failings and strength, and interdependence in the technical sense. This does not include mutual trust—which, as in the case of the leadership, has had its effect on the appraisal process.

Organizational Aspects

These include the infrastructure of the group at all levels. It includes the logistic system, maintenance, and intelligence systems. It also includes the ground rules and regulations, military code, discipline, and routines that form the guidelines for general behavior. These determine the weapons that are preferentially used in given circumstances, the attitude to POWs, the communication and control systems, as well as the command independence at various levels of the total organization.

REAPPRAISAL

The interaction of the combat potential with the facilities, organization, and social domains results in the actual combat performance. As soon as a response is made, reevaluation of the situation occurs; and the process starts again. This is a continuous feedback loop that requires continuous processing. The danger with such a loop (as with all repetitive processes) is the formation of set. Once a pattern of behavior has been proved to be successful, we require much more data to change it than was required to establish it in the first place. Thus, there is an ever-present danger that the appraisal process will lose its efficacy, and follow the already established pattern; the resultant behavior will be rigid, rather than adapting to new situations. Such rigidity or stability on the technical level may have dire consequences; but on the psychological level, it may prove of some benefit: A single negative incident will not necessarily lead to loss of trust in a CO or peers; a single failure need not lead to loss of trust in self. If, however, such psychological rigidity persists in spite of evidence that should affect the appraisal system—as, for example, when an attitude toward the despised enemy should change with new information about his mounting skills—outcomes such as the Yom Kippur War or Pearl Harbor might be the result.

4

What Is Aggression?

"He is behaving rather aggressively" could describe—at least according to the research literature on aggression—such behavior as awarding another low scores on a test; imagining stories that are considered aggressive; delivering electric shocks; successfully remembering stories that are supposed to be aggressive; or the rate of popping balloons, of thumping dolls, or of preventing others from going to sleep. In daily life, this list is extended to types of gestures that, according to a specific group, may be aggressive (for example, the inverted versus the upright V-sign); different ways of expressing political aims; threats; driving speed; as well as to striving after a goal; wanting to answer most of the questions in the classroom; refusing to cooperate; or being determined. In fact, the list can be endless: It can be made to include any act of which we do not approve or are afraid—at least at a given time and setting. I shall attempt to offer a framework for the description of aggression to which the many and diverse approaches can be related.

Ashley Montagu, in his book *The Nature of Human Aggression* (1976), argues strongly (some might even say: very aggressively) the case for the innate nonaggressiveness of human nature. He describes the killing of one member of a small tribe by another in an intertribal conflict as nonaggressive, because killing such as this involves only small numbers and primitive weapons. Only when sufficient numbers are involved (10? 100? 1000?) and sufficiently sophisticated means used (crossbow? rifle? bomb?) can the mutual killing be described as aggressive. Thus, aggression seems to become a matter of quantity, rather than quality. The general who encourages his soldiers to attack, hit, and rout the enemy will be unlikely to be described as "aggressive" by his men, but such saber rattling might well be described and perceived as very aggressive by the opposition. The same act and the same words can be described as aggressive or nonaggressive, according to the context in which they appear and according to the point of view of the actors involved. Further—as Feshbach (1978) points out—the same stimulus, depending on context, can inhibit or facilitate aggression. "Truth is in the eye of the beholder"—a motto that will persist throughout this book—is the guideline for following discussion.

AGGRESSION IN THE EYE OF THE BEHOLDER

It is not to the objective facts of the concrete universe that we react, but rather to our own, highly idiosyncratic perception of the universe. "No action can be identified as aggressive or violent without taking into account the value system of the *observer*" (my italics): So say Tedeschi, Smith, and Brown (1974), who further suggest rules by which an observer will label certain behavior as aggressive. According to their way of describing aggression, it does not matter how the opponents in the conflict perceive or label the action: Aggression is in the eye of the observer. Behavior is labeled aggressive when an observer perceives it as:

1) imposing constraint on another's behavioral alternatives or expected outcomes;
2) detrimental (or assumed to be detrimental) to the target person;
3) antinormative, unprovoked, illegitimate, or disproportional (or considered to be).

It could thus occur that an observer will label behavior as aggressive because he considers it antinormative or unprovoked, while the aggressor considers the action fully justified and appropriate and even the person who is the target of aggression accepts the action as legitimate, appropriate, and nonaggressive. A parent firmly telling off her child who is fully aware of his misdeed might well be described as aggressive by an observer who has one set of values (as in Sweden, where such telling off might even be considered in violation of a very loose law prohibiting violence against children), while another observer relating to other norms would not think of it as aggression, at all. Nor would the actors involved—if this were to occur, for example, in England—consider that any aggression had taken place. A slap to a naughty child might not be labeled as aggressive in one country and might lead to legal action against the parent in another.

What an observer considers to be "provocation" might well differ from what those engaged in the conflict might consider it to be. How many marital and international conflicts have started because of little gestures that no observer in his right mind would consider provocation. Nor can the same act or gesture be considered provocation under all circumstances. A hand placed on the shoulder of a girl as a friendly gesture might well be accepted as such in one setting, or one country, or from one person; while it would create a legitimate *causus belli*—even excusing murder—when made by another, in another country or setting. Tedeschi, Smith, and Brown (1974) criticize much of the current research on aggression because it does not establish the actor's or aggressor's reason for performing in a way considered aggressive. However, even in their own definition of aggression, they do not include the aggressor's reason or aim for behaving as such. They focus on the observer's interpretation of the aggressor's aim, but do not take into consideration the aggressor's reason. Thus, it could occur that an act that is neither felt nor perceived as aggressive by either of the actors involved in an apparent conflict will be labeled as aggressive by an observer.

The observer may be simply misinformed—as one would be who chances upon a scene in which one person is seen to slice the throat of another, and who concludes that an aggressive act has taken place. What he does not know is that, actually, a tracheotomy is being carried out to clear the second person's airways in order to save his life. This may be thought to be a farfetched example, but it is actually fetched from real life: A medical orderly was shot at during action in the field in Israel, because he was apparently intent on slicing a soldier's throat. Under the battle conditions, the orderly's uniform was not clearly seen as friendly; the observer had no doubt as to the aggressive meaning of the act he was observing. Misinterpretation might also depend on the viewpoint and prejudices of the observer. This has often occurred in descriptions of police conflicts with demonstrators or rioters. (Even the word "rioter" is in the eye of the beholder.) When such a conflict was described by those identifying with the students or demonstrators, it was described as violent and brutal. The same scene described by those identifying with the establishment was labeled as restrained and controlled.

WAYS OF AGGRESSION

Some of the behavior that is labeled aggressive by Tedeschi, Smith, and Brown (1974) would not be considered so by Baron (1977), for whom:

aggression is any form of behavior directed towards the goal of harming or injuring another living being who is motivated to avoid such treatment.

Baron focuses on the *goal* of the aggressor's behavior, not on the way his behavior is perceived by others. However, aggressive behavior is here restricted to that aimed to damage or hurt. In their categorization, Tedeschi and co-workers included all behavior that is aimed at either damaging, influencing, controlling, or shaping the opponent's behavior. Baron, however, does not include threats as an aggressive act if their purpose is to deter another, but such threats will be classified as aggressive if aimed at frightening and thus damaging. Aggression is not restricted to physical acts. Causing a person to lose face, causing social damage, degrading him—that is, causing psychological damage—or causing physical damage are all considered aggressive acts if they are aimed to damage rather than to control or coerce.

A mapping of the possible types of aggression has been made by Buss (1961). This is based on three dimensions, each of which is dichotomized:

1. physical/verbal—the means
2. active/passive—the mode
3. direct/indirect—the form

These three dimensions—or, in terms of facet theory and the mapping-sentence construction discussed previously, these three facets and their six elements—make it possible to form eight profiles, each describing a different type of aggression. Table 4.1 below shows how Buss described and exemplified these. The schema describes different types of aggressive behavior. Since aggressive behavior is considered by all theorists as a way of responding to internal or external needs or stimuli, it appears to me justified to refer to the different types of aggression as *strategies of aggression*. Which conditions or circumstances determine which strategy of aggression is the topic of this chapter's discussion. The term "strategy" is used to emphasize that there are many ways of acting aggressively and that these ways are—at least according to some models—a function of the organism's needs. Thus, different strategies might be deployed under different circumstances. An alternative way to categorize the strategies of aggression—a way that is hoped to be more descriptive of all the factors involved—will be offered in the next chapter.

In terms of the strategies described by Buss, Baron's approach excludes behavior that is not aimed at injuring another. Thus, a verbal-active-direct strategy describing a threat—or a physical-active-indirect strategy describing the buildup of a large nuclear weapon stockpile to act as a deterrent—would not be considered aggressive by Baron, while considered aggressive by Tedeschi and co-workers (provided that the observer detected the intent behind these acts). One person might use a verbal-passive-indirect strategy to injure another, while the same person uses a physical-active-direct strategy against another opponent—or indeed the same opponent at a different time: All of which will be described as "aggressive behavior," without differentiation.

A suggestion that one should look at aggression in terms of the intention behind it—rather than in terms of the strategy used for it—comes from

Table 4.1
The Different Types or Categories of Agression Proposed by Buss

Type of aggression	Examples
Physical-active-direct	Stabbing, punching, or shooting another person
Physical-active-indirect	Setting a booby trap for another person; hiring an assassin to kill an enemy
Physical-passive-direct	Physically preventing another person from obtaining a desired goal or performing a desired act (as in a sit-in demonstration)
Physical-passive-indirect	Refusing to perform necessary tasks (as in refusal to move during a sit-in)
Verbal-active-direct	Insulting or derogating another person
Verbal-active-indirect	Spreading malicious rumors or gossip about another individual
Verbal-passive-direct	Refusing to speak to another person, to answer questions, and so on
Verbal-passive-indirect	Failing to make specific verbal comments (as in failing to speak up in another person's defense when he or she is unfairly criticized)

Source: Buss (1961). Modified by Baron (1977).

Zillman (1979). He dichotomizes aggression into two categories: (1) annoyance motivated, which is aimed at reduction or removal of noxious conditions—whether within oneself (such as anger or fear) or external (such as threat or force); and (2) incentive motivated, which is aimed at attaining goals—whether those of intrinsic value (such as feelings of power and superiority—or extrinsic value (such as territorial or monetary gain). The kind of aggression aimed at an incentive gain would not be included in Baron's model, unless the opponent were to be injured in the process of attaining the gain. For Baron, the conflict is always a zero-sum game: One player's gain must always mean the other player's loss. Rappaport (1964) describes the essence of a zero-sum game as that game in which, if one player can do something to hurt another, he will do so. According to Zillman's concept, both partners in conflict might feel they have gained, and yet their behavior could be described as aggressive. Their relationship is a nonzero-sum game.

So far, two major aspects of aggression have been discussed: (1) the means involved, and (2) the purpose or aim—whether conscious or unconscious—of the aggressive act. As we shall soon see, for some theorists, the gain or purpose of the aggressive act is always unconscious; for others, it is conscious. But whichever approach one chooses, the act of aggression is seen to fulfill a need of the organism; thus, I shall use the term *payoff* rather than "aim" or "purpose" to describe the expected gain from the aggressive act—whatever its origins may be. Later in this chapter, I offer a way of describing aggression so as to interrelate both its form and the purpose behind it.

INDIVIDUAL DIFFERENCES IN AGGRESSION: INVOLVEMENT

Individuals (and individual nations) can have different dispositions toward aggression. Individuals with a history of violent behavior were found to be more likely to volunteer for active service and were also found to be those who engage in "unnecessary violence" during war (Yager 1975). Perhaps those soldiers who behave in a way acceptable by the codes of the war (the acceptable codes may well change from war to war) exhibit what Fox (1974) calls "adaptive aggression," while those who behave in a antinormative way exhibit "hostile aggression." The payoff for adaptive aggression is the success of the individual in handling the enemy. Such handling can be achieved through destruction of the enemy—but equally well through the enemy running away, submitting, or surrendering. The aim is control of the enemy, rather than his destruction. The violent, unnecessarily cruel soldier—acting not only against the formal codes of the war, but also against the norms of his society—is the one who seeks in the military a convenient framework for the expression of his hostile, aggressive needs. For such a soldier, the payoff for his aggressive act is the enemy's destruction—hurt and damage to the other. This is the type of soldier who seeks vengeance, whether the need comes as a result of deep inner needs—which might have no bearing on the issues of the war—or as a result of real trauma—such as the loss of a close friend.

I have observed—as have others—that behavior contrary to the rules of war was much more often exhibited by soldiers of the support forces who came to the battle scene after the real conflicts were over, than by the front-line soldiers. The former are much more often responsible for rape, plunder, and killing of prisoners or even civilians. A very easy and convenient explanation for this phenomenon is that the support troops have generally lower social, economic, and educational standards—the higher quality soldiers being selected for the front-line units. The implicit assumption behind such an explanation is that the higher quality troops have the potential for more socialized behavior—for fitting within the expected normative guidelines. Karsten (1978) showed that more cruelty was exhibited by U.S. troops of the lower social classes than by those from other groups. Tempting as such an explanation may be for making sense and structuring our understanding of such behavior, the real explanation might well lie in the situation, rather than in the actors involved. The front-line soldier has a clear task—to win, by whatever means possible. The backup soldier has a supportive task toward his own troops—but no clear payoff, as far as relationship with the enemy is concerned.

The chance for an impromptu investigation of this presented itself on a moonless night, while an infantry force of regimental strength was waiting in the inky pools of total darkness cast by the tall oak trees of the woods at the foot of the Golan Heights. The troops were tense and restless—the tension clear in their whispered voices. The regiment was about to mount an attack against the threatening tower of the Syrian stronghold, which overlooked the fertile valley in the north of Israel. Such a waiting time is the best chance for the psychologist. The soldiers welcome the opportunity to divert their attention from the coming battle; and they also enjoy feeling superior—because they are seasoned combat soldiers—to the psychologist, who is not really one of them. The psychologist (who is more scared than the others) finds great relief in being able to carry out a scientific investigation that will both take his mind off the imminent threat and justify his place among these troops. In a very typical symptom of such high tension, even the soldiers who did not want to talk to each other were only too keen to talk to the psychologist.

So I went from squad to squad, and from platoon to platoon—asking "What do you hope for most as the outcome of this operation?" (phrased differently for different soldiers according to background, education, and so forth). They were all aware that this was going to be a very difficult and hazardous operation. The strategic advantage was on the side of the Syrians, and their attitude toward the Syrians involved more fear and hate than toward the Egyptians or Jordanians. It was clear that the battle ahead might result in heavy losses, and even its final outcome was not at all certain. I cannot report my findings—the distribution of responses—in the acceptable "scientific" way, because I myself was too preoccupied and concerned about the immediate future, and this investigation was carried out as much for my own sake as for any report that would eventually be written.

But a rough description of the responses that I received—which amazed me very much at the time— is justified. I found that about 20 percent replied that, first and foremost, they hoped to return safely. Forty percent stated that their main hope was to gain control of the hill—to rout the Syrians, according to the stated aim of the operation. For about 25 percent, the main hope was to bring relief to the villages covered by the Syrian's guns; and only about 15 percent stated that they hoped to kill, revenge, or destroy the enemy. It became very clear that, for the overwhelming majority, the hope for outcome of the operation was *control* of the enemy, while only 15 percent had the primary aim of *damaging* him. On this occasion, I did not carry out a similar investigation with the support troops; but I formed a strong impression—based on their behavior—that their primary aim was not to control the enemy. By the time the support troops arrived, the enemy was in fact totally—or very nearly—under control, and their real task was the logistic support of the front-line troops. For these soldiers, the enemy was a rather abstract concept—symbolized by the smoking skeletons of tanks, the abandoned army camps, and the sparse and scared civilian population. Their only direct contact with the enemy was either with his wounded in the field hospital or with the prisoners of war safely gathered in prison camps. For the support troops, the enemy offered no real direct threat, but only a threat vicariously felt. Therefore, it was interesting to compare their much more aggressive behavior toward the enemy and their expressed aggressive attitude toward him with that exhibited by the troops who were actually engaged in combat.

An investigation carried out under much more controlled conditions during and immediately after battle used a questionnaire that inquired into the attitude toward the enemy on three dimensions: hate, fear, and respect. Soldiers were asked to rank their answers on a five-point scale (from "very much" to "very little") to the following questions:

1. How much hate do you feel toward the Egyptians/Syrians/Jordanians?

2. How much do you fear these three armies?

3. How much do you respect these three armies?

This questionnaire was administered to infantry and armored divisions on all three fronts—Golan (facing the Syrians); West Bank (facing the Jordanians); and Sinai (facing the Egyptians)—and was given to both combat and support troops. The results are presented in Table 4.2.

A clear pattern emerges. In both groups, there is a consistent order in which fear and hate ranks: Syria, Egypt, Jordan; and respect ranks: Jordan, Syria, Egypt. Comparing the two groups, it is found that the support troops in all cases have significantly greater hate—and lower fear and respect—than the combat groups.

As should be clear from Table 4.2, the rank order for each aspect and toward each country is similar for the support and combat troops. The two groups perceive the relation between the countries in a similar way. But the support troops express more hate toward all enemies than do the combat troops—regardless of the battlefront on which they served. At the same time, the support troops also express less respect and fear toward all enemies. There are many other differences of interest in this data; these will be taken up later. For the present discussion, it is important to note that the support troops express more hate and less respect for an enemy that they do not have to face. Their expression of less fear may reflect the reality of the situation—the fact that they are indeed in less danger from the enemy—but could equally be an indication of the denial of fear, because they feel that they have neither the technical nor emotional equipment for handling direct

Table 4.2

Attitudes toward the Enemy Shown by Israeli Combat and Support Troops on Three Fronts

	Combat troops (N = 1070)			Support troops (N = 913)		
	Syria	*Egypt*	*Jordan*	*Syria*	*Egypt*	*Jordan*
Hate	3.9	2.9	2.2	4.5	3.7	3.0
Fear	3.5	2.9	2.0	2.7	2.1	1.3
Respect	4.0	3.5	4.2	3.2	2.8	3.4

Source: IDF, Unit of Military Psychology, unpublished report, 1972.

Note: The questionnaire was so scored that 1 was given for the least extreme attitude, while 5 was given to the most extreme attitude. All differences in the hate dimension are significant at the .05 level (two-tailed test $t = 1.96$). All differences in the fear dimension are significant at the .05 level. The only significant differences in the respect dimension are between Egypt and Jordan in both groups.

combat with the enemy. If the latter explanation is accepted, one would expect that the support troops will behave in such a way as to counteract the fear and frustration toward the enemy by increased aggressive behavior; while, if the expression of less fear is indeed a true representation of their evaluation of the state of affairs, they should also have less need for aggressive behavior than the combat troops.

Evidence from the battlefield is clear: Support troops engage in more unjustified violence than combat troops. Plundering, cruelty to civilians, and even the murder of prisoners—whether one looks at the cases court-marshaled and brought to public attention or at those not officially noted—occur markedly more often among support troops than among combat troops. Cases of breaking the military code (which, in Israel, is called "purity of arms") both on the formal, legal and the informal, normative levels, are many times higher for support troops. I am tempted to favorably compare—unreliable as such a comparison may be—the overall low rate of such infringements by Israeli troops with those occurring in some other armies. But from the point of view of the psychological processes involved, the comparison should be made from the baseline of each army's and country's norms, rather than in absolute terms. This problem became more acute during the 1982 Lebanon War and will be discussed in Chapter 10. Similar evidence for the more aggressive behavior by noncombatant troops in Vietnam, as well as by German troops in the Soviet Union during World War II, is reported by Karsten (1978).

It has often been pointed out that aggression toward a stranger is much more extensive than toward members of the group. The less similar the outsider is to the group, the stronger is the aggression toward him. As Stouffer et al. (1949) have shown in their study of the U.S. soldier during World War II, hate toward the Japanese was markedly more than toward the Germans or Italians. Would the atomic bomb have been used against the Germans, if conditions had warranted it? Would the murder of millions of Jews by the Germans, the genocide in Biafra, or the massacres in Cambodia have been ignored for so long, if the victims had not been perceived as alien, different, and far removed?

Would a similar massacre of the Swedes or Dutch be glossed over? The nearer and more similar the victim of aggression is, the more we can identify with him, the more involved we are, and the less aggressive will be our behavior toward him. Miron and Goldstein (1979) report that the risk of death for a kidnap victim is much greater if the victim is hooded. They recommend establishing rapport with the kidnapper in order to reduce risk of harm. Israelis generally perceive the Syrians as more different and alien than either the Jordanians or the Egyptians—thus increasing the likelihood of more agressive behavior toward the Syrians. On the other hand, Storr (1968) points out that deviant behavior by a member of our own group is perceived as more disturbing and produces stronger retaliation than that of others with whom we are less involved. One has but to look at the intensity of aggression between different Christian factions in Europe in the past and in Ireland and Lebanon today—or the conflict between Leninist, Maoist, and Trotskyist communists—to realize that closeness or similarity is no guarantee of nonaggressive behavior. (In all fairness, I must admit that this similarity is in the eye of the beholder, while those concerned might feel very dissimilar to each other.) Yet one might also wonder if such feelings of alienation among people who share a great deal is not an induced dissimilarity, developed in order to sharpen and clarify boundaries that were initially very indistinct. The feeling that "there, but for the grace of God, go I"—the feeling that one might very easily behave in a similar manner to that of the deviant—might well be the case for strong aggressive behavior aimed to remove such a similar threat, so as to clarify the difference and set the boundary between "us" and the deviant. If we cannot identify with the other (which would reduce aggression), we must increase our difference (which will increase aggression). The clarity of the structure must be maintained at all times—and all costs.

To compound the problem, in Israel at that time, the support troops had a much higher proportion of soldiers who originated (first or second generation) in the Islamic countries than the combat troops did. Their mother tongue was often Arabic, and their social norms were often more similar to those of the Arab countries than to European norms. One of the most serious problems in Israel is the potential alienation and polarization between the attitudes and norms of Jews originating from the Islamic countries and those from Western cultures. The former are often labeled "Arab-like" by Jews originating from the West (who are of higher status); and, more importantly they often perceive themselves to be more similar to the Arabs than to Western Jews. This uncomfortable feeling of similarity has to be countered by setting boundaries that will allow a clearer perception of belonging to the more Western, high-status group.

It is the very same Jews of Eastern origin—who are psychologically and culturally nearer to the enemy—who expressed the most hate and the least respect toward him. Comparing the "hate" score of soldiers born in Islamic countries or to parents from such countries with the "hate" score of soldiers born in Western countries or to parents from these countries shows the distribution shown in Table 4.3. The differences are similar to—but more extreme than—those shown between the front-line and support troops reported in Table 4.2, and tend to support the fact that the ethnic composition differences between the troops contribute to their different behaviors.

It is interesting to note that soldiers born in Israel and to parents who were born in Israel show a "hate" score somewhat higher than the Western-born Jews, but by far lower than the scores of Jews from Islamic countries. Their scores are 4.0, 2.9, and 2.1 for Syria, Egypt, and Jordan, respectively ($N = 273$).

This difference in hate toward the enemy could be explained by the need of the Eastern Jews to form a more explicit differentiation or structure—to establish a clear and coherent difference between them and the enemy. This need is much less in the "Western" Jews, who have a much clearer perceived difference between themselves and the Arabs. The need for such differentiation—for a clear self-concept formation—is one that will lead to aggressive behavior. Magnanimity and tolerance can only be achieved from the position of perceived superiority; destruction and damage to the other must be

Table 4.3
Comparison of "Hate" Scores of Israeli Soldiers from Islamic and Western Countries (1973)

	Syria	Egypt	Jordan
Islamic ($N = 1000$)	4.7	4.0	3.3
Western ($N = 1000$)	3.8	2.7	2.0

Note: All differences are significant at the .05 level (two-tailed).

Source: IDF, Unit of Military Psychology, unpublished report, 1972.

the means by which self-realization can be attained when there is but a poor border between the groups concerned. The one who has a secure base can afford to achieve his aims by controlling the opponent, while the one who is insecure in his base must achieve his aim by destroying the opponent.

A factor that might also contribute to the greater hate among the Eastern Jews is learning. They or their parents actually suffered under Arab rule, while none of the Western Jews suffered directly from the Arabs. One might expect the latter to behave more aggressively in a fight with Germans—for example—than would the former. But since not in all of the Islamic countries did Jews suffer under Arab rule—nor was such suffering extreme in most cases—this is probably just a factor of marginal importance.

To summarize: All troops engaged in a war must exhibit aggressive behavior, but their strategies differ to fit with their ultimate aim. The combat soldier aims to win; and it does not matter whether victory is attained through capturing, routing, or killing. An enemy's surrender is as welcome (for some, even more so) than his death. The support troops have no need to win; by the time they arrive, the battle has generally been won. Their aggression is based on attitudes and feelings, rather than on concrete results that must be attained. The enemy is already under control, but the trooper has to discharge his aggression. He must do so by "putting the enemy in his place"—vicariously, at least—by destructive behavior, plunder, rape, and murder.

As is the case in Israel, this can be further compounded by the need to differentiate oneself from the enemy. It is a remarkable tribute to the effect of the prevalent social norms in Israel that such aggressive behavior rarely occurs. In Chapter 10 this issue will be viewed in the somewhat different perspective of the 1982 Lebanon War.

A practical implication of all this is that the role of the support troops who come after the battle has been fought should not be structured only in support terms (such as supply, clearance, and maintenance), but should include enemy-oriented tasks that allow them to formally control the enemy. The tendency is to leave the more sensitive tasks—such as contact with the enemy and the enemy's civilians—to the combat troops, because they are seen as more reliable and more likely to behave in a becoming manner; but delegation of such tasks to the support troops is the way to allow them to adopt controlled and aimed aggression, instead of destructive aggression.

INDIVIDUAL DIFFERENCES IN AGGRESSION: RESPONSIBILITY

The idea of substituting a milder form or a more restricted form of aggression for total war is not new. In the less civilized times of the Middle Ages, conflicts between nations were sometimes settled by combat between their representing knights. This, in turn, must have been a development of the earlier mode of settling conflicts in which the leader of a group fought the opposing leader, and the outcome determined the outcome of the total conflict. How tempting it is to imagine Reagan and Gorbachev or Khomeini and Hussein locked in combat. How many wars would not have taken place, if those deciding to go to war had to do the fighting themselves? Such speculation is not just mere fancy; Evidence shows quite clearly that the farther the initiator of aggression is from the outcome of his decision, the more aggressively he will act. A person who feels directly responsible for the outcome of his decisions and has to immediately face the consequences of his acts is always much more reticent to make a decision than if there is a long chain of events between him and the final results. Escalation of aggression can be predicted as a result of the alienation between the aggressor and the target of aggression. The same principle that predicts greater aggression toward the outsider who is more alien also predicts greater aggression toward the person who is farther away. Distance is often increased by the chain of command and by delegating responsibility, but it can be equally increased by absolving from responsibility. Dramatic experiments by Milgram (1963; 1974) showed that ordinary people, when given an order to administer electric shocks to others—to strangers toward whom they had no special feelings—were capable of very aggressive behavior indeed. When absolved from responsibility for their acts, people are potentially much more aggressive. War is one of the most obvious cases, where soldiers have to obey orders and there is explicit legitimization of aggression—both according to the social norms and as a consequence of the direct orders received. On the other hand, there is evidence (Kilham and Mann 1974) that people are less aggressive (deliver less shocks) despite direct orders to do so, if they have to deliver the shock directly rather than through an intermediary.

Marshall (1947) reports that only about a third of the soldiers in World War II shot at the enemy; and while others (see Keegan 1976) report a larger proportion, it is still clear that many soldiers do not shoot directly at the enemy. Many reasons are given; one of them—which, oddly enough, is not often discussed—may be the reluctance of the individual to act in a direct aggressive way.

INDIVIDUAL DIFFERENCES IN AGGRESSSION: POTENTIAL

While examining volunteers for commando units, I asked candidates if they were willing to become snipers—a task that clearly demands direct aggression. Several factors differentiated those who were willing to become snipers from others, but the most pertinent difference lay in their potential aggression. This potential was measured by means of their responses to the TAT—a test in which somewhat ambiguous pictures are presented, and the subject is asked to tell a story about the picture as he perceives it. The underlying hypothesis behind this test (as in all projective tests) is once again that "truth is in the eye of the beholder": those who interpret the picture as portraying an aggressive situation (for example, two people fighting each other) have a more aggressive disposition and are more inclined to appraise situations as requiring an aggressive response, than those who will perceive the picture as nonaggressive (for example, one person supporting another).

Members of the group that had volunteered to be snipers ($N = 187$)—those who were willing to act aggressively and directly against the enemy—were found to have a significantly greater tendency (Mean aggressive score of 15.9, SD 2.8, as compared with Mean 8.9, SD 2.1; $Z = 2.0$, $P = .05$) to interpret the pictures aggressively.

One can wonder if the expression of aggressive fantasy is a reflection of the potential for actual aggressive behavior, whether those who had or expressed more aggressive thoughts would indeed be capable of more aggressive acts. However, the fact remains that those who expressed more agressive fantasy were willing to volunteer for the more aggressive tasks. The aggressive fantasy stimulated by the TAT pictures is not directed at any specific person and cannot be a response to anger or frustration caused by a specific person portrayed in the picture; it must indeed be a reflection of an aggressive potential, a drive, or a state of mind of the individual. The theories we have discussed would predict that such a person would react more aggressively to all circumstances—at least in the presence of an aggressive cue or legitimization for an aggressive act.

Another investigation which was carried out on Israeli youth just before their enlistment (Shalit 1970), shows that aggressive fantasy—as reflected in the content of TAT stories—is reduced by vicarious participation in aggression. It was found that the aggressive fantasy of youth enlisting shortly before the outbreak of the 1967 war was higher than those enlisting a year later—after the war—and that it rose again to its initial level in those enlisting two years later. The Six Day War created very intense involvement for all the population of Israel—being perceived as a very intense and immediate threat to its very existence. There cannot be any doubt that, for these 17-18-year-old-boys—although they did not actively participate in the hostilities—the war caused a very real—if vicarious—participation and identification with aggression. The drive reduction theory would predict that such a reduction in aggressive fantasy would be associated with reduction in aggressive behavior (see Feshbach 1956), thus termination of hostilities should reduce the aggressive fantasy. But such a reduction in aggressive fantasy may also be a result of a reduction in the perception of threat, as experienced after the overwhelming victory in that war. That the perception of threat increases the content of agressive fantasy has been shown by Bourne and Coli (1968) in soldiers under threat of attack; thus, the reverse process is also probable.

In Israel at that same time, a change in the aggressive fantasy level, which is viewed by some (see Green and Berkowitz 1967) as a change in arousal or readiness for potential for action, occurred—on the average—in the whole population tested. Thus, it seems reasonable to assume that the rank order of individuals remains: Those who were previously the ones with the most aggressive score remain in that position even after the overall reduction in the aggressive scores. These individuals will always be the ones who are willing to act most aggressively, relative to the norms of the group.

A certain base level for what is considered legitimate or acceptable aggression must exist in each group at any given time. This "acceptable aggression" may be the insistence on one's rights, the use of angry words, or the use of physical force. These acceptable aggressions are the social norms that differentiate groups or people. Thus, the driver who overtakes, or the person who uses derogatory remarks to another will be perceived as aggressive in Sweden, while it will require much more violent driving or more brutal words to be perceived as aggressive in Israel. Aggression is not to be assessed in absolute terms, but rather in terms of deviation from the norm. The change of aggressive fantasy noted in the study above does not reflect reduction of absolute aggression, but the lowering of the acceptable aggression norms. After the 1967 war, there appeared to be a general lowering of the baseline for aggressive behavior. What was previously perceived as nonaggressive or mildly so, was now perceived as more aggressive. The fact is that Israel was swept by feelings of goodwill and a genuine desire for cessation of hostilities—which, alas, were not reciprocated and did not last long.

Because the Israeli-Arab conflict continued, the level of acceptable aggression rose again; and advocated retaliation toward the enemy—that is, escalation in military responses—clearly indicated that such an increase had occurred. Fluctuations in the level of individual aggression obviously do occur, but a remarkable level of stability can be noted: "Not much lower than the stability typically found in the domain of intelligence testing" (Olweus 1979). Thus, although the group's aggressive level may shift, individuals seem to retain their relative position.

Like most relationships affecting human behavior—whether between motivation and learning, stress and performance, or vigilance and perception—the relationship between aggression and adjustment appears to take the form of an inverted U-curve. Robinson (1971) concludes that too much aggression in an individual (relative to the society's norms) will lead to crimes of violence, tragedies, and nonproductivity. On the other hand, too little aggression (again compared to the norms of the group to which the individual belongs) will lead to poor adjustment—both on the personal and interpersonal level—through the inability to achieve dominance or control.

The presence of acquired or normative strategies of aggression will ease their deployment. Like with all other situations that require problem-solving behavior, one tends to approach a new problem by utilizing the skills with which one is most familiar. So, with aggressive behavior—which is aimed at solving a problem (internal: the need for drive reduction; or external: the need to counter frustration)—we adopt the mode of response with which we are most familiar or the most acceptable one from the normative point of view.

USES OF AGGRESSION

Much in the same way that it is possible to grade intensity of aggression by the strategy used, one cannot grade intensity of frustration by the means deployed when responding to it. Harsh words or the spreading of nasty rumors might well be perceived as more aggressive or more frustrating than a slap in the face. Escalation of aggression or of its frustrating antecedents can occur by intensifying a particular strategy used, such as switching from mild swearing to vicious slander or from mild shoving to a knife attack. But escalation can also occur by switching from one strategy to another—from verbal to physical, or from passive to active. When frustration of sufficient intensity occurs, it leads to a response. The initial level of the aggressive response may well depend on past experience, habits, and social norms. If the aggressive strategy fails to produce the desired effect (to control or destroy the frustrator), escalation of the aggressive response—either by intensifying the previous strategy or by changing strategy—will occur. The choice of the strategy initially deployed—as well as its intensity—is probably guided by the presence of an aggressive cue. Mild frustration will lead to an aggressive response earlier when in the presence of information indicating what the approved strategy is. Similarly, aggression that does not stem from frustration but from the need to dominate or to establish structure will preferentially take the form of the strategy suggested by an aggressive cue—whether in form of an instrument or indicated by social norms. In a society in which aggression is predominantly verbal, physical aggressive strategies are less likely to be initially deployed; while, in a group in which physical strategies are predominant, an individual is less likely to utilize verbal aggression.

Because nations have a need to dominate one another, they behave—according to Lorenz (1966)—in an aggressive way toward each other. By substituting the geopolitical sphere of domination for that of the sports field, Lorenz believes that one can reduce the aggression between nations. The need for domination seems to be perceived as an undifferentiated drive—the actual area in which it is achieved is of no importance.

As long as the individual or even the group feel that they dominate in one critical aspect, this is sufficient to reduce the need to dominate in all others. Montagu (1976) quotes an investigation by Sites, who compared the war history of different countries with their preoccupation with aggressive sports. He found that the countries that had a more aggressive, warlike history favored more—not less—the aggressive, competitive sports. Thus, the investigator draws the conclusion that aggressive sports do not successfully divert aggressive behavior from the international sphere, and that dominating in sports will not reduce international aggression—as Lorenz had suggested.

The purpose and aim of the sporting competition is to win—to be better than the opponent. The aim of wars is to win by damaging—or at least controlling—the opposition. The aims of war are to make the enemy obey orders, or withdraw—or, at the very least, to prevent him from acting contrary to one's wishes. In sports, the aim is to show how much better one is. In fact, the better the opponent over whom victory is gained, the higher the value of the victory. War's payoff is always the enemy's loss; the payoff in sports is always the challenger's gain.

The aims of aggression used in war and aggression used in sports are different; it is therefore not surprising that they cannot be substituted for one another. It is not sufficient to find a common denominator between the two forms of aggression—the "need to dominate." One has to differentiate between the different payoffs for that domination. "Dominate" here describes means rather than an end; and these means can be differentiated into physical and verbal means, and into direct and indirect means. This differentiation will be further discussed later; but the main point is that domination in any form is one of the possible aggressive strategies aimed either at controlling or at damaging the opponent.

SUMMARY

Aggression is viewed as the force that an individual or a group deploy to establish their self-perception in relation to a specific environment seen to be threatening their integrity. A further development of this concept will be made in the following chapter.

The stronger the perceived need to establish one's rights or self-perception—physically or psychologically—the greater is the degree of involvement to be expected in pursuing this goal. The very perception of a state in which one feels the need to establish oneself is a potential threat situation; success in coping with it must depend on the effectiveness of the appraisal process.

The second level of the perceptual process depends on the kind and degree of emotional involvement ("Is it relevant? Do I want it?") and committal. The greater the involvement, the greater will be the investment in coping with the problem—and, hence, the aggressive behavior. The aggressive behavior will deploy different strategies depending on its purpose—whether to control or destroy the potential threat—and depending on the norms for the individual's reference group, as well as on his own disposition.

5

Origins of Aggression and Its Evaluation

One should not discuss the payoff for aggression without some analysis of the theories describing the roots of aggression. Very roughly, there seem to be two major viewpoints about the origins of aggression. The first is exemplified by Freud (1933), Lorenz (1966), and Ardrey (1970 a;b), who view aggression as stemming directly from an innate need or drive of the organism. These authors differ in their view of the form that aggression takes, but are united in viewing it as resulting from a basic biological drive or state. The other approach is exemplified by Berkovitz (1974), Feshbach (1970), or Baron (1977), who view aggression as a response to external stimuli or conditions—a response acquired by and essentially related to the stimulus that triggered it.

SELF-PERCEPTION AND INTERNAL DEMANDS

Lorenz and Ardrey describe aggression in terms of its payoff. For both, aggression is behavior aimed at dominating the opponent—their emphasis is on the control aspect of aggressive behavior, rather than on the damage inflicted on the opponent. According to Ardrey, aggression does not necessarily involve physical violence; and much of Lorenz's descriptions of aggressive behavior are devoted to the control of the opponent by means of nonphysical cues. He shows that much physical violence is preferentially avoided, rather than engaged in. Lorenz distinctly states that there is no need for war in men—that there is no innate need to engage in violent behavior—but that there is a clear and innate need to dominate others. (These statements are selectively ignored by Montagu [1976] in his attempt to prove his anti–innate aggression argument.) Only when external conditions prevent or frustrate attempts to gain control or dominate—then and only then—are violent physical strategies of aggression resorted to. In other words, two types of aggressive strategies are available to an individual: The first is an innate and nonviolent strategy aimed at control; and the second is a violent strategy, which might be triggered if the first fails, and might be either innate or acquired. As Desmond Morris says in *The Human Zoo* (1969), "The goal of aggression is domination not distruction, but this goal has been blurred because of a vicious combination of attack remoteness and group cooperation." Later, we shall return to these aggravating factors mentioned by Morris.

In Lorenz's view, the need to dominate is primarily attained through the control of others by establishing self. The focal point is the struggle for territoriality—for establishing clear boundaries between what is "mine" or "me" and what is "his" or "him." Clear labeling is required of both the individual and his standing in the social hierarchy and of the territory possessed by the individual. The aggressive act is aimed at establishing such clear demarcations for oneself, and is not aimed at affecting the other or even placing him in a particular position for its own sake. Thus, there is no attempt to force on another a certain status of territory, but only to clarify one's own standing—a process that might accidentally affect the other. Behavior aimed at eating others is not considered aggressive; and one could argue that this process is also aimed at establishing self, rather than at dominating the other (who is just accidentally chewed up). This rosy picture does not seem universally true. In a fascinating account, Kruck (1972) describes some scenes from the animal kingdom, apparently showing that senseless and wanton killing does occur—for instance, the slaughter of gazelles by hyenas, in quantities way beyond their need or capacity to eat; or the destruction of gulls which could not fly in a stormy night and thus were "sitting ducks" for foxes which proceeded to kill them beyond any possible need for food. These types of reports—as well as observation of human behavior—tend to throw doubt on the model that claims aggression to have only the aim of domination or food. However, it should be noted that such senseless violence in the animal world—as well as most of the violence in the human domain—is shown by groups, rather than by individuals. This problem— like others before it—will be returned to later in this chapter.

Let us return now to Lorenz's concept in which the payoff for aggression is the establishment of clear boundaries that allow physical and social differentiation between the individual and his environment. This is closely reminiscent of the importance in differentiation of the individual as expounded by Witkin et al. (1962; 1979). The individual who has a clearer differentiation—who has a better articulation of himself and of himself in relation to the environment—can also cope better with all internal and external stresses, can function better, and is healthier. In a very similar vein, we can view research on the concept of the strength of body image (see Fisher and Cleveland 1968), showing that those individuals who have a stronger and more distinct image of their body boundary—who have a clearer demarcation between the "me" and "out there"—are those who function best psychologically, socially, and even physically. Thus, the need to differentiate oneself—to establish the relationship of the individual to the system in which he perceives himself to belong—is a primary need, for the fulfillment of which aggression may be used. Or aggression will be used whenever a threat to one's integrity (physical, social, or psychological) is perceived.

Somewhat more diffusely, Ardrey suggests that aggression stems from our basic need to seek self-fulfillment—to attain a state of satisfaction that "will inform us why we are born" (1970a). According to Ardrey, individuals clash because they try to establish themselves to attain fulfillment—not for social or physical or other (external) rewards. To me, this appears another way of describing the payoff for aggression in terms of clear differentiation and boundary formation by the individual within himself and toward his environment. The primary need is to obtain a clear picture of who we are and where we stand, as well as our relation to others. In fact, this is the basic perceptual requirement—structure appraisal.

Aggressive behavior is not to be viewed as irrational behavior—as aggression for its own sake. Aggression reflects purposive behavior aimed at attaining a goal, of which one may or may not be aware. Dengerink, Schnedler, and Covery (1978) have shown that, when individuals can avoid or reduce shock to themselves by reducing shock to their opponent, they do so. Then again, if they can reduce shock to themselves by increasing shock to their opponent, they also do so without hesitation. Behavior is rational—even if, according to some, it might be described as selfish.

Feshbach (1970) suggests that inflicting injury on another is not the principal goal of aggression—which is, rather, the production of pain in an opponent in order to restore the aggressor's self-esteem and sense of power. The payoff for aggression is clearly the gain in self-perception; and the need for clear self-perception appears to be innate, even if aggression used to fulfill this need is but one technique with which to attain the goal. The innate need for self-establishment is also proposed by Deci (1975), from a completely different point of view. According to him, there is an innate need for attainment—to establish one's self-perception and the perception of one's relationship to others in a clear and coherent way. Such a drive can be fulfilled by many strategies, from intellectual processes to a generalized drive for achievement. Obviously—at least in some cases—fulfilling the drive for achievement might involve the domination of others, and possibly even their destruction. Such destruction would not be the desired payoff for the behavior—but rather an accident, while pursuing the self-fulfillment goal (which is no comfort to the one so treated). The strategies deployed in attaining self-fulfillment can be either physical or nonphysical. "Man is not so much violent or aggressive by nature [or] exceedingly ambitious, his primary ambition within his group is to assert his self-identity" (Priestland 1974).

All aggressive behavior discussed up to this point has this clear payoff: the structuring of a coherent relationship and differentiation by the individual to his environment, and stems from the organism's inherent need to attain a coherent perception of its interaction with the ecological system in which it finds itself.

For Freud, aggression is not a drive aimed at a payoff that could be described as goal attainment (which, in turn, could be assessed by an achievement of any kind). Aggression (if it is a drive, rather than the outcome of a conflict between two drives—Eros and Thanatos—as appears to be the concept reflected in his later writing—see Freud 1933) is a means of releasing tension, and the direction this takes is of secondary importance. Thanatos—the death wish present in all human beings, which is aimed at termination of life and the dissociation of the individual—is a catabolic process dictating the breakup of the individual. This is the instinct that leads to the destructive type of aggressive behavior—both toward the individual himself (expressed by masochistic behavior), and toward the world in general (expressed as sadistic behavior). In a letter to Einstein in 1932 (quoted by Bramson and Goethals 1964), Freud writes, "War is due to a destructive instinct—instinct aimed at returning things to the inanimate state and which can work both inside and outside the body."

The payoff for the aggressive behavior is a reduction in the tension of internal conflict, but the final outcome of that behavior will be a compound of the losses and gains resulting from the actual aggressive strategies deployed by the individual on himself and his environment. This outcome appears to be dependent on chance factors and the temporary constellations in which the individual finds himself.

EXTERNAL DEMANDS

In the theories discussed above, aggression was viewed as an expression of a state or need within the individual, rather than as a response to external demands. In contrast, one may look at the model of Dollard et al. (1939), which describes aggression as a response to frustration. It is viewed as a potential drive built up within the individual as a response to external forces that prevent him from attaining a desired goal. This drive needs reduction, and such reduction is attained by aggressive behavior. Aggressive behavior can be expressed by a wide range of strategies: from a passive-verbal-indirect strategy such as aggressive fantasy, through mild verbal expressions of annoyance, to the direct-active-physical strategy involved in a barroom fight. Since (according to Dollard et al.) the constrictive impact of environmental conditions—such as punishment or its threat—can affect the expression of aggression but not reduce the basic drives behind it, it can be expected that the strategy of aggression deployed will be adapted to the individual's appraisal of the forces on him. The authors state that the optimal strategy of aggression is the one most directly aimed at the frustrator: Aggressive fantasy about the frustrator will be less effective than an aggressive verbal response, and will also be less effective than a direct physical attack made on him. But we cannot tell whether a direct verbal response will be less effective in reducing the aggressive drive than a direct physical attack aimed directly at the frustrator. Since we are not offered a hypothesis that will further differentiate the efficiency of the strategies used for drive reduction in terms related to their impact on the frustrator, we cannot discuss payoff other than in terms of the strategies' effectiveness in reducing the frustration potential. Thus, the payoff depends primarily on the perceived impact on the aggressor, while the actual consequences to the target of aggression are of but secondary importance. The individual who feels that he has adequately hit back at his frustrator will be equally satisfied whether his victim feels or does not feel hurt by the act. A child hitting the parent who frustrated him does not require the parent to be hurt; a person making derogatory remarks about another may find this sufficient relief of frustration, even if the subject of the remarks remains entirely unaware of them.

Berkowitz and Turner (1974)—further modifying the concept of frustration—view aggression as a response to anger, which may have been aroused by frustration—but not only by it. If occurring in the presence of an aggressive cue, anger—for whatever reason it was evoked—will produce aggression. Aggressive cues are the physical, social, or psychological stimuli indicating that an aggressive strategy may be used. They can take the form of social norms approving aggression, or the presence of a weapon—even if irrelevant to the expected behavior. A rifle lying in the room in which a person—within the framework of a learning experiment—is allowed to administer electric shocks to another will tend to increase the degree of the shocks given (Berkowitz and Le Page 1967). There is no relationship expected between the type of aggressive cue and the aggressive strategy used. However, Berkowitz states that the payoff for the aggression is in harming the subject as a response to his anger-arousing behavior. Unlike Miller's (1948) approach, diversion of aggressive behavior from the frustrator to another object is ineffective, since the actual frustrator has to be harmed in order to achieve anger reduction. Unlike Lorenz's model—which allows for reduction of the drive for aggression by means of controlling and dominating the other—Berkowitz's approach requires damage to the opponent. However, such aggression is not innate; the need to destroy is not the result of a biological drive in the individual. It is a response to anger aroused in him by environmental conditions, such as frustration or fear. In the absence of anger, there would be no aggression. There is no connection between the aggressive strategy deployed and the opponent's behavior or needs; the strategy is not aimed at modifying the opponent's behavior, but at satisfying the aggressor's needs.

LEARNED RESPONSE

Aggression can also be viewed as an acquired behavior, following the same learning laws as other behaviors. According to Bandura (1973), aggression can be learned directly through instrumental learning, and by conditioning; and it can be acquired by social modeling—by following the example set by a person one identifies with—or by the norms of the group. The aims of the aggressive acts, as well as the strategies deployed, are viewed as acquired skills. The payoff for aggression will be the attainment of the goal for which aggression was used, whether the aim is to control or to destroy. Success of the aggression is directly related to its aims, and not—as in some of the other models discussed—in the actual process of aggression. Aggression is defined as behavior that results in personal injury—mental or physical—or destruction of property. However, it requires social judgment to decide whether a specific act that leads to an injury is to be classified as aggressive (as, for example, in the case of a surgical operation). Just as in the theory of Tedeschi, Smith, and Brown (1974), the observer or the social norm is the standard by which the aim behind the act—and, hence, the presence of aggression—is determined.

Baron (1977)—after a comprehensive and impressive analysis of the literature on aggression—concludes that only severe frustration leads to aggression, while mild frustration does not. The effects of mild frustration can be increased when it occurs in association with an aggressive cue; thus, a violent cue may produce aggression, even under conditions of only mild frustration. But what makes for severe or mild frustration? One becomes frustrated when one cannot obtain a desired goal, but the frustration must depend on the nature of the goal, the degree of its attractiveness, and the context in which the situation is set. Being unable to leave camp might be frustrating for the soldier, but it will be more so if he knows that his girlfriend is waiting. If the soldier is prevented from leaving by a hostile MP, this may prove to be more frustrating than if he is stopped by a friend doing guard duty—and even more frustrating when he is stopped because of unexpected operational needs. The same frustrating act—the same constriction of behavior—will be experienced differently not only because of the different importance of the desired goal, but also because of different attitudes toward what stands in the way of attaining the goal ("the enemy"). Further, the same person preventing the attainment of the same goal may be perceived as being more or less frustrating, according to the means he uses to control behavior. Baron shows that verbal interference may cause more frustration, and generate stronger aggression than a physical act aimed at the same construction of behavior.

I suppose that one cannot conclude a discussion on the definition of aggression without reference to the formal dictionary definitions of the term. The British *Chambers Dictionary* defines aggression as "the first act of hostility or injury," while aggression is "making the first attack or prone to do so; offensive as opposed to defensive." In rather similar vein the Swedish *Academy Dictionary* defines aggression as "attack" or "assault" (*angrepp, överfall*). Both these dictionaries—presumably representing the norms and way of perception of their respective cultures—view aggression in wholly negative terms. An aggressive act or behavior is always bad behavior. War is not necessarily aggressive, if one describes the acts or retaliation as self-defense—only "making the first attack" classifies such behavior as aggressive. The American *Standard Dictionary* has a somewhat more liberal viewpoint: "Aggressive implies the disposition to dominate, sometimes by indifference to others' rights but now more often by a determined forceful prosecution of one's end."

In the European views, aggression involves damaging the opponent; according to the U.S. approach, an attempt at domination is sufficient to categorize behavior as aggressive. But even selfish prosecution of one's ends is to be classified as aggression. Thus, to dominate another in business competition, in a knowledge quiz, or the striving for some legitimate aim may well be classified as aggression—and yet not necessarily be perceived as negative. Some such aggression is not only to be tolerated in some circumstances, it might even be viewed as a positive characteristic. Naturally, within the military, aggression will often be viewed as a positive attribute—not only because what the military and neurotics have in common is the need to be aggressive (at least according to Markowitz 1972), but because a positive evaluation of aggressive behavior is likely in any group that approves of competition and the struggle for differential achievements.

ASSESSMENT OF AGGRESSION

Aggression is usually investigated in laboratories and under closely defined conditions. In most of these investigations the subject is allowed only one form or strategy of aggression, such as verbal responses or physical action. The relationship between the cause of aggression and the aggressive behavior is expressed by the degree or intensity of the particular strategy investigated—the intensity of the electric shock administered by the aggressor, or the nastiness of his verbal expressions.

One paradigm, for the assessment of aggression—developed by Buss (1961) and by Berkowitz (1964)—uses a shock machine. The subjects are told (one way or another) that they must give shocks to the target person in order to assist his learning process. These shocks were not administered in reality; but the subject was nonetheless convinced that he was shocking and aggressing against the other, for the latter's own good. From the subject's point of view, the desired outcome—the payoff for the aggression—is in the target person's improvement on a specified task. The aim is to control and direct the target person so that the aggressor will gain credit for a job well done.

Another approach—modifying the shock technique—has been developed by Taylor and Epstein (1967). In this paradigm, two persons partake in some sort of competitive game. The rules of the game demand that the winner shock the loser. However, the shock intensity can be determined by each player. Naturally, giving a strong shock to the opponent (who is—without the subject's knowledge—a collaborator of the experimenter) might entail receiving a stronger shock from him when the tables are turned (again, the schedule of wins and losses has been fixed by the experimenter, without the subject's knowledge). The formal aim of the situation is to win; and one might say that, for some aggressively inclined individuals, the aim might even be to be able to shock the other. But probably the primary aim is to avoid shock, gain relief from shock, or receive a lesser shock (by reducing shock to the other)—rather than to shock the other. The payoff, then, is gain through control of the other.

Wheeler and Gaggiula (1966) looked at verbal, rather than physical, aggression—measuring aggression by the nastiness and bellicosity of expressions used to describe a person who made very offensive statements. They recorded such expressions made following a verbal provocation. The expressions had no consequences, and were effective only in venting the subject's feelings and relieving his anger. The aim of aggression in this case was retaliation toward the offending person—not in order that the aggressor would gain anything (as was the case with the above shock experiments), but rather that the opponent would be hurt in retaliation for his offensive behavior. The payoff was the enemy's loss achieved through damaging him. The aggressor gains relief for his presumed frustration, but such relief is most effective only when the verbal response is made toward the offender—thus, symbolically at least, damaging him.

To my knowledge, there are very few laboratory investigations that do not restrict the strategy of aggression to be used by the aggressor; aggression is then measured in terms of the stipulated strategies. Diener, Dineen and Endersen (1975) permitted the subjects to aggress in any way they wished toward a person who was a passive and accidental recipient of the aggression. No guidance or aim for this act of aggression was given, but the subjects were encouraged to express themselves in any way they wished. Subjects were primed into an aggressive attitude by experiences that occurred before they were allowed to act, but these experiences were unrelated to the subsequent aggressive behavior. The different behaviors—such as hitting a person with sponge balls, or pushing him—were ranked as representing various degrees of aggression, but not categorized into strategies. Nor were the acts discussed in more specific terms, other than their expression of the subject's need for aggression.

It has only been within the framework of field experiments in a real-life setting that subjects were able to respond with any strategy that they saw fit, and that fit the occasion. Harris (1974) and Harris and Samerotte (1975) conducted such an investigation in which collaborators harassed innocent and naive persons who were standing in queues, walking in the street, or shopping—by pushing them, pushing in front of the queue, or annoying them by other means. The reactions of the annoyed victims were recorded and scored according to their aggressive responses—from mild verbal to strong physical responses. Since some subjects deployed several forms of aggressive response, the final "aggression score" was the sum total of all responses given. Equal weight was accorded to all forms of aggressive strategies. One exception to this was the case of a lady who reponded to the provocation of the experimenter by spraying him with an aerosol gun—for this effort, she received an extra point! (Harris and Samerotte 1975). Since no interview with the assaulted took place, one cannot know how they experienced the aggressive act; thus, we cannot relate the strategy used by them to their expected payoff—whether it was to control or to damage the aggressor.

One other investigation (Leyens et al. 1975)—somewhat more controlled, but nevertheless in a real-life setting—aggressive strategies used without constricting the subjects' range of responses. Leyens et al. studied the effect of films òn groups of children in a school, and reported change in aggressive behavior as the impact of aggressive films, dependent on interaction with other factors. Aggressive behavior was taken to be in one or more of these possible categories: physical attack or threat (verbal aggression)—each of which could be other directed, self-directed, or not directed. Other behavior was also recorded—such as active and passive social interaction. All categories of behavior were given equal weights, and recorded on the basis of time sampling. The observed change in behavior as a result of the aggressive films was an increase in aggressive forms of behavior.

Thus, it is seen that measurement of aggression is generally confined to recording a carefully guided, predetermined mode of response. This mode is chosen by the experimenter to suit his instruments or interests, but is generally unrelated to the aggressive (provoking) stimuli and never related to the subject's perception of that stimuli and his purpose or aim behind the aggressive response.

SHAPING OF AGGRESSION

In his survey of the literature on aggression, Baron (1977) describes many factors or conditions that can affect the degree of aggression exhibited: physical factors, such as noise and temperature; social factors, such as crowding; the setting within which orders are given; and psychological factors, such as frustration and alienation. But all these investigations measure the effects of various conditions on the *degree* of aggression, not on the type or *strategy* of aggression shown. Nearly all investigations relate to the aggressive behavior of an individual, and not of a group—with the exception of studies (mainly observational) of the behavior of crowds or mobs. The investigations differentiate aggression according to the stimuli that provoked it, whether external—such as a threat or frustration—or internal—such as needs for dominance or for hurting another. They focus on the *cause* of aggression and on the *expression* of aggression, but they do not—or very rarely—investigate the *aims* of aggression.

As shown previously, the same aim may be achieved in many ways, (for example, by using verbal or physical aggression), and it may be a response to different causes (for example, frustration or innate drive). To describe the process of aggression, one must describe the means as well as the cause. But the cause for a particular response might well not be the objective environmental factor(s) that the experimenter designated as "provoking" or "frustrating" stimuli. The cause behind an aggressive response is in the eye of the beholder. The response of the individual is aimed at the cause that he perceives, and is made in order to affect the cause in a way that he feels will lead to the best outcome. One might be able to judge the perceived cause of an aggressive response by understanding the payoff expected. One cannot deduce the expected payoff from an objective description of the cause.

Fraczek (1977) suggests that "aggressive actions are partly regulated by emotions but cognitive processes mainly effect their cause by determining situational orientation and assessment and anticipation of the effects of own behavior." The intensity of the aggression is determined by emotional involvement—the degree of frustration or threat perceived, or of anger experienced. But the strategy of aggression is determined by an appraisal of the situation and an appraisal of the relationship of the person to the situation. This appraisal process—which has been discussed previously and shown to be the focal point of all adjustment processes—determines the coping style to be deployed, including the aggressive strategy with which the opposition is tackled. Coping behavior—behavior aimed at structuring, attaining coherence, and establishing an equilibrium between the individual and his environment—may take many forms, one of which is aggression. Aggression deploys strategies aimed at attaining coherence and structuring through control or destruction. Storr (1968) says that we must "accept that idea that achievement of dominance, of overcoming obstacles, the mastery of the external world, for all of which aggression is necessary, is as much a human need as sexuality or hunger." Intensity of coping behavior depends on the degree of perceived incoherence or imbalance and on the extent of the need to restore equilibrium and to structure the perception. The intensity of the aggressive response depends on the perceived disturbance of equilibrium caused by the opponent or threat, and on the extent of the felt need to offset this disturbance and to cancel the impact of the opponent or threat. In the next chapter, I will further discuss the concept of the opponent.

Durbin and Bowley (1938) attributed the causes of fighting in general and war in particular to three main causes.

1. *Fight for possession.* When we want something that another has, the motivation is clear. What we covet may be concrete and tangible—such as territory or markets—or intangible—such as authority or goodwill. One may fight for something that was of no initial intrinsic value until coveted by another; only the opponent's desire to possess imbues our possession with value in our eyes. This is a case where truth was not in the eye of the beholder until it is reflected in the eye of the observer. The best way to make the grass look greener is to build a fence across it.

2. *Intrusion by a stranger.* What is defined as "stranger" is related to how we define ourselves and our environment. A tightly knit homogeneous group will notice and react to a newcomer who shows slightly divergent norms more than a heterogeneous group that contains a wide range of diverse behaviors within itself. Durbin and Bowley point out that the stranger must have some aspect of similarity to the group, in order to be perceived as a threat: A child is more of a threat to a group of children than an adult is, because the completely unrelated cannot be perceived as a threat.

In fact, the differentiation between Durbin and Bowley's first and second categories seems rather unclear. To their mind, the similar stranger is more of a threat, because he is more likely to compete for a common possession. Surely, the panic reaction to the famous broadcast of the Martian invasion was not because Welles's description of the Martians protrayed a picture of manlike creatures (they were, in fact, described as most alien and unhumanlike), but because they threatened us and our earth. The triggering of a conflict may not be related to the degree of perceived similarity of the threatening opponent, but the degree or strategy of agression deployed against him might indeed depend on the degree of perceived similarity. Catholics versus Protestants in Ireland; Leninist, Maoist and Trotskyite communists; as well as the more intense hatred of Eastern Jews toward Arabs—all appear to me to indicate that similarity between opponents often serves to intensify conflict. The deviant behavior—the threatening behavior of one who is similar to us—is responded to with greater intensity not because he offers a greater threat to our possessions, but because his threat is greater to our self-concept. As has already been suggested above, the perceived threat is: "There, but for the grace of God, go I." The prison warden who comes from the same socioeconomic conditions as his ward is more likely to behave aggressively toward his charge, in spite of potentially being more familiar with the prisoner's problems. The relationship between similarity and aggression seems to form the usual U-curve. One is more aggressive to what is similar and to what is very different (for example, U.S. reactions to Japanese versus Germans in World War II). We are most aggressive to what threatens our self-perception, or the coherence of our picture of ourselves; and we are most aggressive against the very different, because—by its very strangeness—it threatens the coherence of our understanding and the clarity of our structure of the world around us. The strange, unknown animal or culture is as much a threat to our orientation in the world as what is very similar to us and yet behaves in a way we cannot understand or accept.

To increase the aggressive potential toward another, we must either increase the perceived similarity and then emphasize the danger of "contagious" behavior—"you must not behave like that; otherwise, you will be like him"—or decrease all similarity. Dehumanizing the enemy by means of derogatory verbal labels (such as "wogs," "huns," or "goons"), by means of cartoons, or by attribution of degrading social or moral qualities is a very common way of increasing the dissimilarity between the enemy and ourselves. Gault (1971) studied the behavior of soldiers who slaughtered Vietnamese beyond the needs of battle, and found that dehumanization of the enemy (as well as dilution of responsibility) contributed greatly to facilitation of such behavior. White soldiers showed substantially more violence to the Vietnamese, "whom they seemed to regard as not fully human." Black U.S. soldiers in Vietnam were more ready to—and often did—attack their White officers and buddies (Kroll 1976). They felt more similar to the Vietnamese than to the White peers (Finan, Borus, and Stanton 1975). The Vietnamese offered no threat to the self-perception of the Blacks—nor to their concept of the world—and did not even compete for a common possession. Their White peers and—especially—officers offered a threat to the place of Blacks in the world—similar, in the everyday struggle for existence; and, at the same time, perceived as dissimilar in many ways. Thus, the White became a more likely target for aggression, from two viewpoints. After seizing the U.S. embassy in Teheran in November 1979, the Iranians released first the women and the Black Americans—possibly because the Blacks were perceived as nearer (more similar, but not competing), and thus evoked less aggression.

Those who are dissimilar elicit less aggression, unless their dissimiliarity is very great. But once aggression is initiated against them, there will be less inhibitions about carrying it out. Increasing the distance between the partners—whether by emphasizing their differences or by increasing the chain of responsibility between the aggressor and his victims (see Milgram [1963; 1974] and others, discussed in Chapter 4)—allows for an increase in the degree of aggression. The strategy or aim of the aggressive act differs, according to the perceived threat.

Stanger (1977) explains that violent behavior is associated with egocentric and ethnocentric thinking—focusing on oneself as an individual or a group—while less violent behavior is associated with altracentric thinking—thinking that does not differentiate boundaries between self and others. It appears to me that one cannot afford to have an altracentric approach—that is, disregard the boundaries between oneself and others—until one has established very clear and precise boundaries. Only the individual or the group that has a very strong and clear boundary can afford to tolerate others who might be a threat. Those who focus on their boundaries—who feel them to be insecure—must react more aggressively to defend the borders. Aggression can be used to control the opponent, or to damage him. Aggression aimed at controlling is likely to be less extreme than that aimed at destroying, even if the same methods are used (a harsh word instead of slander; a shove instead of a knife thrust). Those who have a clear perception and coherent structuring will primarily aim at controlling the threat, while those who have an insecure base will probably aim at destroying rather than controlling.

3. The third and last cause for fighting—as listed by Durbin and Bowley—is *frustration—external or internal*. This cause has been previously discussed at length. The point it so important that it should be summarized again by noting Storr's comment (1968) that the base level for aggression is frustration—a state that evokes the need for self-actualization and mastering of the environment.

To sum up the discussion so far: There are different approaches to the causes of aggression—viewing it as a result of an internal need, or as a response to environmental demands. Aggression can be viewed as a primary mode of behavior, or as an acquired style of response. The intensity of aggressive response has been shown to depend on the level of need as well as on the type of stimuli that triggered it, and the context within which it occurred. These discussions generally do not relate to the purpose or perceived payoff that the aggressor has for his action, and do not directly relate to the strategy of aggression used to gain that payoff.

PARAMETERS OF AGGRESSION

I shall make an attempt to outline the parameters of aggression discussed up to this point: Although the models discussed above do not focus on the aims that lie behind aggressive acts (even though a term offered by Tedeschi, Smith, and Brown 1974—"coercive aggression"—does indicate that attention has been paid to the purpose of aggressive behavior), it is possible to study these theories and make assumptions about the aims that are appropriate to the behavior described.

1. *The relevance of the target toward which aggression is directed.* Is the target just chosen by chance, or because of availability, familiarity, and so forth? Is there a need for the aggression to be channeled toward a specific object because of its specific characteristics, or is the object totally irrelevant? Clearly, for theories that assume aggression to be an expression of an internal conflict or drive, the target's characteristics are of no—or of only secondary—importance. For theories that view aggression as a response to an environmental condition—whether a frustrating or threatening factor—the target is of primary importance and directly relevant to the aggression.

2. *The relevance of the strategy used in the aggressive behavior.* Does a model specify that a certain strategy of response is the most likely or the most appropriate

toward a particular kind of stimulus? Is a different aggressive strategy associated with response to internal or external stimuli? Are strategies chosen on the basis of past learning, disposition, or feasibility, or in accordance with some innate requirements? Apparently, all theories in which aggression is viewed as originating from a drive that can be reduced or displaced treat the strategy deployed as of secondary importance: If one strategy fails, another will do equally well.

3. *The expected payoff for the aggressive act.* The outcome or impact of the aggressive act can have as its primary aim either the effect on the aggressor or the effect on the aggressed. The effect of aggression can be expected to lead to a change in the aggressor—to make him more powerful or more threatening. The effect can be expected on the target of aggression—to make him run, damage him, or control him. The payoff affecting the aggressor can be described as the aggressor's gain; the payoff affecting the aggressed can be described as the opponent's loss.

Aggression might well involve both aggressor's gain and opponent's loss. However, such a combination is not necessary. In aggression aimed at aggressor's gain, it is sufficient for him to gain, while the opponent's loss is irrelevant—and vice versa. Table 5.1 summarizes the theories we have discussed in terms of the three aspects listed above.

The actual aggressive act can be divided into a simple dichotomy, as offered by Buss (1961): physical and nonphysical aggression. Buss also offers two further dimensions: the active and passive, as well as the direct and indirect. The first dimension (physical/nonphysical) is the commonsense one used in everyday speech: "Sticks and stones will break my bones, but words will never hurt me." The other two dimensions cover—besides a description of the aggressive act—also some of its aims. I am going to suggest that, for the purpose of characterizing aggression (as will be done below), it is sufficient to differentiate the means of aggression as physical or nonphysical.

Table 5.1

The Parameteres of Aggression as Represented in Some Theories of Aggression

Parameters of the Aggressive Act	Theories of aggression				
	Freud	*Dollard*	*Berkowitz*	*Lorenz*	*Bandura*
Relevance of target	irrelevant	irrelevant	source of anger	threat to dominance	following learned aims
Relevance of strategy	irrelevant	irrelevant	irrelevant	irrelevant	to fit norms
Payoff: aggressor's gain	balance Eros/ Thanatos	reduce frustration	—	control	according to problem
Payoff: opponent's loss	—	—	hurt source of anger	—	according to problem

Source: Author.

Buss also suggests that, according to the evidence, nonphysical aggression often leads to the physical strategy, rather than vice versa: Physical aggression is the stronger aggressive strategy.

To sum up the discussion on the parameters of aggression so far: We seem to be primarily concerned with three aspects or dimensions. Althought they do not describe all possible parameters of aggressive behavior, these aspects serve to differentiate between different aggressive strategies, and thus might assist in understanding which factors lead to and motivate aggressive behavior in general and in a military setting in particular:

1. Means   m1 nonphysical aggression
                 m2 physical aggression

2. Mode   aggressive behavior will be utilized in order to:
                 d1 attack   — act directly on the opponent
                 d2 deter   — act directly on self to coerce opponent (for example, by acquiring weapons or skill development)

3. Aims   the ultimate payoff for the aggressive act is:
                 a1 destroy — to hurt or damage the opponent
                 a2 control — to shape the opponent's behavior according to the aggressor's wants (for example, by making him run, obey, or cooperate)

The means dimension is identical to that offered by Buss. While Buss classifies the mode dimension into active/passive, I have analyzed (in the previous discussion) the mode in terms of its purpose, rather than in terms of its dynamics. While the elements active/passive differentiate between the extent of investment or involvement in the aim, they are only indirectly related to it. "Attack" and "deter" can also be placed on a dynamic continuum, but are more directly linked to the way of attaining the goal than the active/passive description. In fact "attack" and "deter" describe—at least partially—both the mode and form dimension of Buss's classification. Thus, active-direct equals "attack" and active-indirect equals "deter" while passive-direct and passive-indirect describe milder forms of "attack" and "deter," respectively.

The third dimension—aim—is used to describe the purpose as well as the degree of aggression—thus containing all the information in Buss's analysis, but focusing attention on the aims of aggression. This emphasis (as the foregoing discussions should have clarified) is made so that aggression can be analyzed in terms of strategies of behavior—reflecting an individual's way of coping with a problem, as he perceives it.

These dimensions and their elements can be described by means of a mapping sentence. The purpose of the sentence is to relate the impact of the interaction of all these factors to the ultimate strength of aggressive behavior. Thus, the sentence describing the domain of aggression reads:

The Extent to Which an Individual (X) or a Group (Y) Responds to a Perceived
Opponent at Time (*t*)

	Means		*Mode*		*Aim*
by	m1 physical	a response	d1 attack	in	a1 destroy
	m2 nonphysical	in the form of	d2 deterrent	order to	a2 control

high

an opponent ⟶ ↕ **aggression**

low

A hypothesis included in this mapping sentence is that all elements listed
as first (number 1) are stronger in their effect on aggression than those listed
as second (number 2). Thus, physical means, the attack mode, and the
destroying aim are each more powerful in affecting aggression than the
other elements in their respective dimensions.

A further assumption or hypothesis with regard to the relative impact of
each dimension on aggression can be made: The aim has a stronger impact
on determining the strength of aggression than the mode—which, in turn, is
more powerful than the means.

Formally stated:

$$A > D > M \text{ and } 1 > 2$$

The above sentence generates eight possible profiles (2 × 2 × 2),
which—in view of the hypotheses above—can be listed in rank order of
degree of associated aggression:

1.	m1d1a1	physical	acting in order to destroy
2.	m2d1a1	nonphysical	acting in order to destroy
3.	m1d2a1	physical	deterring in order to destroy
4.	m2d2a1	nonphysical	deterring in order to destroy
5.	m1d1a2	physical	acting in order to control
6.	m2d1a2	nonphysical	acting in order to control
7.	m1d2a2	physical	deterring in order to control
8.	m2d2a2	nonphysical	deterring in order to control

These are profiles describing the eight basic strategies of aggression—strategies to which I will refer again and again throughout this book.
To help in remembering these strategies (as a kind of label), I have attempted
to describe them with words associated with aggression. These labels are by
no means semantically accurate, nor will their interpretation be unanimous;
but hopefully they serve to differentiate the eight strategies (Ag 1–8).

m1d1a1	Ag 1	ERADICATE (some street fights; some cancer operations)
m2d1a1	Ag 2	COMBAT (brainwashing; desensitization)
m1d2a1	Ag 3	FIGHT (siege; immunization)
m2d2a1	Ag 4	RESIST (some spying activities; Mahatma Ghandi–type resistance)
m1d1a2	Ag 5	STRUGGLE (wrestling; some military or police actions)
m2d1a2	Ag 6	COERCE ("educational processes"; psychological warfare)
m1d2a2	Ag 7	STRIFE (mountaineering; weapon development)
m2d2a2	Ag 8	THREAT (acquisition of skills or knowledge)

All the profiles containing an a1 element (destroy) can be described as violent strategies (Ag 1–Ag 4), while all the profiles containing the a2 element (control) can be described as hostile strategies (Ag 5–Ag 8). *Violent strategies are aimed at the opponent's loss, while hostile strategies are aimed at the aggressor's gain.* Thus, the differentiating point lies between Ag 4 and Ag 5. The former describe resistance against; the latter, struggle for.

From the examples given, it is clear that not all strategies of aggression are necessarily "negative," in the usual European normative sense. *Aggression is defined as any action or withholding of action that aims to affect a factor perceived to behave or affect us in a way incongruent with the state we wish to attain or maintain.*

Any threat to our perceived equilibrium—physical, social, or psychological—or any threat to our attaining such equilibrium will result in deploying at least one of these aggressive strategies. *Whenever we cannot attain coherent structure, a clear perception, or a stable organization of ourselves or of ourselves in relation to a specific environment, a threat to the need for equilibrium occurs, and an attempt to redress the balance follows.*

A murder aiming to maintain the Mafia leader in power would be described as Ag 5, as would the developing of good physical condition to avoid a heart attack. A murder by a jealous husband of his wife's lover is Ag 1, as is removal of a tumor. The international police force advocated by Janowitz and referred to as a "surveillance force" by Schelling (1962) would deploy Ag 6, since the force is supposed to attain its control by means of observation (like the UN force in Lebanon and the Israel/Egypt observation forces in the Sinai), rather than by physical means. While the subjects in a Milgram-type paradigm (1963; 1974; see also Chapter 4) utilize Ag 5, Swedish behavior during World War II can be described as Ag 6—deploying nonphysical methods (declaration of neutrality) to control the potential German attack. Swedish declared policy today can be described as Ag 7—being based on the development of sufficient deterrent power to make it not worthwhile for an enemy to invade. A similar strategy describes the U.S. strategy in developing its deterrent forces.

The attempt to exterminate the Biafrans, and the Nazi extermination of the Jews—as well as eradication of malaria—would be described as Ag 1.

The Six Day War initiated by Israel in response to imminent threat by the joint Arab forces—with the aim of deterring such an attack, not of destroying the Arabs—can be described as Ag 5. At the same time, the openly declared aim of Syria to destroy and wipe out Israel is to be described as Ag 1.

Religious and messianic movements (whether deist or political) that aim at conversion and gaining souls can be described as Ag 6, if they use nonphysical means to convince or coerce. However, often (especially if strategy Ag 6 fails) such movements tend to switch to Ag 5—using physical means to attain their aim of controlling others. It may also happen that, if Ag 5 fails and they do not succeed in controlling others, they will escalate to Ag 2 or Ag 1—aimed at destroying what they cannot control. Other groups (such as anti-nuclear power movements or the "moral rearmament" movement) deploy Ag 2 from the start—aiming to destroy the opponent (or at least his policy) by nonphysical means. But when this strategy fails, it is often seen to escalate the utilization of physical means.

ESCALATION OF AGGRESSION

The mapping sentence—producing profiles that can be ranked in terms of the intensity of aggression associated with them—describes the sequence in which escalation of aggression will occur. The sequence of escalation triggered by the effectiveness of aggressive behavior can be summarized in a formal way:

The Laws of Escalation of Aggression

1. Escalation will follow this sequence: nonphysical to physical; deter to attack; control to destroy.
2. The failure of one strategy will lead to the deployment of the higher strategy on the scale.
3. The initial strategy deployed depends on the appraisal of the situation, as well as past habits and needs.
4. The degrees of aggression utilized within each strategy depends on the degree of the perceived conflict or threat.
5. Change of strategy follows failure of the strategy deployed.

A schematic presentation of the escalation routes is presented in Figure 5.1. It is seen that the initial strategy determines and restricts the subsequently available strategies, if and when escalation does occur. Thus, if the initial strategy was nonphysical acting to control (Ag 6), escalation will bring on physical acting to control (Ag 5), and then physical acting to destroy (Ag 1); and strategies described by Ag 2, Ag 3, and Ag 4 will not be deployed. In other words, if a physical attempt to control fails, one will not attempt to deter in any way, nor to destroy by nonphysical means—but will attempt to destroy by physical means.

Figure 5.1
Flow Chart for Aggressive Strategies

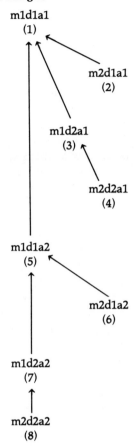

Source: Author.

GROUP AGGRESSION

So far in the discussion, I have not differentiated between group and individual aggression, even if such a difference were implied. This differentiation is essential when looking at factors that escalate aggression. "War," says Rousseau (1962), "is never fought between individuals but between heads of organisations, which have the power invested in them by the organisation. War is a social evil, and can only be cured by severing the bonds which hold society together, since only the social organisation can create the ruler who can lead to war." To the historian Howard (1978), this comment seems to be sardonic comment, not to be taken too seriously. I, however, cannot dismiss it so lightly. The effect of the group—the behavior generated by a number of interacting individuals—is so clearly different from that of the separate individuals, that it is clear that the breakup of a group is bound to be reflected in changes in behavior of its members. Any police force knows that it is essential to break up a crowd when attempting to control riots, or when trying to reduce the threat of a violent outbreak. The "critical mass" concept is as viable for human behavior as for radioactive isotopes. Much as when the physical mass of radioactive materials exceeds a critical point and the interactions of the liberated particles reinforce one another in an ever-escalating energy release curve, so does the presence of a human group increase its energy output by mutual reinforcement—until it erupts in an uncontrolled and violent way. Freedman et al. (1972) have stated that all crowding has an intensifying effect. If aggression exists, it will become more so as a result of crowding; if joy exists, it will also be intensified by the crowd. It has been shown by some studies (see, for example, Wicklund 1979) that a mirror in front of an aggressor tends to increase his aggression—if he was disposed to be aggressive. However, if this individual were not so disposed, the effect of the mirror would be to further enhance his nonaggressive tendencies. The effect of the crowd seems to be much like a mirror, reflecting each individual's behavior in those around him and thus intensifying the existing pattern of behavior. Besides the mirror effect, the crowd also—according to Zimbardo (1969)—has the effect of increasing the anonymity of its members and reducing their responsibility—thus increasing the dehumanization that "transfers men into beasts."

Morris (1978) points out that only under crowding conditions does one see animals fight to destruction. As a rule—says Morris (1969)—animals fight, but do not go to war (Ag 5, not Ag 1). Aggression escalates from the aim of domination to that of destruction due to a vicious combination of attack remoteness and group cooperation. Lorenz (1966) says that the individual is not a killer, but the group is. "The control of human warfare is not going to be achieved by the methods which are effective in modifying the fighting behavior of individuals," concludes Scott (1971), following an investigation of the conduct of U.S. soldiers in Vietnam.

Koestler (1978) offers a model for human behavior—in fact, a model for the interaction of all systems in an organism or an organization—according to which each individual is continuously affected by and affects two opposing forces: (1) the self-assertive force, which is directed toward self-maintenance and defense of the existing structure or equilibrium of the individual in relation to himself and to the higher organization; and (2) the self-transcending force, which is directed at establishing new relationships and developing new structures. These two forces—one maintaining and stabilizing; the other developing and disrupting—are always present and maintain an unstable equilibrium with each other.

To Koestler's mind, the act of identification with the group—an act by which the individual "sacrifices himself" by losing his self-identity through adopting the group's norms—is a result of the self-transcending force. The loyalty that the individual develops toward the group is what, in its turn, reinforces the self-assertiveness of the group—which will strive to maintain its basic character and stability, force all newcomers into its pattern, and ensure the loyalty of its members at all costs.

The group will thus act more violently against outsiders—having increased its aggression as a result of the individual's loyalty and sacrificing for the group. As Koestler (1978) states, "The egoism of the group feeds on the altruism of its members." Innate aggressiveness is—for Koestler—also a result of the (innate) self-transcending drive, which leads to integration in the group and—in turn—to abrogation of the individual's responsibility, depersonalization, and submission to the group's norms. These create conditions that allow for such extremely violent group behavior as is commonly associated with lynch mobs or race riots, as well as for the ecstasy of carnivals.

Reflecting on political behavior Priestland (1974) says that political violence evolves from the individual to the group. Such change brings about escalation in aggression in quantity, as well as a real change in quality. Violence in the group is a substitute for religion in offering a definition to "who we are." It is because a clear self-concept is missing that violence is deployed to attain it. One might also suggest a reverse causality—that religion destroys the meaning of man and weakens his self-concept by making him subservient to superior and unchallengeable forces, and thus leads to violence. The history of human warfare certainly indicates that religion was—and is—very frequently the cause of the most extreme violence.

Milburn (1980) suggests that the description of violence and aggression should be along two axes: planned–spontaneous, and individual–systematic. The planned and systematic type of violence is generated by institutions in order to attain their goals (for example, lynching to control Blacks). This is violence generated in a detached and distant way—impersonal and thus more aggressive than spontaneous person-to-person behavior. This is the violence typical of group violence; and, thus, group violence is always more extreme.

The military is interested in increasing rather than decreasing aggressive behavior. Thus, the reduction in aggressive behavior that results from the collapse of a group is of major importance. A group's effective firing power can be reduced to a much greater degree than expected, by the loss of the firing capacity of some of its individuals. A loss of 30–50 percent of the objective firing potential of a group has been shown to reduce the group effectiveness to a level much below these figures, and to even render it completely ineffective. According to Keegan (1976)—summing up evidence from the UK, French, Italian, and Russian troops in World War II—the break in the will to fight occurs when the number of casualties and deaths in a unit roughly equals the number of effective soldiers remaining: The "critical mass" was about 50 percent. However, this critical ratio did not hold true for the German troops, who continued to fight in spite of greater losses. According to Keegan, they continued fighting because it offered the line of least resistance for them.

Investigation by Shils and Janowitz (1948) showed the German's organization to be much more cohesive than the Allies—thus contributing greatly to their fighting effectiveness and to their resistance to loss of fighting capacity. The average figure of about 50 percent losses as the critical point for maintaining group effectiveness—although remarkably consistent for many countries—must hide quite a large variation within each force. "Better" troops must have been able to tolerate such losses more than "poorer" troops; and group cohesiveness—with its very high predictive power for morale and combat effectiveness—cannot be attributed to chance.

However, the term "group" used here cannot be defined exclusively in organizational terms. The primary organizational unit of the military is the squad; but, when referring to the critical loss of 50 percent of the members of a group, does one inevitably refer to the squad—or does it relate to the platoon, company, and so on? Clearly, the first requirement for defining a group is that each of its members know about the others in it. Thus, a brigade cannot be viewed—at least by the ordinary soldiers—as "a group," but a platoon is likely to be viewed as such. A military group should be a rough equivalent of the sociologically defined "primary group"—one that has a face-to-face relationship. Such a group is not necessarily of one particular organizational character, and may indeed be formed across several organizational units—such as infantry and panzer platoons acting together. The primary unit described in *The American Soldier* (Stouffer et al. 1949) was the platoon; but what seems to have been relevant during the Korean War was much smaller: the squad (Janowitz 1964)—or even a group of two, described as "the buddy system" (Little 1964). It follows that, in Vietnam, the loss of one soldier would immediately affect the fighting capacity of another; in the earlier wars, it required the loss of several to affect the fighting capacity of others in the group. Asking soldiers in the field in Israel "Which group do you belong to?" revealed that, at times, the reference group was given as the squad; others referred to the platoon (the most common reply); while yet others referred to their company and even their battalion. I had a strong impression—never conclusively confirmed—that, when the battalion was of high status, the tendency was to give it as the reference group. The lower the status of the military unit, the smaller or lower down in the hierarchy was the reference group chosen.

Greenbaum (1979) summarizes military and other literature on the effects of small groups on combat efficiency by explaining that the better units will be characterized by:

1. Strong identification of its members with one another
2. Its members using one another as a standard of comparison for competence, value, emotions, and well-being
3. The members of the group adjusting to the group's norms and perceptions with regards to values, emotions, and so forth. Good leadership will enhance this process, but is not in itself sufficient to create a good group.

To conclude: from a military point of view as well as from a nonmilitary viewpoint, a group will behave more aggressively than an individual; and the more cohesive the group, the more aggressive it will be—hence, a more effective military instrument.

It appears obvious that, when describing the parameters of aggression, one must also describe the context—individual or group—in which the aggression takes place. The mapping sentence offered above related to the reaction of an individual (X) or a group (Y). This should now be modified thus:

AN OPPONENT WHICH IS PERCEIVED, AT TIME (t)

	Context		*Means*		*Mode*
by	c1 a group c2 an individual	to require	m1 physical m2 nonphysical	response in the form of	d1 attack d2 deterrent

	Aim			
in order to	a1 destroy a2 control	$\longrightarrow$	high $\updownarrow$ low	aggression

Sixteeen profiles are generated by this sentence: the eight listed previously, each of which can now occur in group or individual context. More aggression will be associated with c1—group aggression.

To the five laws of escalation of aggression listed above, one more law must be added.

6. Whenever the aggressive act is switched from the individual to the group, escalation will occur.

The mapping sentence describes aggression in terms of perception of the "opponent." This was used as a generic term denoting individuals or groups that the aggressor wants to affect in some way. However, since "opponent" is also in the eye of the beholder, some discussion must be devoted to the question of who or what an opponent is—or, in military terms, who is the enemy? This will be done in Chapter 6.

A MODEL OF AGGRESSIVE BEHAVIOR

Bandura (1973) diagrammatically describes the relationship between the different theories of aggression, as presented in Figure 5.2.

Figure 5.2
Diagrammatic Representation of Motivational Determinants of Aggression in Instinct, Behavior (Reactive Drive), and Social Learning Theories

INSTINCT THEORY
<u>   </u>
           AGGRESSION   AGGRESSIVE BEHAVIOR

BEHAVIOR THEORY
<u>   </u>
    FRUSTRATION   **AGGRESSIVE DRIVE**   AGGRESSIVE BEHAVIOR

SOCIAL LEARNING THEORY
<u>   </u>

FEELINGS OF DISCOMFORT	**EMOTIONAL AROUSAL**	DEPENDENCY PERFORMANCE WITHDRAWAL AND RESIGNATION
EXPECTATIONS	**REINFORCED MOTIVATION**	AGGRESSION PSYCHOSOMATICIZATION SELF-ANESTHETIZATION CONSTRUCTIVE PROBLEM SOLVING

Source: Bandura (1973).

According to the behavior (reactive drive) theory approach, frustration—thwarted expectation; the inability to reach a desired state—is the cause of aggression. According to the social learning theory approach, an aversive experience—which leads to a desire to terminate it—produces arousal. Frustration or anger also produce arousal; but—as Bandura shows—not all arousal produces frustration or aggression, yet all frustration produces arousal. The instinct theory—viewing aggression as a primary drive that initiates behavior—would surely also accept that arousal must occur in order to translate the drive state into actual behavior. Aggression with the aim to dominate (described by Lorenz) or the aggressive behavior in the Freudian approach must trigger the same sequence—arousal followed by behavior—regardless of whether the initial stimulus was a signal from another animal or an internal imbalance.

Arousal can be accounted for by accepting the concept of a basic curiosity drive. The need to know—to make sense of the world around us and our position in this world—could in itself account for arousal, whenever incoherent perception of an individual and his environment occurs. As Berlyne (1971) explains it, a state of uncertainty produces a specific exploration drive: "Specific exploration is connected with reward through arousal reduction, since it resolves [the] aversive condition of curiosity." Lowe and McGrath (1971) have shown arousal to be high whenever uncertainty is high—especially within a situation perceived to have marked consequences, such as any combat situation might involve. Thus, signals challenging the territorial imperative, the desire for stability of existing mores, or the thwarting of needs—all trigger the need to reestablish equilibrium to attain a coherent perception.

The need to establish a coherent perception of a situation—the structure appraisal—has been previously shown to be the most critical point in the appraisal process. Failure to attain this will produce the highest degree of arousal, and all behavior will be aimed at coping with this potential threat. Coping with this threat will be by either adapt or attack strategies—the latter as described by the eight strategies of aggression. The model presented in the previous chapter showed that the strategies of aggression play their part between coping appraisal and morale; and, indeed, it is in this phase that their impact on combat behavior is felt. However, the same disposition for aggressive behavior affects behavior when tackling the primary threat—ambiguity and uncertainty.

Taggert, Carruthers, and Somerville (1978) have shown that adrenaline excretion—a clear index of arousal—is associated with both aggression and uncertainty. One can assume that such arousal must also be associated with other coping strategies.

Looking at the seven examples of coping behavior listed by Bandura, we see that three of them would be classified as "aggressive" according to the mapping of aggressive strategies: aggression, performance, and constructive problem solving. Four styles of behavior have in common the avoidance of conflict and aggression: dependency, withdrawal and resignation, psychosomaticization, and self-anesthetization. The first group is aimed at the modification of the aversive stimulus; the second, at adapting to it. A rather similar dichotomizing is offered by Friedman and Rosenman (1974), who classified individuals into types A and B. Type A were those predisposed to utilize competitive behavior, time urgency, and hostility as coping strategies; while type B used opposing strategies. As Cummings and Cooper (1979) conclude, type A individuals (in contrast to type B) prefer to control their environment, and their behavior is aimed at asserting such control. Which coping approach is chosen to deal with a specific situation depends on biological disposition, ability, and past experience, as well as on available resources and the attitude toward these means. But all these modes of behavior could be aimed at structuring the situation and attaining coherence, as well as dealing with an external protagonist.

SUMMARY: AGGRESSION AND MORALE

Aggression is defined as *a form of coping aimed at restoring or maintaining an equilibrium perceived as desirable by the organism. When the coping behavior is directed toward affecting the state of another—whether by action or inaction, regardless of the other's needs or desires—it is called aggressive behavior.*

Aggressive behavior can be characterized by its means (physical or nonphysical), its mode (attack or deter), and its *aims* (control or destroy). The choice of the initial strategy of aggression to be deployed depends on past learning, biological and technical potential, the context, social norms, and an appraisal of the situation. The intensity of the aggressive response within each strategy depends on the extent of the perceived threat. Escalation from one strategy to another—following a predetermined sequence—occurs when a strategy fails or the context of the aggressive behavior changes from individual to group involvement.

Two kinds of morale were proposed and discussed in Chapter 3: A, mood—labile and changing; and B, resilient—the ability to persist in the initial committal. Mood is based on a superficial emotional evaluation—a willingness to act on stage 5 in the SAM process. Resilience—on the other hand—depends on a more developed perceptual process, which includes a full assessment of coping capacity (stage 6) as well as skills (stage 7). Thus, resilience also includes the appraisal of "how," not only of "I want."

To be able to answer "how," we must have access to a coping strategy. The discussion in this chapter focused on the possible aggressive coping strategies. Combining the feeling of "willingness to respond" with—for example—a disposition of Ag1 ("acting in order to destroy") will lead to aggressive combat behavior. If this is combined with a good coping assessment, the resultant behavior would be labeled as "high morale" in the military context.

6

What Is the Enemy?

I have attempted to describe aggression in rather technical terms, as being a strategy of behavior aimed at attaining a state of equilibrium or of establishing one's self-perception. In real life terms, this is not a very edifying definition; and each and every one of us knows quite well when he or she is or feels like being aggressive. We know aggression to occur when we quarrel, when we push our way in front of a queue, as well as when we kick a door that will not open, or swear at a car that will not start. We always aggress against another person or—if we react to "that bloody car that will never start"—against an inanimate object as if it were a sentient being. As we perceive it, the most extreme form of aggression is against another human being who deliberately opposes our aims; but, we at times, also feel aggression against inanimate things, which—having no will of their own—still frustrate our aims. Some factors—physical or mental—in our environment are perceived by us to have qualities beyond their objective biological, physical, or abstract characteristics. Thus, we relate to them in terms that we would relate to a purposeful human opponent. One fights aggressively to eradicate ignorance, to exterminate disease, to establish ideas, or to destroy beliefs. We aggress and fight against what we feel "opposes" us.

ENEMY IS IN THE EYE OF THE BEHOLDER

Different people have different ways of classifying the factors in their environment as "opponents" and "nonopponents"—into factors that they react aggressively toward and those that they might indeed try to affect, but not by responding aggressively. For some, "opponent" is a matter of direct conflict; for others, this category can be extended to faraway authorities with whom one has no direct contact—"them," "the establishment," "communists," "fascists," and so on. Some extend their circle of perceived opponents to more abstract concepts such as "devil," "god," and "evil spirit"; while, for others, even more abstract concepts such as "ignorance" and the rule that "one always misses the bus" or "a watched kettle never boils" are included in the category of opponents.

The initiation of aggression does not require a clear challenge from a perceived source; it is sufficient for us to perceive something as threatening to our desired state. To quote Jefferson: "I have sworn upon the altar of God eternal hostility against every form of tyrany over the mind of men." The nature of the threat differs if it arises from an outside source acting on us, or if it arises from our actions (or the blocking of our actions) aimed at the outside source. A person who passively blocks our way might constitute a different threat then a person who actively gets in our way. The difference between these two types of challenge is important for they might evoke different strategies of coping and aggression. More precise definition challenges is thus called for.

Opponent is that animal, vegetable, mineral, or abstract element perceived to be behaving in a mode that is incongruent with our aims. An opponent stands in our way, passively. *The effects of an opponent are felt in proportion to the extent of our actions on it, when we act on it.*

Enemy is an opponent perceived to be behaving in a mode that actually threatens our aims. *An enemy actively challenges our desired state or actions, and his gain is perceived to be our loss.*

The extent of the interaction with the opponent is determined by our action, and the relationship can be described as either a zero- or a nonzero-sum game. The interaction with the enemy is perceived to be initiated (directly or indirectly) by him, and the relationship must be described as a nonzero-sum game.

An opponent becomes an enemy when he or it is seen to threaten us actively. The person who happens to stand in our way is an opponent; if he refuses to move, he becomes an enemy. A math problem is an opponent; but, if failing to solve it will lead to failure in an exam, it becomes an enemy. A foreign ideology is an opponent so long as it does not threaten us, but it will become an enemy if we perceive a danger in its influence on us. The military rules that govern the soldier's life are an opponent to be avoided and dealt with. They become an enemy when wielded directly by the military police who have caught the soldier in the act of breaking the rules. The military regulation—like a difficult mountain climb or the strategic plans of the other country—are opponents that one wishes to overcome. The military police, the falling rocks, and the military outmaneuvering are the actual enemies that are a threat to us. The most obvious enemy to the soldier is the soldier of the opposing army. But the term "enemy" is not restricted only to the uniformed agent of the opposing country. "Enemies" can be civilians—whether "partisans" in resistance movements, "terrorists" (a term that depends on time and place and the attitude of the reporter, rather than on the content of their actions), or "fifth columnists." Even in such a clear context as a state of war between two countries, the perception of what is an enemy is subject to rapid fluctuation. A dramatic example of this change in perception occurred in Lebanon after 1982 when women and children—because they also deployed weapons—were newly perceived as "enemy" by the Israeli soldiers.

CHALLENGE IS IN THE EYE OF THE BEHOLDER

The level of probability that each individual grades as likely or unlikely varies with individuals and events. Thus a 0.01 percent chance of winning the pool can be perceived as a reasonable chance, while a 10 percent probability of a car accident can be perceived as unlikely. All expected events—like injury in war or false decisions—are classified into three psychological domains: likely/possible, unlikely/not possible, and unclassifiable. Events that fall into the last category cannot be perceived as positive or negative—desirable or unwanted. As has been emphasized in the previous discussions, any event that cannot be classified—one that cannot even be evaluated as to its possible outcome—is always perceived as a threat. It is only after a stimulus has been appraised as noxious or benign (by valence appraisal) that the relevance of the probability of its outcome is included in the next stage—that of coping appraisal.

A transition must occur between perceiving an event as likely—one that must be considered—and "unlikely"—one that can be ignored. This transition does not occur at any rationally fixed point (as, for example, at the 95 or 99 percent probability level commonly used in formal statistical evaluations). What determines the actual transition point must depend on the event, its context, and the disposition of the perceiver. But the basic intolerance of ambiguity—the need to achieve a coherent structure—exerts pressure on the perceiver to dichotomize events into positive or negative—certain to occur or certain not to occur. The tendency will always be to leave as few events as possible in the range of ambiguity.

Events or stimuli become "real" only when classified in the extremes of the probability perception. Stimuli that fall in the range of ambiguity are treated as "nonstimuli." Behavior may be aimed at removing this ambiguity (that is, at establishing their coherence), but it will not be aimed at handling the stimulus until it is classifiable as an event or a nonevent.

One cannot treat a threat as a "maybe threat." A challenge classified as a possible challenge will be either responded to as a challenge (even while accepting that it might not occur) or ignored. As far as coping behavior is concerned, we will either respond or not respond; we do not have a third alternative. What we can vary is the degree and strategy of response; but, if any response does occur, it is made only to a stimulus perceived as real—regardless of the objective or subjective probability of its occurrence.

HIERARCHY OF ENEMIES

The different armies opposing Israel were perceived with different degrees of hate and fear. They were all enemies, but were not rated equally (see Tables 4.2 and 4.3). Although we might face many enemies or opponents at any given time, one of these must be given priority at any given point, and be seen as the most critical enemy—the one whose threat is most critical. The opposing soldier who shoots and pins you down is likely to be perceived as your most important enemy at the time, and all attention is focused on dealing with him and the threat of being hit. But, if the enemy succeeds in enforcing a siege—preventing you from obtaining food or water over an extended period—hunger or thirst might become the primary enemy. The need for water might become so strong that you are willing to risk being shot—a risk you were not willing to take before—just in order to obtain water. The hierarchy of enemies has thus changed. The "official" threat of shooting deserters is an attempt to create a hierarchy of enemies in which the opposing army is seen as less threatening than the actions of your own officers. Mass desertion shows that this method is not inevitably effective, as is also demonstrated by the fact that crimes are not stopped by the threat of punishment.

This failure to restructure the perceived hierarchy in accordance with the aims of authority might depend on the fact that the threatened punishment is not perceived to be likely: The probability of being caught is perceived to be too low to bother about. But failure of punitive systems also occurs because the threatened punishment is not perceived as being worse than abstaining from the behavior that it tries to prevent: The consequences of the threatened punishment is not placed in the highest position in the hierarchy. For many soldiers the threat of sitting in prison as a punishment for improper conduct in the battlefield—or even during peacetime service—is not perceived as a punishment at all. The safety of the prison and its relative comfort and security offer much less threat than the discomfort and dangers of the field. It is for this reason that, during the wars in Israel, detention in military prisons for disciplinary (rather than criminal) offenses was nearly discontinued. The prisons turned out to be an attractive way to avoid arduous service in the field. For a punishment to fit the crime if the aim of the punishment is to deter, it must be perceived as worse than the crime. The perceived hierarchy of threats or enemies can be changed by the introduction of a more severe or threatening enemy. The well-known sergeant major (a character in every army) who promises the troops that they will be more afraid of him than of the enemy creates a clear hierarchy of threats designed to relegate the "real enemy" to a position of lesser importance, and thus reduce his threat value.

CHANGES IN EVALUATION OF THE ENEMY

The perceived challenge or threat value of an enemy can be reduced by presenting a still more threatening enemy, but it can also be reduced by a change in the evaluation of the enemy or by a change in the evaluation of our potential for coping with the enemy.

Acquiring better weapons is a simple way to reduce the perception of threat by the enemy. In fact, it is not the actual acquisition of better weapons that will reduce the perception of threat, but rather our feeling that better weapons have been acquired. A soldier who feels he possesses the better weapon feels less threatened, and vice versa: The feeling that one has the poorer weapon is sufficient to reduce the effectiveness of the soldier, regardless of the real effectiveness of the weapon. In the 1973 war, the Israeli armored forces met the Sagger and Snell hand-guided antitank missiles for the first time. These infantry-operated, highly mobile and effective missiles were a completely unexpected development in the battle tactics and put an entirely new dimension on infantry versus armor warfare. The invulnerability of the tank to the infantry soldier had been a very important aspect of the tank crews' perception. Not that these crews were not aware of the danger of antitank weapons operated by the infantry such as the bazooka, but their possible effects were seen as an accident—a chance factor of low probability, which could be avoided. However, the new hand-guided missiles were an obvious, clear, and real threat—part of the normal course of events, their effects unavoidable, and their consequences disastrous. The tank, which had been perceived as the protector of the infantry, suddenly required the infantry's protection. It took some time (depending on the circumstances and the effectiveness of the leadership) before reorganization of the perception of these weapons occurred. As awareness of countermeasures developed, and realistic evaluation of the missiles' effectiveness developed, their subjective threat value decreased. The objective effectiveness of the weapons did not change. However, their psychological impact—and, thus, their impact on combat performance—was reduced; and the challenge value of the enemy, reduced. This led to a very clear improvement in morale and combat ability—due to better self-evaluation (as well as better countermeasures), rather than due to a change in evaluation of the enemy. The hierarchy of enemies did not change (the missiles were still the biggest threat); only the missiles' impact as the most critical factor was reduced. The Lebanon War placed similar demands for reappraisal of the enemy—demands that were not met equally successfully. This will be taken up again in Chapter 10.

Belief in the enemy's faulty equipment, lack of ammunition, and poor morale will reduce the impact of his threat—regardless of the real facts—for as long as such a belief persists. The laws of dissonance predict that, when forming the basis for some organized structure leading to coherent perception, such beliefs—even if faulty—will be remarkably resistant to any change—even under the impact of real facts. Once we have an organized and structured picture of the environment, we will tend to resist all data or changes that might cause a reorganization of our perception. "I know the truth, so do not confuse me with facts" seems to be an important rule guiding our perception of the world around us.

This certainly appears to have been the culling rule by which some of the most senior decision makers in Israel operated during the summer and autumn of 1973. A very detailed and soul-searching investigation carried out in Israel following the Yom Kippur War concluded that the available signs (and even clear indications) that the Arabs were preparing for an all-out attack against Israel had been ignored and denied. Information that such an attack was about to be mounted—that the Egyptian armies had reached both strength and readiness to be able to mount such an attack—had been either completely disregarded or so downgraded as to be dismissed as irrelevant—"as of extremely low probability." Perception of the Arab enemy remained in line with the picture that Israelis had had of their opponents in the past. Their firm and fixed ideas of Arab inability, lack of daring, and inefficiency were clear and well structured—a derogatory picture that had to be maintained at all costs. It was so important to keep this coherent perception that psychological defense mechanisms distorted perception of reality, with disastrous consequences.

Perceptual distortion seems also to have occurred before the Pearl Harbor attack, when evidence clearly warning about oncoming attack was ignored (Janis and Mann 1977). Such distortions happen in daily life, when we ignore or misperceive information—whether it be criticism by fellow workers or a spouse, or cold statistical evidence on the likelihood of the outcome of the football pool or the efficacy of prayers.

Janis and Mann (1977) list the main sources of error (or perceptual distortions, similar to those described above) that lead to faulty decision making:

1. Looking only at one of the possible alternatives, and ignoring the others. Choosing only the outcome or threat that fits the existing structure (such as: The Arabs will not attack: They have never had the courage, and they are too disorganized"; or, "A car accident will never happen to me")

2. Allowing for only one or a few alternatives. Not accepting that other possibilities could occur—thus, not having to consider them in the first place. The

alternatives that do not fit into our structure—the alternatives that lead to a result too frightening or difficult to contemplate—are ignored ("Even if the Arabs attack, we cannot lose"). The alternatives are considered (unlike the case above, where they were not even perceived), but the likelihood of some is rated so low as to legitimize their dismissal.

3. The ordering of the alternatives. The assigned probability and importance is fitted with the existing need structure. Alternatives of which one is aware but does not wish to contemplate or cannot handle are not excluded a priori from consideration, but are assigned such low probability or low importance that one is justified in not investing resources or efforts in dealing with them ("We have our defense line. It is so good that it is not worthwhile investing in alternative systems"—regardless of the cost of a mistake in this evaluation.)

4. Testing of the alternatives. The criterion by which we judge the outcome of possible strategies is so tailored as to support the model to which we have committed. Thus, for example, if we decide that the most important criterion for our actions is the security of the state, one does not have to evaluate the possible consequences of certain strategies on the freedom of the individual. By deciding that monetary gain is the only relevant criterion, one does not have to consider the consequences to the happiness of the individual.

All these mechanisms reorganizing perception are aimed at maintaining and supporting an existing structure of perception—at maintaining and supporting the values and rank order of the perceived enemies, as well as our own explanations and needs. We do all we can to attain coherent perception. Once a stimulus is classified as an enemy of a certain potential, there will be a tendency to organize perception so as to confirm and support this classification and evaluation. It will require much more pressure—of facts or of subjective needs—to reclassify the evaluation of this enemy (or any other stimulus) than was required to classify and evaluate it in the first place. Initial categorization is much easier than the reclassifying of information into new categories.

In order to overcome such perceptual traps, Janis and Mann suggest a routine that forces the decision maker to consider all possibilities and outcomes. In Israel, following the 1973 debacle, a "devil's advocate" department was formed within the intelligence community. Its official function is to dispute all evaluations and question all agreements, so as to force consideration of any accepted evaluation of the enemy.

IDENTIFICATION WITH THE ENEMY

We have seen that coherence of structure can be maintained by changing the appraisal of the enemy's potential threat. However, extreme situations do occur, in which the enemy is perceived as being so overwhelmingly powerful that another method of evaluation of the threat has to be sought.

Bruno Bettelheim (1960)—a psychologist who experienced Nazi concentration camps—described a process called "identification with the aggressor." He explained the occurrence of *capos*—Jews (and other inmates) who actively collaborated with the Nazi guards to enforce the rules of the camps, and who identified with the jailors' aims, as a process of identification with the aggressor. The basic factor behind this process was explained to be the need of the prisoner to make sense of his world. He was faced with a situation in which the Germans had total and absolute power over his life. His cultural background often supported the principle that "might makes right." Therefore, because of its very existence, such power must be right, and must be justified; thus it cannot be evil. Such absolute power over men's lives can only exist in the hands of the Lord and his agents or another coercive father figure—and, thus, it must be right. If the power is right, the Germans are right. Thus—as one accepts the absolute power of a father, identifies with him, and tries to emulate him—so does one identify with the Germans. Anna Freud (1937)—who coined the term "identification with the aggressor"—describes this process as one of incorporating the frightening characteristics of the aggressor, and thus neutralizing them. Whether one accepts these psychoanalytical interpretations of the phenomenon or not, evidence that such a process does take place has been very clearly shown in other contexts.

As mentioned before, during the 1973 war, an extensive questionnaire was administered to a very large proportion of the armed forces. This questionnaire included questions pertaining to various attitudes toward the different Arab armies. During that war, a number of Israeli soldiers were captured by the Egyptian and Syrian forces. These soldiers were eventually returned after about a year, when the final exchange of prisoners occurred.

On their return, the soldiers were faced with an extensive battery of psychological tests and interviews, as well as attitude measures similar to those administered to all the soldiers during the war. These assessments took place before any other investigations (other than the most rudimentary medical checkup) were made. They were made before the returning prisoners talked to their families, their comrades, or any other contact in Israel. The purpose of this rather drastic order of priorities was to minimize the impact of the tendency we all have to relate experiences and organize our feelings in such a way as to fit the norms and standards of our environment, as well as in accordance with our own self-concept and ideals (again in order to attain coherence).

The data collected from the returning prisoners of war formed the basis for an evaluation of their attitudes toward their captors. This evaluation was based on two aspects:

1. Comparison of their responses to attitude questions in the standard questionnaire. Comparison was made with the mean responses given by other soldiers who

had not been captured, and which were made at the same point in time at which the ex-prisoners were captured. Thus any attitude shift that might have occurred in the soldiers who remained at the front was discounted. The POW group was matched on the bases of age, type of service, rank, education, ethnic origin, and place of residence (town, village, or kibbutz).

2. Comparison of the POWs' responses to TAT pictures with responses of other soldiers enlisted after the war, and matched for background data as above. The comparison was made on the hostility and anxiety indexes of the TAT, using the same method as discussed in Chapter 4 (see Shalit 1970).

The POWs were examined in two separate groups and on two occasions (since the soldiers were returned by Syria many months after those who were returned by Egypt). Treatment of the POWs in Egypt and Syria had been very different. Those held in Egypt were treated more or less according to the Geneva convention. At any rate, they were not treated in a way that was not according to the accepted norms the Egyptians have for treating their own prisoners. The Israelis held in Syria were often tortured, beaten up, burned, deprived of food and drink, isolated from one another, and treated in ways that can only be described as inhuman. The Israeli attitude generally and the attitude of the soldiers specifically had always reflected more hate toward the Syrians than toward the Egyptians (in part, probably because of the expectation of worse treatment by the Syrians), and the general reaction toward the Syrians' mishandling of the POWs was naturally very hostile.

The findings of the investigation into the attitude change caused by imprisonment came as a shock, for it showed very clearly that, while the POWs from Egypt showed no substantial shift in attitude toward their captors, the POWs from Syria showed a significant and *positive* shift toward the Syrian (see Table 6.1). Exposure to real torture, deprivation, and utter helplessness—rather than generating hate toward the capturers—caused an increase of identification and understanding and a decrease in the initial level of hate.

Such a finding was very upsetting to the coherence of the structure of our own prejudices (in Israel), and, in fact, there was a tendency to deny such data and ignore it. It is not easy to accept that cruel behavior can induce liking; it appears completely irrational and against all common sense. However, if one remembers that the primary aim of all adjustive behavior is to make sense out of a situation—at whatever cost to representation of reality—this unexpected shift of attitude does make sense. To borrow from psychoanalytic terminology, what occurs is regression (in terms of ability for reality testing) in the service of the ego (in terms of success in attaining coherence).

Since that investigation, kidnapping has become very common in the world, and has often offered further demonstrations of this process. What is

Table 6.1
The Differences in Attitudes toward Their Captors among Prisoners Returning from Syria and from Egypt

	Syria		Egypt	
	POW *N = 23*	*control* *N = 69*	*POW* *N = 87*	*control* *N = 250*
Hate	3.5	4.3	2.9	3.1
Fear	2.5	3.0	2.8	2.8
Respect	4.4	3.8	3.5	3.3

Source: Author's research based on unpublished reports.
Note: The scores were given on a five-point scale (1 = least; 5 = most). Only the differences in the Syria group are significant, at the .05 level (two-tailed).

now known as the "Stockholm syndrome"—referring to an incident in which two captured bank clerks identified with, willingly cooperated with, and helped their kidnapper—has often been repeated, sometimes in very extreme form, such as in the case of Patty Hearst. In all these cases, appraisal of "who is the enemy" has shifted by shifting the reference point. The enemy ceased to be "out there," but became incorporated in—and approved by—the reference system of the person, and thus ceased to be an enemy. Others—initially part of the reference system—were ejected and rejected and became outsiders; they were now the enemy to be fought against—sometimes actively, as in the case of Patty Hearst; at other times, passively, by showing and feeling sympathy with the aggressor.

The other part of our investigation related to perception of aggression and hostility. It was found that the POWs returning from Egypt did not differ from the comparison group of soldiers who did not partake in the war. Those returning from Syria, however, had a higher anxiety score and a lower aggression (hostility) score (see Table 6.2).

The POWs who identified with the aggressor—who solved the incongruence and inconsistency of their appraisal by restructuring their perception and accepting the aggressor and his aggressive acts—had a lower need for aggression or hostility than others who had to function in a less structured environment, in which the aggressor was still perceived as the threatening outsider. The Syrian POWs successfully coped with the threat at the expense of their ideological structure. Their increase in anxiety can be explained by (objective) worries about health and homecoming, as well as by possible fears due to their being aware that the very fact that they did not hate the Syrians would come in conflict with feelings they were so obviously

Table 6.2
Distribution of Mean Anxiety and Hostility Scores in
Israeli POWs Returning from Egypt and Syria

	Syria $N = 23$	Egypt $N = 87$	Control $N = 1366$
Anxiety	12.0	9.8	8.4
Hostility	7.2	10.3	11.9

Note: Significance of difference between the Syria
POWs and the control group is .01 ($t = 2.9$), while the difference between the Egyptian POWs and the control group
does not reach the .05 level of significance.

Source: Author's research based on unpublished reports.

expected to express. The shift in the Egyptian POWs was in the same direction although statistically not quite significant. The fact that their hostility
toward the Egyptians was also reduced—without any apparent identification with the aggressor—seems to show that familiarity in itself has the effect of reducing aggression.

I have no evidence as to the persistence of these attitude shifts; but interviews carried out during the following months indicated a general reduction
in anxiety, but no apparent increase in aggression toward the Syrians. It must
be emphasized that this shift in attitude did not occur as a result of systematic
and organized "brainwashing" such as the Russians used during the 1950s. No
attempt had been made to break down the existing frame of reference—such
as is achieved by the sensory deprivation used by the Russians, or by a
breakup of all social structures as used by the Chinese in Korea. Systematic
brainwashing aims to destroy the existing frame of reference. This
breakdown is followed by instilling a new frame of reference, which those
"brainwashed" eagerly adopt because they cannot survive psychologically
without having some framework by which to structure the world. The
Syrians carried out random torture, cruelty, and deprivation without offering
any alternative. The captors' need to form a coherent perception—a
framework for handling the universe— was sufficient to shape their attitude
in a way more similar to that of their capturers than to their own initial attitude, or the normative attitude of their past group.

APPRAISAL OF THE ENEMY

When facing overwhelming odds, one often stops struggling; one accepts
and submits and explains that "it is fate" or "it is the will of God."
Fatalism—whether by justifying the cause of the event ("We deserve this

punishment"), or by creating explanatory laws ("Every bullet has a name on it")—does not only mean that we delegate responsibility to another agent; it also means that we restructure our perception of the environment. Whatever these laws are and whether we understand them or not, if we feel that they exist, things make sense; and then we can hope, try to understand, or avoid. It is the random, unstructured environment that we cannot handle. Thus, under the impact of war—which, from the individual soldier's point of view, is often total chaos—many develop their own codes and laws for structuring events. The use of mascots, signs, and superstitions is very common; prayers and belief in organized religion increase; and it should be noted that this increase occurs predominantly in those soldiers who are less self-confident, as well as less intelligent (Stouffer et al. 1949). To conclude in Stouffer's words: "The threat is unexpected and unpredictable, is brought into acceptable bounds when the unexpected is redefined as the inevitable."

Appraisal of the enemy or opponent can be cognitive or affective—on the basis of some assessable qualities, as well as on the basis of attitudes. Most likely, appraisal will be mixed, looking at both the capacity of the enemy and the feelings one has—fear or respect—toward him. Much in the way that a hierarchy of threats or enemies is perceived, so one organizes the perception of different aspects of the enemy into a hierarchy. Some characteristic—such as his intelligence or the quality of his equipment—will be perceived as the most critical or important aspect of the enemy; other characteristics—although considered—will be evaluated to be of less importance. The feature or characteristic that is the most critical—on which our attention focuses—may shift under different circumstances. An enemy country might be mostly perceived in terms of its air force or its economic powers. The "tank" may be perceived by the infantry soldier in terms of its size, noise, and firing power; or it may be predominantly represented by the image of its cannon. But that same soldier—sitting in a ditch toward which that tank is rolling—may perceive the tank as nothing but the spinning treads, the grinding sound of churned earth, and the moaning metal avalanching on him. The war, the opposing armies, the opposing soldiers, and the tank—all are represented and encapsulated in the sight, sound, and vibrations of the links of the advancing treads. For a practitioner of yoga, the contemplated naval might represent "universe"; and any other single feature—concrete or abstract—chosen from a large complex universe might be "the enemy" for a threatened person.

It is in the interest of the military system to identify the representing characteristics of the enemy. For it is through modification of the perception of these critical characteristics that the attitude toward the enemy can be changed. Weapons acquire effectiveness due to one critical and frightening characteristic, much beyond their objective effectiveness. Bombs and shells that whistle are rated as more effective and frightening than those that don't. The dive-bomber was reported by Stouffer to be more frightening than the horizontal bomber, regardless of objective data to the contrary. The German dive-bomber—the crank-winged *stuka*—which always started its attack with a half roll followed by a near-vertical power dive, inspired fear way beyond its objective efficacy. In fact, the plane used air brakes to slow its speed, but the Germans enhanced the impact of the plane by designing it so that it emitted a heart-chilling whistle during its apparently immensely fast dive.

By shifting attention from a critical characteristic that cannot be avoided—such as the noise effect of the bomb—to another that can be dealt with—such as its blast effects—one can actively reduce the potential threat of the weapon. The aim should be to structure perception of the enemy in such a way that he or it (this includes all weapons and other possible dangers) is seen to be characterized by a feature that can be handled—that can be included in a perceived means of response. Propaganda that builds up the enemy as cruel—making cruelty his trademark—creates a critical characteristic that cannot be handled. Characterizing the enemy as clever might appear to support the opposition and threaten one's own morale, but it offers a clear feature that one can tackle and deal with. Thus, the potential threat value of the enemy is reduced.

To conclude: an enemy is perceived as actively challenging our desired state of equilibrium. An opponent contains the potential for such a challenge, but will become relevant only when and if we attempt to act on it. Possible enemies or threats are organized in hierarchies and our adjustive behavior is primarily aimed at dealing with the most salient enemy—reducing its threat value, either by restructuring our perception of it or by modifying our self-evaluation in relation to it. An enemy is usually perceived in terms of multiple cues, structured hierarchically. Our response will be primarily aimed at the most salient cue characterizing the enemy at any given time and place.

7

Courage

THE MEANING OF COURAGE

After the war of independence in 1948, Israel awarded only ten medals for supreme courage. At that time, it was felt that such awards and medals were not really becoming to the pioneer spirit of the new country, in which each was naturally expected to do his or her utmost. The picture of the chest of a strutting general covered with ribbons and medals was unpalatable. From that date up to 1973, no further medals were issued; and the only public acknowledgment of acts of valor was a citation in dispatches. But inflation seems to have taken its toll in this, as in other walks of life. After the Yom Kippur War, more than 300 medals of three different grades were awarded. This does not indicate that soldiers were braver during this war than in previous campaigns, but that (it was felt) such acts needed more attention and acknowledgment—perhaps because they were no longer taken for granted, or indeed because the objective battle conditions were the hardest encountered in Israel's history.

Amongst the ten awards given in 1948, there was one awarded to a soldier who cast himself on a barbed wire fence so that his comrades could step on him and over the fence. The platoon was attacking a well-defended Egyptian machine-gun post that was effectively preventing a critical attack on a strategic hill. It proved impossible to penetrate the defense, and the platoon was repelled time and again. At this point, one of the soldiers in the platoon cast himself on the barbed wire, thus formed an effective spring-board over which the rest stepped, and led a successful attack against the defended post. For this act, the highly exclusive and outstanding award—the medal of courage (*Ot Ha'Gvura*)—was given. Today, a routine part of any basic infantry training includes training on how to cast oneself on such wire and form a living springboard over which others can step. Not only is the act not considered specially heroic anymore, but it is very likely that not doing it will lead to disciplinary measures.[1] To paraphrase George Bernard Shaw's reputed statement that "pornography is a matter of geography," it would appear that courage is a matter of time and place—rather than the nature of the act itself. *Courage is the right act at the right time and in the right place.* It must be an act that is perceived to be outstanding in a setting it can drastically affect. The same act in a different setting may be even perceived as cowardly. Not only is the setting of the act critical for determining its heroism; the evaluation by the beholder also determines its perception. Placing a bomb in a crowded street or a bus will be described and perceived as an act of valor by the underground movement fighting for the liberation of its country, but will be perceived as an act of cowardly terrorism by those so attacked.

The usual look at various dictionaries serves to emphasize the different interpretations that "courage" can be given. The Israeli *Ben Shushan* dictionary describes courage as "strength, power, might." Therefore, it relates courage to traits of the individual—rather than to active and dynamic behavior. The Swedish dictionary lists several characteristics: "masculine, manly; dashingness; confidence; daring, fearlessness." These also are descriptions of traits or attitudes (and they are worded rather to the disadvantage of the female sex). On the whole, the Swedish characteristics are more diffuse and possibly less dynamic than those described by the Hebrew dictionary; but nonetheless they only describe the individual's potential, rather than explain his way of perceiving or handling demands.

The British *Chambers Dictionary* describes courage as: "the quality that enables men to meet danger without giving way to fear; bravery, spirit." Bravery is defined as: "courage, heroism; to brave—to meet boldly, to defy, to face." This definition looks at courage as an interaction—an interplay between the perceived threat and the ability (or rather appraised ability) to handle the threat. Threat must first be appraised (instead of "giving way to fear"), and then must be met. Strength or manliness are not sufficient to define a person as courageous; these traits must be applied in a situation that appears to involve a threat to the individual.

The American *Standard Dictionary* elaborates further: Courage is

The quality of mind which meets danger or opposition with intrepidity, calmness and firmness; the quality of being fearless, bravery.

And it goes on to explain:

The brave man combines confidence with firm resolution in the face of danger. Courageous is more than brave, adding the morale element. The courageous man steadily encounters perils to which he may be keenly sensitive, at the call of duty.

It would appear that we are dealing with three levels:

1. The bold or daring—having self-confidence regardless of circumstances, as explained by the Israeli and the Swedish dictionaries

2. The brave—showing the characteristics of the bold, but combining this with awareness and appraisal of danger, as defined by the British dictionary

3. The courageous—showing the characteristics of the brave; but with, in addition, elements of drive or motivation for tackling the situation (drives that go beyond the immediate needs of the individual), as explained by the U.S. dictionary

Obviously, all three kinds or levels of courage involve a valence appraisal that leads to the need for action; and it is the coping appraisal process that differentiates them:

1. The bold individual bases his appraisal on his own potential; his cognitive appraisal shows his abilities to exceed the demands, and thus will produce a high combat potential. The type of individual who seems to emerge is one who, on the affective side, never doubts his abilities. The motivation for action is based on his own needs and the dispositon is best described as endocentric.

2. The brave individual's cognitive appraisal is not predetermined; he might even conclude that the congruence between the threats and his ability is to his disadvantage. But, like the bold, he is backed by a positive appraisal on the affective side; he has a feeling of confidence with an aggressive disposition—high morale, which leads to high combat potential.

3. The courageous individual—on the other hand—has not got this predisposition to a positive appraisal, either of the cognitive or affective side. His appraisal is strongly affected by his sense of duty and obligation to others or by values he shares with others. He has the ecocentric disposition.

A similar differentiation—if from another viewpoint—has been offered by Larsen and Giles (1976), who talked of social courage and existential courage. Social courage was defined as "performing in the pursuit of socially valued goals where the risk primarily involves threat of physical injury and destruction." While existential courage is seen to be "the ability to face or confront anxieties which are derived from the finiteness of the individual." This type of courageous person will be guided by his self-concept and thus less likely to be affected by social pressures. To put it in Aristotle's words: "The man . . . who faces and who fears the right things and from the right motive, in the right way and at the right time, and who feels confidence under corresponding conditions, is brave, for the brave man feels and acts according to the merits of the case and in whatever way the rule directs."

From the foregoing discussion, it is clear that the three categories of courage are viewed along a continuum: One cannot be courageous if one is not brave, and one cannot be brave without at least some boldness. Nonetheless, the dichotomy into the endocentric and ecocentric precursors of courageous behavior appears to have some explanatory value. The same acute behavior may be the final outcome, but it was brought about by different processes. Perceiving only the act of courage, we might appreciate it for its own sake; but, given information about the process behind it, acts known to involve self-sacrifice will be deemed to be more courageous than those based on the need for showing off, or worse—on ignorance of the danger that lies in the situation. The Victoria Cross, the highest medal for military courage awarded in Britain, has sometimes been described as one earned by fools or madmen—that is to say, by those who could not appraise the situation as dangerous, or who disregarded danger for pathological reasons. This may do injustice to many who have earned the medal in circumstances in which they were fully aware of the danger and its consequences; but, nonetheless, it serves to point out that, in this context at least, courage is not necessarily a description of a psychological attribute. Rather it is an evaluation of an act that, at a given time and place, proved of great benefit to the group. Therefore, it can easily happen that an act perceived to be courageous by an individual will not be so perceived by the group, or vice versa—an act heralded as courageous by the group will be not in the least perceived as such by the hero.

What we require for an act to be classified as courageous is that it involve a threat to the well-being of the individual who performs it or to those he closely identifies with. I use 'well-being' rather than 'life' to emphasize that an act such as speaking out against the group's norms—although not necessarily involving any physical danger—might nonetheless be considered to involve a threat to one's well-being. Although we use courage to describe a state of mind, it is most often deduced from an overt act and not because of the attitude behind the act. In fact, the comment that "only fools or madmen earn medals" shows the tendencey to deduce a state of mind from the act, rather than vice versa.

The following discussion of heroism and courage will look at acts of courage, their etiology, and their possible training. But whatever aspect is being discussed, it will be dichotomized into an endocentric or ecocentric viewpoint. Included in that dichotomization is also the observer's viewpoint: Under endocentric will come behavior deemed to reflect the individual's needs or motivation; while under ecocentric will come behavior judged according to the society's needs, norms, and so forth.

MYTH OF HEROISM

Modern Israel has not generated many heroes. I do not mean the ones formally cited for heroism; I mean the names that form part of the national lore. One of the few names famous or infamous is that of Meir Har-Zion. This individual, together with others in a special commando unit led by Arik Sharon, carried out very daring and unconventional raids on the enemy in the 50th (1950)—a period in which Israel was much less powerful than it is today. His actions—although daring—were often without any regard to the formal conventions of warfare, or even the norms of his country. At times, he disregarded orders and the military code; yet his behavior has often been heralded as heroic, and publicly defended as courageous. His escapades have become part of Israel's mythology.

Undoubtedly, the most outstanding act of heroism in Israel's mythology is that of Mazada. This is an example of heroism of the group, not of individuals. To this desert fortress escaped the unsuccessful defenders of Jerusalem in the year 73 A.D. The Romans laid siege to the defenders and their families. When it became clear that all hope was lost, the defenders decided to commit mass suicide. Fathers killed theis sons; sons, their mothers—until no one was left alive to fall into Roman hands. This behavior of the whole group ('normative behavior,' by definition)—"the spirit of Mazada"—is often given as an example of ultimate heroism—an example to follow when facing enormous difficulties: Follow not because of the ultimate outcome, but because it shows determined behavior and the ability to disregard personal safety for the sake of higher values. Act at controlling the enemy by physical destruction of self—which (to return to the strategies of aggression previously discussed) would be described as Ag 7.

Being able to carry out such an unconventional act (rather than the obvious or conventional one of surrender)—an act against human nature, or at least the culture's norms and its religious laws—must have required a great deal of courage. But, at the risk of upsetting many, I feel that one can question whether the act—when analyzed on the individual level—was indeed so courageous as described. In Mazada, the whole group decided and presumably accepted the need to commit suicide. It might even have had the support of the religious code that calls for "dying for the glory of the Lord." This decision created a new norm for the group—a norm so powerful that families saw it as their responsibility to assist each other in the act. Under such circumstances, a person would have to be very powerful—indeed, extremely courageous—not to commit suicide. Thus, it may well have been endocentric behavior that lay behind that group act.

It is interesting that this act of self-sacrifice, rather than another historical example—that of Samson—is taken to be the ultimate heroism, in Israel. Samson—who was captured by the Philistines and tied to their temple's pillars—brought the house down on himself and killed all its occupants, while saying, "Let me die with the Philistines" (Judg. 16:30). Indeed, he committed suicide, but he made the enemy pay dearly for his death. Samson's heroic act was aimed at the enemy; the payoff was the enemy's loss—an ecocentric act that would be described as involving aggressive strategy Ag 3. Mazada's act was heroic because of its effect on those carrying it out; the payoff was their gain, and not the enemy's loss. Even if one views this as having been done in order to serve the glory of the Lord, it is still behavior aimed basically at personal emotional gain, rather than at the enemy.

In a discussion of Jewish heroism, it would be unfair to omit the Maccabeans—especially Judas Maccabaeus, who led a rebellion against the Seleucid army and freed Jerusalem in 164 B.C. His valor—much heralded in the Books of Maccabees—is often lauded in modern Israel. Nonetheless, it is "the spirit of Mazada" that is held to be the epitome of courage; and Mazada, revered more often than Judas's burial place: Modl'in is the place most associated with initiation of new troops and other military ceremonies. "The spirit of the Maccabee" is often associated with the battle of the few against the many. This story led to the development of the myth of the ability of the Israelis to cope with their overwhelming enemies. This coping appraisal has formed the basis for aggressive coping strategies—but just because the historical act was based on a positive appraisal it does not necessarily mean that the resultant behavior was courageous. Discussing the Maccabee myth, Bar Kochba (1980) points out that—in fact—the war was between armies of matched strength, and the false historical picture of the few winning against the many has led to the kind of false coping appraisal that resulted in the excess of self-confidence shown by the Israelis when assessing the Arab strength and threat potential in 1973.

Another national hero in modern Israel is Trumpeldor, who was the defendant of a Jewish settlement in Palestine before the founding of the State of Israel, and who is best known for the fact that, when fatally injured, he stated: "It is good to die for our country." Again, the basic theme is the benefit to the hero—regardless of the consequences for the enemy. It is considered heroic that he appreciated his death and was not afraid to die (for the sake of others), rather than adopt the attitude expressed by General Patton, who stated: "No one ever won a war by dying for his country; he makes the other bastard die for his." The Jewish history of the past hundreds of years is rich in examples of heroic acts of the self-sacrificing kind—the ecocentric act. It is much rarer to come across acts of heroism in which the motto is "It is good to have the enemy die," rather than "It is good to die" (although many that are not so much heralded must have occurred). It is only after the return of the Jews to Israel that this balance seems to have changed: Many more acts of the Ag1 and Ag3 type are cited, and fewer that involve Ag7 behavior are heralded. The endocentric model has become the prevalent one.

This shift in the model for the heroic act seems to be congruent with the general shift in behavior of the Jews in Israel. As described in Chapter 4, Israelis seem to have a high aggressive potential. Intuitively, as well as on the basis of some historical observation, I feel that the aggressive level of Jews outside Israel—and, especially, the strategies of aggression deployed by them—is lower than that of the Israelis. It is not within my competence to offer historical explanations for such differences and developments (if, indeed, there are such); but, if such a change in the general group's aggressive strategies has occurred, it is not surprising that a congruent shift in the model for heroism has also occurred.

Kloskowska (1970), also, argues that examining the types of heroes of a given people or nation helps to understand the character of its culture, and that we can deduce changes in national group characteristics by looking at changes in national heroes.

Most of the above discussion focused on ecocentric or group-oriented acts of heroism. It is interesting to look at a British hero, T. E. Lawrence, as an example of an endocentric—if not egocentric—hero. As Mack (1969) describes him: "Lawrence's struggle for heroism, to give value to the Arab cause, to turn a beleaguered struggle into a glorious triumph, may be regarded psychologically as a displacement—an attempt to redeem his fallen self-regard by elevating alien people. By helping them to fulfill their idealistic needs." It was chance that Lawrence's struggle for heroism was associated with the Arabs; it could well have been with other people or problems. "Already as a boy he put himself through dangerous ordeals to test what he can endure," says Mack. In fact, Lawrence's heroic behavior (that is, his behavior assessed by others to be extraordinary and courageous) was the fulfillment of a deep need of the individual—a drive for action, which required no courage. Indeed, it would probably have required more courage or exerted greater pressure on Lawrence to abstain and control himself—to behave in a normative way—than to cater to the powerful needs of his soul. In a comment on Mack's article, W. L. Langer (1969)—after looking at Lawrence's motives—concludes that: "Lawrence is really a pathetic rather than heroic figure."

Actions explained to originate from deep internal needs—rather than from appraisal of the situation—are now downgraded; their heroism and courage, evaporated. Gal (1980) reported that Israeli post-1973 war medalists showed somewhat higher scores on personality characteristics of "leadership," "devotion to duty," and "perseverance under stress" than the general population, but did not differ from the control group on "sociability," "social intelligence," and "emotional stability." Thus, in opposition to Trites and Sells's (1957) conclusion, it appears that some individual personality traits—rather than social characteristics—are of primary importance for determining who will show heroic behavior, but only under conditions that tend to generate such behaviors. The environment—especially the social environment—is the precursor or prerequisite for heroic behavior, and will presumably have the strongest impact on the ecocentric individual.

But other personality factors interacting with this perception of the environment will determine the final heroic act. It may also be the case that some—like Lawrence—will seek out these "heroism generating" situations, because of their own needs.

THE QUALITY OF COURAGE

The Symptom of Courage

Courage can be viewed as originating in the individual—as being a quality or characteristic of a person that will come forth when the situation warrants it. Thus, Lord Moran, in his book *The Anatomy of Courage* (1945) about his World War II experiences, defines courage as a "morale quality": "It is not a chance gift of nature like aptitude . . . it is willpower that can be spent—and when it is used up—men are finished." "Natural courage" does exist; but it is really fearlessness (that is, "bold," as defined above), and is opposite to the courage of control. Lord Moran describes four types of persons:

1. knew fear but did not show it, and carried on with the job
2. knew fear, showed it, but carried on with the job
3. knew fear, showed it, but did not carry on with the job
4. knew fear, did not show it, and did not carry on with the job

In terms of mapping sentence, it is possible to describe a person's behavior in combat as characterized by:

a1 fear	b1 show	c1 do job
a2 no fear	b2 not show	c2 not do job

bold behavior is: a2 b2 c1
courageous is: a1 (b1 b2) c1

Sooner or later—says Lord Moran—all men will know fear; they differ in their threshold—how much they will take before they know fear (and, presumably, also differ in the point at which they will show fear). The real issue is how they will *function* in spite of their fear: It will be overt and observable behavior that will generally classify behavior as courageous.

A similar differentiation between courage caused by indifference to danger (that is: passive, and not from pathological reasons) and courage in spite of perceived danger was made by Bartlett in 1927, studying experiences from World War I. "Normal courage seems to be sometimes the genuine control of fears by ideals and morale, and sometimes the mere indifference to danger, which is more a matter of intellectual and emotional lethargy than anything else." Courage is not viewed as a trait—not even as "morale quality" to which Moran refers—but rather as an accidental circumstance of personality factors, not of environmental circumstance. In fact, in the index to his book, one finds a listing for "fear," but not for "courage."

Lieutenant Colonel Browne (1976) views courage as an innate characteristic. For him, fear is the absence of courage. The majority of men come into battle without fear, or have overcome it; thus, they are courageous. It is those who have fear of fear who fail. But, according to this author, not all men are similar in this innate quality: "The armies of the pre 1914 era were largely recruited from men of stronger fiber who were less influenced by cultural and soft social conditions, and often lacked the faculty of deep thought, which drew no picture of danger or feeling of fear. It might be said that such men possessed a natural courage, which really was a courage of insensibility to danger."

The courageous soldier seems to be the one who is unaware of danger, not the one who can overcome it. But, like Lord Moran, Browne also views courage as an exhaustible resource, which might run out after long exposure to battle strain. According to Moran's model, exhaustion will eventually lead to an incapacity to act; while, according to Browne, it seems that even fools will eventually realize the real dangers.

That different groups of people have different levels of courage—or at least different fighting spirit—had already been pointed out by Bartlett in 1927. He refers to nations—like the Gurkhas—who are better at attacking, while others are better at withstanding attack.

Marshall (1947) considers courage to be more than an innate quality: "Courage and cowardice are alternative free choices that come to every man. Overriding all emotional stress, that . . . man simply chooses which he prefers and [can] be . . . courageous if he is told he must." Fear—assumes Marshall—is general. But men try to hide it from each other. It finds its expression in specific acts called cowardice. Group pressure against such acts—against deviation from the expected norms—can prevent acts of cowardice. Group pressures actually reduce the free choice of the individual and act on him so that he must "choose" the courageous act.

Blake (1978)—analyzing the "altruistic suicide" acts of soldiers throwing themselves on hand grenades to save their peers—show this act to be more common in the more cohesive group, and among enlisted men than officers. "Group pressure" does not necessarily mean conforming with the overt demands of the group, but may refer to the pressure it exerts by bringing about the individual's total identification with the group—"the subjugation of self for the good of the group." At the same time, it might be argued that to act against group pressure involves as much courage as to act against an enemy threat. But such an act would often be labeled "cowardice" since it is opposite to the group's norms and goals. All of the above approaches look at courage as a personal attribute, to be applied whenever required. It is not determined in relation to a situation, and it seems to be equally available to a person at all levels.

The Profile of a Hero

Are you a man of slightly above average intelligence, around 20 years old? Are you unmarried and without children, and an NCO or midlevel officer? Israeli born and of Western origin? If so, than there is a good chance that you can be an Israeli war hero in the next war.

This is the conclusion drawn by Gal (1980), who investigated nearly 300 Israeli soldiers who were cited for bravery following the 1973 war. His investigation included the two lower grades of awards (*Oz* and *Mofet*), but not the highest award (the *Gvura* medal). It was clearly shown that the soldiers winning awards did not possess special or outstanding personality characteristics. In fact, their personality profile was very similar to that of the top 25 percent of all recruits. Gal used the matched pairs method, in which he compared each of the soldiers who was awarded a medal with another of a similar military rank and stationed in the same unit. Controls were also matched for demographic characteristics (age, personal status, and origin), personal characteristics (different measures of intelligence and attitude), and military variables (training and past operational experience). The author further looked into the nature of the situation in which the act for which the citation was given occurred. The situations were analyzed to show whether:

1. The soldier was a formal commander and acted in terms of his position in the group, or whether he was an informal leader in the group
2. The act was carried out by the soldier himself—independent of other members of the group—or whether several soldiers were directly involved
3. The act occurred under fire
4. The soldier was killed as a result of his actions
5. The act involved saving of wounded soldiers

The personal characteristics and the situational characteristics were analyzed together, using the Multidimensional Space Analysis (MSA) technique (a technique related to that of the SSA discussed in Chapter 9) in order to obtain a structure or typical profile for the person/environment interaction characteristics of heroic acts. Four situations that tend to "generate" heroic acts were described:

1. *The isolated group fighting with their back to the wall*. This is the "no choice" situation (accounting for 27 percent of the cases), where danger—although clearly perceived—cannot be avoided by any means other than an attack, despite what would logically be considered unreasonable odds. But when there is no alternative, odds cease to be unreasonable; and against the certainty of death, an act that appears to have only 1 percent chance is more reasonable than no act at all. However, it must be emphasized that the perception of no alternative is not necessarily restricted to physical alternatives. Psychological imperatives—such as "no surrender"— act as equally powerful constraints on the availability of responses. The history of Israel up to and including the Six Day War was characterized by the phrase "we have no choice," for any war was literally a fight for the very existence of every person in the state. It was only after 1967 that their strategic position allowed the Israelis to consider wars as military campaigns—battles that must be won, but under circumstances allowing for certain setbacks. Each battle became less critical; and the direct threat on the population centers, farther removed. It may be that this alteration in the perception of danger made acts of heroism less self-obvious, which changed the perception of normative behavior and thus led to the introduction of citations—which were previously deemed unnecessary, and even unbecoming. Gal further points out that it is usually the commander who displays the courageous behavior, because he feels an obligation to his men. The physical threat of extinction must have been equal for all members of the group; but the situation is perceived as even more threatening by the commander, who feels responsibility for the well-being of others. It is primarily the environment that forms the reference for this ecocentric behavior.

2. *Face-to-face combat* (accounting for 18 percent of the cases), in which the hero spontaneously assumes command from a wounded or killed commander or comrade. The structure of the military situation has been upset by the commander being incapacitated. This structure is reinstated—and the organization, maintained—by a person who has sufficient grasp of the situation and an ability to analyze and structure it. His behavior can probably be described as being on the intellectual or cognitive level, rather than the emotional. It is interesting to note that the hero in such a situation usually survives to tell the tale. This situation was labeled "last remnant and savior." It is probably determined primarily by endocentric orientation.

3. *A self-sacrificing situation* (10 percent of the cases), in which a few men are surrounded by a numerous enemy and one soldier gives up his life to save the rest. This is a situation in which it is most difficult to ascertain the motivation behind the act. It may be clear that the act resulted in saving members of the group; and in some of these cases—like when a soldier casts himself on a grenade that fell into the bunker—such motivation is self-evident. But there may well be such acts resulting from a miscalculation by the hero—not due to deliberate, premeditated behavior. Such acts may also reflect a pathological need of the individual (Blake 1978); thus, both endocentric and ecocentric orientation could lead to the same behavior.

4. *The hero fights to the last bullet* (13.9 percent of the cases), knowingly carrying on to the point where he must inevitably be killed. This situation seems to me to have a lot in common with the first. In both, "no alternative" is the deciding factor. The difference mainly lies in that the first situation describes the effect a group can have

on individual behavior, while the latter is an act of an isolated individual. The first situation implies that the whole group (or its majority) has a similar perception and appraisal of the situation—which characterizes a cohesive group—while, in the latter situation, the appraisal (right or wrong) depends on one individual only. The first situation will affect the individual with ecocentric perception; the latter, only one with endocentric perception.

Gal's conclusion was that, since all cases—but for about 20 examined (7 percent)—could be classified into the four groups and since a prior differentiation between heroes and nonheroes could be made on the basis of any personality or biographical data, the situation—rather than the person—generates acts of heroism, even though certain personal characteristics are more likely to contribute to such behavior.

If we attempt to classify these four situation types in terms of the aggressive behavior strategies suggested in Chapter 4, we find that:

- Situation 1 (*back to the wall*) involves the Ag1 strategy—physical action aimed at destroying the enemy.
- Situation 2 (*face-to-face*) involves a mixture of Ag1 and Ag6—nonphysical action on self (taking control of the situation and group) in order to control the situation.
- Situation 3 (*self-sacrifice*) is described by Ag5—involving physical action on self in order to control the enemy (that is, neutralize him).
- Situation 4 (*fight to the last*) again involves Ag1.

The same aggressive strategy can be used by individuals with ecocentric and endocentric orientations. The aggressive strategies deployed are a result of an interaction between the personal disposition of the individual and the demands imposed on him. It is not surprising that neither the situations described by Gal nor others described below involve nonphysical strategies aimed at control. The situational demands of the battle limit the possible coping strategies—regardless of the individual's disposition. A possible case where Ag6 strategy—nonphysical in order to control—might be deemed to occur is that case of a soldier refusing a palpably illegal order by a superior officer—to shoot prisoners, for example. This act of courage and its implications will be discussed later. To conclude in Gal's words: "As a situation becomes more stressful and threatening, there will be more situational related factors than person related factors that will account for the observed behavior."

Situations 2 and 4 are both endocentric situations in my terminology, while situation 1 and 3 are ecocentric situations. Gal—who predicts the increase of the importance of the situational factors with the increase in stress—would expect more ecocentric behavior. However, such behavior or change in orientation is only likely if the individual can perceive himself as part of the environment or group. As stress increases, we can indeed expect members of a cohesive group to become more cohesive—to be more willing to sacrifice themselves for one another. But in the case of a non-cohesive group, we expect further desolution of the group, and more selfish (endocentric) behavior. This will be further discussed in relation to morale in the following chapter. Gal's analysis is based on Israeli troops and—in fact—mostly on the better troops, which are fairly cohesive. In their case, "the situation" for the individual also included—besides the external threat—"his group" in the concept of "self," and, thus, stress did indeed increase their importance.

A study in a somewhat similar vein was carried out by Blake and Butler (1976), investigating the highest U.S. military award—the Congressional Medal of Honor. The authors classified the acts for which the medal was awarded into six groups:

1. Rescue, which—in terms of the model of strategies of aggression—can be described as Ag5 (struggle; physical acting in order to control)

2. Extra aggressiveness, such as charging the enemy: Ag1 (eradication; physically acting in order to destroy

3. Grenade acts, referring to actions of absorbing full enemy power (such as grenades): Ag5 (fight; physical deterring in order to control)

4. Rear defense, staying behind and holding the enemy: Ag5 (physical acts in order to control)

5. Refusing medical aid: Ag8 (nonphysical deterring in order to control)

6. Leadership: Ag6 (nonphysical act in order to control)

On the basis of this classification, two combat orientations were isolated: war winning and soldier saving. A basically similar dichotomy was found by Gal. The former category was most frequently associated with officers (about 70 percent, compared with 30 percent enlisted men), while the latter award was more associated with the enlisted men (69 percent in the lower ranks, compared with 30 percent of officers).

It would appear that the same situation affected the perception or orientation of the soldiers in different ways. Because of that difference, different strategies were utilized. It is clear that the formal position of the soldiers in the organization—their formal rank in the military—affected the pattern of their behavior. While it seems logical to argue that the opportunity for heroic acts within the category of leadership is much greater for officers than enlisted men, no such argument can be presented for the "grenade" or "medical refusal" categories. Different acts of heroism involve different risks—or at least so it would appear, judging from the different rates of posthumous awards. In the group of enlisted men, 82 percent received the award posthumously, as compared with 25 percent among the rank of captain or above. Blake and Butler offer the possible explanation that men and officers have a fundamentally different orientation or appraisal of the battle situation. The primary loyalty and identification of the enlisted men is with their peers—their buddies—while that of the officers is with the organization. The implication is that men will act first and foremost to help their peers; while officers, to support the organization. This differential value system would lead the enlisted men and the officers to perform different acts of heroism in the same battle situation. However, the authors conclude on a rather more cynical note. It is not that men and officers are differentiated by their choice of action, but that the organization—or more explicitly, the committees responsible for the awards—tend to reinforce the behavior they expect and see as fitting for the different kinds of soldiers. Thus, the soldier-saving activities are deemed appropriate for the enlisted men, while leadership or aggression are more appropriate for the officers.

The difference in expectation by the organization can also be described as endocentric—the expectation that the men primarily look after themselves and their own level—and ecocentric—the expectation that officers identify with the greater organization and its more abstract values. Such expectations by the establishment—especially if they are so obviously expressed and reinforced, as suggested by Blake and Butler (1976)—must shape behavior. However, I doubt if the Israeli military system tends to similarly differentiate heroisms appropriate to the different ranks. All the same, one of the ten citations given in Israel in 1948 was to the commander of a naval operation. In this operation, tiny boats loaded with explosives were driven toward the Egyptian flagship, which threatened the port of Haifa. The driver of the boat had to guide it into near proximity of the target and then—at the last minute—abandon the boat, which carried on to hit its target. It was not the driver of the boat that sank the ship—but, rather, the officer in charge of the operation—who received the citation.

The British are even more explicit in their differentiation between courage and courage, according to the formal status of the soldier: The Distinguished Service *Cross* and the Military *Cross* are awarded to officers only; for the same acts and in the same place, enlisted men will receive the Distinguished Service *Medal* and the Military *Medal*, instead. This is in line with the tradition started by Cromwell (1590), who awarded the Dunbar Medal to all ranks—but in gold for officers, and silver for other ranks. I suppose this is better than the later development during the Peninsula Wars (1807-14), in which the army offered gold medals for courage only to officers of the rank of lieutenant colonel and above. The first medals to be awarded to other ranks were presented in 1816, after the Battle of Waterloo. It is interesting that, at about the same time, Napoleon commented, "It is astonishing what men will do for a 'bit of ribbon'." While devaluation of medals seems to have occurred over time—since they are now available to all—some medals have actually increased in value. For example, when first awarded in 1856, the Victoria Cross could be earned by saving another's life or by capturing the enemy's standard. After World War II, much more stringent requirements were set, and the medal was only awarded for outstanding behavior in the face of the enemy.

Even more explicit differentiation of the different impacts of the same battle stresses on officers and men (this sounds as if "officers" are more that just "men") is seen in the United States: Pay for "extra hazardous duty" in Vietnam was $110 for officers, and $50 for their comrades in arms who did not have the right epaulet tags.

By now, it must be clear that cultural or social norms determine what is labeled as courageous behavior—and thus, indirectly guide or assist in the development of such behavior. Other behavior, which might be described as equally courageous by other cultural norms, will tend to be discouraged. The individual will find it easier to take risks and act daringly along lines that the culture approves (for example, forms of attack) than those that it disapproves (for example, forms of restraint).

When Israel decided to reintroduce citations, committees deliberated for a long time on how many citations—and of which grade—should be awarded. Rather prolonged haggling went on, while each branch of the armed forces and the units within them were given a ration of awards (at least of the lower two grades). It was up to each authority to distribute their portion, and I know of no case where awards were returned because no suitable candidate could be found. A final committee had to approve all awards; but, in fact, the desire of each separate authority for its share of glory determined the evaluation given to many of the outstanding acts. Thus, the same act might or might not have received its official citation, depending on how many other soldiers had displayed similar behavior in the same branch of the service at that time.

In a most interesting account, Major Newman (1967) describes how the heroic behavior of a U.S. sergeant was upgraded from meriting "only" a Silver Star to the highest award—the Congressional Medal of Honor. The author describes how, with paperwork only, he managed to change an administrative decision, and thus create a new hero. Heroism is not only in the eye of the beholder (and more often than not regulations require at least two beholders to classify behavior as heroic); it is also in the pen of the administrator.

Notwithstanding these rather cynical comments on the formal meaning of courage, the fact remains that some men do act in ways that most would not follow—not out of stupidity or depravity, but out of deep conviction and with full understanding. It is such men—or the circumstances forming such behaviors—that we have to discuss, because it is these men and their acts that often sway the battle—and even the war.

THE MAKING OF A HERO

The Unconventional Personality

Cultural norms and expectations have been shown to determine what behavior is labeled heroic or courageous. At the same time, "the norm" of the average expected behavior of the average soldier is not to be heroic. It requires unusual—and therefore "not normal"—behavior to be perceived as heroic. Thus, it is the deviant who might be the hero.

Significant breaking with norms can occur both in the quantitative aspect (for example, charging onward while others take cover) and in the qualitative aspect (for example, being the first to think of using a body as a bridge across barbed wire). The element of daring or bravado is important, but equally important is the element of originality. One could argue that originality always requires some daring. Galileo's new concept of the universe required daring—not only in proposing a theory in direct opposition to that of the Catholic church, but no less in his own ability to break away from a well-established "truth." Our psychological—and often physical—safety and security lie in operating within frameworks and structures that we know. The stronger the stresses on us, the more we tend to rely on well-proved and well-known reference systems. To be able to abandon such security, especially under stress—to break new ground, apply new methods, and develop new concepts—requires at least as much courage as to pursue well-known patterns of behavior against high odds.

Koestler (1964) describes the decisive phase of the creative process as "when the rational controls are relaxed and the creative person's mind seems to regress from the disciplined thinking to the less specialized more fluid way of mentation." In a way, it appears that discipline and courage are opposite ends of a stick. While discipline seeks to codify patterning and predetermine behavior, courage—or at least one aspect of it—involves the breaking of known and accepted patterns, rules, or norms of behavior. (The following chapter will be more concerned with these aspects of discipline.)

A term often used in association with "creativity" is that of "breaking set"—the ability to free and separate an object or a concept from the setting or association in which we are accustomed to perceive it or use it. This is followed by the transfer of that object or concept into a new setting and a new application. Koestler describes such a process as one that "implies a temporary suspension of the 'rules of the game' which control our reasoning routines; the mind in labour is momentarily liberated from the tyranny of the rigid, overprecise schemata [and from] its built-in prejudices and hidden axioms."

By definition, practically, an act of courage is an unusual or original act—an act that many others, faced with the same situation, did not carry out. Often, they did not do so because they had not thought of it; while, at other times, they might have thought of it, but did not dare to do it. People differ in their ability for creative thinking, but those who have this ability are unlikely to confine its application to the killing of the enemy—to battle. It is not only the approved opposition that might be attacked in original ways; some of the basic assumptions, tenets, and holy cows in the home pastures might also be questioned and set out for original criticism. Thus, it is perhaps not surprising that the soldiers who do not take kindly to discipline; who are troublesome for the establishment; who doubt, question, and rebel against authority and the established way of doing things are often also those who prove to be most effective when the established system breaks down. Rocking the boat in smooth waters is frowned on, but often rewarded with medals when the seas are stormy.

A person capable of the most original and unconventional strategies—as General Dayan showed himself to be (in military strategies, as well as in opening Israel's borders to citizens of enemy countries after the 1967 war, in order to normalize relationships)—is also a person capable of disregarding established rules and order (as in Dayan's treatment of rules concerning archeological digs and possession of archeological finds). It may well be that a search for the unconventional—and thus, daring—personality lay behind the German attempt to recruit submarine crews from the jail population, which had already shown disregard for the laws of the land. This attempt—like similar ones in other countries that were building special task forces—seems to have failed. Probably, those involved—although capable of breaking the rules—did not feel motivated to restrict this ability to the goal prescribed by the authorities. Thus, they rejected the framework in which they were placed in the military, just as they had rejected the framework of their civilian life. An even more explicit association between heroism and pathology is offered by Rank (1909), who shows that many of history's famous heroes were driven by paranoid needs and other psychological disturbances. Such explanations might describe the genesis of unconventional heroic behavior, but does not detract from the value of such behavior for the group.

I have never studied acts of heroism; but, while selecting candidates for special commando forces and other unconventional tasks, I became aware that those who would be formally classified as having sociopathic tendencies often proved themselves later to be the most outstanding soldiers. Clearly, too many or too strong sociopathic or psychopathic tendencies (a tendency toward behavior that disregards the codes or conventions of a given society) will raise doubt as to the soldier's reliability and motivation to act in the services of his society. But having some such tendencies seems to increase the likelihood of that soldier's being eccentric, original, and creative—a potential that, in the right circumstances, might prove of great value. Also, in the right circumstances, this potential might generate acts of heroism and courage. It may seem to be a rather risky business to rely on the selection of psychopaths for heroes. It may be scientifically doubtful, as well as morally objectionable. The critical question then remains whether it is possible to train for at least this important aspect of heroism.

In adults, the ability for creative thinking seems to be a fixed quantity. Although it may be further developed in each individual, the actual potential is either innate or has been determined during the early developmental phase. Many techniques for developing such a potential are available. Essentially, they have in common the development of a critical, questioning, and even doubting attitude. But such an approach is in direct opposition to a basic tenet of the military institution—obedience, discipline, and unquestioning acceptance of the orders of the commanding officer. The military spends an enormous amount of time and effort in shaping the soldiers' behavior into following and accepting unchallengeable rules (see the next chapter for a further discussion of this). Attempting to generate a doubting and critically questioning attitude within such a framework leads to a direct conflict of interests. In fact, one could well conclude that the conventional military system is directly biased against the development of original thought—at least on the lower level—and thus creates antiheroic conditions, rather than fosters acts of courage. When they occur, such acts happen in spite and not because of the military system. Luckham (1971) equates heroism with initiative: Freedom of action and initiative are necessary for heroism—action that organizations in general, and military organizations in particular, often abhor above all.

However, this discussion has considered only one aspect of the act of courage. The other—involving daring and disregard for self in order to help the group—is indeed encouraged by the military organization. The more cohesive and interdependent the group is, the more is the individual in it willing to sacrifice himself for his peers; and it is the military organization that often succeeds in forming such cohesive groups (Janowitz and Little 1974).

Risk Taking

What must be conspicuous by its absence in the above discussion is the element of motivation. Clearly, it is not sufficient to be able to have original thoughts and unconventional ideas to become a hero. Neither is it sufficient to land in a situation that calls for heroism. One must also want to act in such a way, and be ready to do so even at a risk to oneself. One must be willing to take risks. Himmelstein and Blaskovics (1960) showed that ROTC candidates selected those of their peers as "best for combat" who obtained the highest scores on a risk-taking scale, and vice versa. It was also those candidates who scored highest on that scale who elected to serve in active combat units. The image of the good fighter seems to be the risk taker; but can one therefore conclude that the best fighters—and indeed heroes—are risk takers? I know of no investigation that has looked into a general combat behavior of soldiers who earned medals, but my strong impression is that medal earners do not come exclusively from the best all-around soldiers. However, it should be mentioned that Gal (1980) found no case of AWOL among medal earners, while the control group had a mean of .98 absences. It is even more certain that not all outstanding soldiers are awarded medals. Some might even argue—as did Shakespeare's Falstaff—that "the better part of valour is discretion." Much is determined by chance, circumstances, and opportunity—as shown by Gal—as well as by the personal disposition interacting with these conditions. Which of these variables will have the critical impact on the appraisal process must depend—among other things—on the endocentric or ecocentric disposition of the individual.

Watson (1978) reports that soldiers who committed atrocities in Vietnam were also the type most likely to volunteer to high-risk missions, to gravitate to the more risky positions in a platoon, as well as to be three times more likely to earn medals than other soldiers. Watson argues that the tendency for such deviant (and, and this case, pathological) behavior is clearly a personality trait interacting with circumstances allowing for such behavior. The tendency for risk taking is clearly a personality characteristic (see Chapter 5). The level of probability of outcome that, for some, will be sufficient to be interpreted as certain or justifiable will be considered by others as inadequate. As pointed out in Chapter 2, not the objective probability of an event—but its subjective appraisal—determines its perception, and therefore the action taken toward it. Thus, what is appraised by the observer to be "risk taking" may not be so appraised by the actor himself. For an act to be heroic, it must involve risk in the eye of the hero; and, if the act is not so perceived—whether due to inability to see the risks involved, or because of having a very high risk threshold—the act is not really courageous.

Each group determines its own level of what behavior—under what circumstances—becomes risky. As one becomes accustomed to certain conditions (for example, the handling of explosives), one considers them less risky. This baseline shift affects all members of the group, and the risk taker will increase his real risk taking as the group's baseline changes—a phenomenon known as "risky shift." Thus, the same act—involving the same objective risk—will cease to be viewed as risky (and consequently, not be potentially heroic) when others perceive it as involving only a reasonable risk.

THE NEED FOR COURAGE

We tend to assume that it requires more courage to fight than to flee—that the natural tendency of the untrained soldier is to escape from the battlefield, but that his sense of duty and loyalty keeps him going in spite of that basic desire to escape. But, as Keegan (1976) points out: "The dynamics of battle, forward surge, mechanical and topographical features [lack of coverage] make it easier to fight than to flight. Basically there is a strong resistance to movement in the modern army, partly material, partly psychological. This resistance might be as strong as the enemy's opposition."

Other conditions of modern warfare—such as the sudden close engagements with massive firepower, where survival depends on having immediate and overwhelmingly superior striking impact; the ever-increasing reliance on small independent groups and the pressure they generate—probably also make flight the greater of the two evils. Thus, "courage in the face of the enemy" is much supported by external conditions, which could lead to the fact that one type of act of real courage (as previously defined) is in direct opposition to the aims of the fighting group—the refusal to fire when all others do so, in cases where the order is believed to be immoral. Courage is unusual—even deviant—behavior aimed at overcoming what is most stressful to the individual. As I have often pointed out, what is most stressful depends on subjective appraisal. Danger to life and limb may be most stressful to one; while danger to those who rely on him, the most stressful to another. In terms of courage, there may be no difference between physical and moral courage—provided each demands this unusual behavior from a person who is most threatened by physical or moral stress, respectively.

According to Richardson (1978), the threat to one's comrades is perceived as the primary stress (an ecocentric disposition). Thus, acts of sacrifice for them will be the primary motivation for the fighting spirit, and presumably also for acts of courage. In a somewhat similar vein reasons Field Marshal Lord Slim (quoted by Richardson), who assumes that the regimental colors inspire more immediate loyalty than duty to king or queen. According to Richardson, even loyalty to the commanding officer is secondary to that of loyalty to peers. An investigation carried out in Israel during the 1973 war confirms the enormous importance of loyalty to comrades in inspiring the will to fight; but it shows that the primary factor was identification with the direct commanding officer, rather than identification with peers.

This difference in emphasis may be an artifact of the development of modern warfare. Whereas in the past, great emphasis was placed on close formation, mutual support, and close contact—that is, on support and interaction with the surroundings—the trend today is the use of smaller and independent groups, dispersed and out of direct contact with each other. The modern basic military group is so small that it becomes equated with "the primary group," and is thus very similar to the concept of self. This is why, in the model, actions and attitudes that relate to the small group are described as endocentric. At the same time, the individual soldier has to rely much more on his commanding officer for orientation in the fog of battle, for he receives much less direct visual information about the overall battle situation. If identification with the CO is high and the CO is part of the group, the importance of endocentric information increases again. The shift to emphasis on endocentric appraisal might also lie in different cultural orientations. In Israel, the role of the leader is epitomized by the words "Follow me." The leader is in front; he is the one who sets the example, is first to do what he demands of his men, and is to be followed at all times as the one who sets the norms for the group's behavior. He is referred to by his function (for example, company commander) rather than by his rank (for example, major).

This is the optimal modern leadership model (Gabriel and Savage 1978) but is not always followed. In contrast, one can take the Swedish orientation. Here, at least as has developed after many generations of a peacetime military system, the leader is a reflector of the group's norm rather, than the creator of it. A good leader is one who can represent, reflect, and structure the group's attitude and desires; he is not the one who forms them. He is the manager referred to by his rank, not the director. His role is ecocentric—rather than endocentric—from the group's point of view, because he is an outsider (however much admired) and not an integral part of the unit. In fact, I suspect that a leader who sets out to give an outstanding personal example that is in some way deviant from the group's norms will be completely rejected. While in Israel the leader's primary function in easing the stress of battle is to lead the group by structuring the environment, in Sweden it is to guide the group by structuring the group itself. This difference may well be a result and adaptation to circumstances (more than 180 years of peace), and might disappear if Sweden were exposed to real threats. It may be that such differences also exist between the British and Israeli perceptions of a leader, or possibly even exist between different subcultures and even between different military units.

Bourne (1969) has pointed out that differences in the perceived stress of the same situation by different soldiers depends on the coherence of perception of the threat: "Nor can the objective threat of death and mutilation be interpreted as a stress without consideration of the manner in which the individual perceives the threat." When Muslims declare a jihad—a holy war—the believer is guaranteed a place in heaven if he dies in the war. This removes much of the threat of death, and might even make it an attractive outcome. Similarly, the Japanese kamikaze pilot's fear of death must have been largely neutralized by the honor and positive consequences of such a death. Bourne goes on to say: "It is that each subject utilized very extensive and effective psychology defences to handle the events with which he is faced. The defences enable the man to perceive reality in such way that he minimizes the dangers it represents, as well as creates for himself a feeling of invulnerability and omnipotence."

Lazarus (1976) sums up: "Death is feared in different ways and for different reasons, depending on the *motivation patterns* of the individual. Its psychological effects on people can only be fully understood by considering the impact of death on their most important personal goals or commitments" (italics in the original). As men can minimize the perception of danger by selective perception, they can enforce the perception of confidence by their evaluation of their own abilities in different areas. When the threat is seen as a physical one (requiring great strength or endurance) and the individual appraises himself as having great physical ability, the threat value is decreased. Courageous behavior is more likely in those areas in which the individual feels most competent or has high self-esteem. It is not surprising that, as shown by the medals awarded, men excel in the area of instrumental performance; while officers, most in leadership. Military training as well as social pressures lay different emphasis on the values and self-concepts of men and officers, and these must affect the areas in which they are both able and willing to show outstanding behavior.

TRAINING FOR COURAGE

A critical question remains to be answered: Can we train for courage? One may be able to train to overcome fear. This—suggests Bowman (1973)—could be done by making soldiers climb dangerous rocks or handle snakes. It seems to me that such methods might increase the confidence of soldiers in handling specific frightening situations (if, indeed, they happen to be frightened of snakes), but it cannot guarantee that they will also be fearless when facing a dissimilar situation. However, it could be argued that what is being trained is general self-confidence—the development of trust in one's ability to handle difficult situations. According to the model, such basic confidence in one's abilities relative to environmental demands is one of the foundations for coping—but, although it is a prerequisite of courage, it does not guarantee it. One can—and must—guarantee every element (cognitive and affective) in the system leading to combat performance. But even that offers no more than the prerequisites for courage.

The factors that differentiate courageous behavior from generally effective combat behavior are the unusual situation, and the ability to be able to construct a new solution to the unusual situation. One can train for many unusual and unexpected situations; but when one learns to properly respond to them, they cease to be unusual and unexpected—and thus, by definition, reactions to them are not courageous. What remains is to train for the ability to think in an original and independent way, either as an individual or as a member of the group. This ability one can train—each within his potential.

Such training is not situation bound and is a skill that the individual can apply to any situation, if he is so motivated. But such skills are—again, by definition—aimed at breaking concepts and at disregarding norms and rules; and, thus, they are very likely to come into direct conflict with the demands of discipline in the military system. In Israel at any rate, such explicit training is allowed only in a few choice units and task forces, who are encouraged to ignore conventions; and the price of their (at times) antidisciplinary behavior, passively accepted. It is in these units that one can observe outstanding courageous behavior (which, however, is often not considered so heroic within the norms of the units themselves). The time factor is the most critical decision-making element in battle. It takes courage to make decisions when one lacks data and is under the pressure of time. However, one can train for fast decision making—which then increases the effectiveness of a less courageous decision maker to that of a more courageous one, by virtue of the acquired skill.

One could select individuals who would be more likely to perform in a "courageous" way—for example: in the face of death, by selecting those who are not afraid to die. Such might be an effective way to achieve a goal, but it would be false to describe such behavior as "courageous." Selection of heroes is impossible—what one can do is strive to have maximal combat effectiveness by guaranteeing congruence of appraisal, morale, and motivation. This—coupled with both training of skills and encouragement of original and unconventional thinking—increases the likelihood that, when the right circumstances occur, a person will react in a courageous way.

SUMMARY

An act of courage is an act that involves a new original response on the part of an individual, under conditions perceived to offer a threat to his value system and perceived a risk to himself. It is not the act itself that determines courage—but the way an individual or a group perceive the circumstances, and their response to it. In practice, formal recognition of courage is given to those acts that contribute to the goals of the group, regardless of the meaning of the act to the individual. To create a greater potential for courageous actions is possible by increasing the ability for unconventional thinking. But the real aim of the military (and others) is to assist brave behavior, rather than create heroes. Such can be achieved by reducing the perceived incoherence of the situation, increasing the individual's perceived ability to cope with the situation, and—in addition—increasing his potential for original thought. The more structured the situation is perceived to be and the more coherent the information about it, the better the fighting potential and the less need there is for heroism. This offers a strong argument for a more generalized training of soldiers: For example, the infantry soldier should have some training in the basis of tank warfare. By this means, many of the threats of unfamiliar methods of attack are reduced; the power and time scale of these methods begin to make sense and can be better appraised—and responded to. For the infantryman, "the tank" then ceases to be a diffuse threat that only heroes dare tackle, but becomes a weapon that can be dealt with by skills and understanding available to all.

I have deliberately not included some detailed and concrete descriptions of heroism to illustrate my points. The trouble is that one cannot illustrate these points by anecdotes showing a clear case of heroism—even by citing such apparently heroic and self-sacrificing acts as casting oneself on a grenade to save buddies. Glass (1953)—for example—explains that the process of group identification and pressure "deliberately forces" and "compels" a person to such acts. It follows that any acclaimed act of heroism can be "explained away": The hero acted because of selfish needs or stupidity. This sort of analysis debases the importance of the act to the group and the individual, while adding no general explanatory value.

The importance of understanding the perceptual framework that leads to heroism is so as to encourage and stimulate such behavior in the future, and not to make light of past acts. There is no point in attempting to quantify and measure heroism. The above analysis is an explanatory concept, not an assessable one. Like love and pain, heroism is a subjective concept, which nonetheless—when it affects the environment—can lead to very concrete and objective results.

NOTE

1. In fact, such behavior was taught in the British forces during World War II, and was introduced by General Laskov in the first Israeli officer's course; but, nonetheless, it was not a routine part of a soldier's basic training, nor was it expected under such conditions.

8

Discipline

THE MEANING OF DISCIPLINE

A question often asked by visitors to Israel—and I have often been asked the same abroad—is: "How is it that the Israeli military, which so obviously lacks overt formal discipline, is such an effective fighting machine?" As a matter of fact, the same question has often been asked within Israel, when comparing the very informal discipline of the paratroopers and that of the much more formal discipline of the armored service—while appreciating the effectiveness of both. It is often thought that this lack of discipline is a survival of the partisan origin of the Israeli military. However, as Rothenberg (1979) writes: "He [Dayan in 1953] de-emphasized outward appearance, ceremony and formal discipline, and instead stressed the primacy of the combat mission." When appointed commander in chief, Dayan faced a demoralized and poor army. It was his unconventional and highly pragmatic approach that raised the level of the army to such an effective force. Over the years, the norms have changed again, but differently in different branches of the service. I well remember how, on my first visit to units in the Sinai after my appointment as commander of the military psychology unit, I discovered that I had to adapt to these different norms. Entering the tent of a paratrooper battalion commander, I saluted—which, besides earning me a rather disdainful look—also served to alienate me from the gathered officers and label me as a General Staff Pen Pusher! Several miles further down the road and a few hours later, I omitted the salute when meeting with an armored battalion commander—which nearly resulted in my expulsion from that unit. In fact, I was probably forgiven by both commanding officers only because I was clad in naval uniform—which automatically explained my ignorance of proper behavior, to both of them.

Later, I often discussed the concept of discipline with the paratrooper battalion commander, who was—and is—one of the most oustanding leaders in the Israeli Defense Forces (IDF). For him, discipline had to be strictly functional:

It is a poor policy to make the soldier go through acts for which he cannot see any reason, just because orders say so. If one cannot explain the purpose for a way of behavior it is best not to demand it. Occasionally one has, without explanation, to give orders which appear illogical. These will be followed by a soldier who knows that his commanding officer is not in the habit of behaving illogically, that he must have a reason for such orders. Trust has been built up and the commanding officer can call upon this credit when it is needed. But if the soldier has never seen and accepted the reasons behind orders and particular discipline, he will treat all orders as compulsion and coercion, to be avoided whenever possible.

The paratroopers did not salute; their encampment did not have all its stones arranged in geometrical patterns; nor were all nonmovable objects in them whitewashed. But they kept meticulous time, looked after their equipment, gave accurate information, and obeyed operational orders to the letter. However, one of their most famous officers—Arick Sharon—and another outstanding officer—Moshe Dayan—disobeyed direct orders from the commander in chief when they thought that their assessment of a battle situation was more correct than that of the highest commander. I suppose navies can also point to Nelson, who was well known for his insubordination. This might well turn out to be the thin edge of the wedge, when a soldier allows himself to disobey an order because he feels it to be patently wrong. It would appear to be the most fundamental breach of the basis of all military operations, and yet—as we shall later see—there are circumstances where blind obedience is considered a worst fault than disobedience.

The armored divisions—whose encampments were always much neater, their uniforms tidy and correct, and their salutes impeccable—were not less efficient for all that. However, I wonder what would have happened to their efficiency if discipline had been according to the paratrooper's norms, just as I wonder how the paratroopers would have functioned under more rigid formal discipline. The operational mode of the paratroops is based on small units with a high degree of flexibility and autonomy. Each individual is directly involved in action and can often personally affect the results of the troop's actions. He often has to make independent decisions; and, although the general plans are laid out, he has to adapt and extemporize a great deal in varying conditions—and show a great deal of individual initiative. In contrast, a tank crew has a much more rigid framework in which to operate. The technical and mechanical parameters are critical limiting factors affecting all members of the crew—as a unit. Exact routines and rigid procedures are required by the machinery on which they depend. Electronic and mechanical limitations predetermine their ability to act as a unit, and their interactions with others as a larger group. Each member of the crew has restricted and predetermined functions, which must be rigidly followed so that the unit may function as a whole. Their freedom of individual choice—as well as their chance for individual initiative—is much limited, compared with that of a paratrooper or even an ordinary infantry soldier.

These restrictions are even more extreme for members of a ship's crew, not to say a submarine crew. Each member of these crews has strictly predetermined functions that he has to carry out with little or no knowledge of what the rest of the crew are doing. He has to blindly follow orders, knowing that each deviation from them might well lead to disaster. Only the captain has an overall knowledge of the situation; only he can decide what is to be done, or initiate action. Absolute obedience—perfect discipline—are essential for the survival of the individual. There is no way in which an individual can cope or come through a battle in a ship, other than by perfect discipline. An infantry soldier can always feel (however mistaken he may be) that, by disregarding an order and taking the initiative, he may succeed better or survive better than by following the order. No crew member—be it tank or submarine—can feel that he, as an individual, can escape or survive without coordinated action with the rest of the crew.

Thus, separate units and the services themselves place different demands on the soldiers and often do require different modes of behavior—from the very rigid and restricted to the more varied and unexpected. To have the optimal effect, training or education must be congruent with the demands. Rigid, unthinking discipline may well be the most appropriate behavior for the submarine or tank crews, but may be disadvantageous and counterproductive for the paratrooper. The difference between discipline as a means (acquisition of specific patterns of response aimed at handling specific situations) and discipline as an end (obedience without question to all orders) decreases as the situational demands impose greater restrictions on the options of behavior. Conflict as to the meaning of discipline occurs when one tries to generalize the optimal discipline required to handle one situation to all other situations, however different.

Discipline has clearly different meanings for different individuals and different groups. A rather superficial—but nonetheless instructive—look at different dictionaries might serve to illustrate the point.

The Swedish *Academy Dictionary* defines discipline as:
    Obedience, in good order, regular, tidy

The Hebrew *Ben Shushan* dictionary definition is:
    1. Listening (accepting) another's orders, attention
    2. Acceptance of authority, the duty of obedience to established order or norms

The American *Standard Dictionary*:
1. A systematic training or subjection to authority, especially the training of moral, mental or physical powers by instruction or excercise
2. The result of this: subjugation: habit of obedience
3. Punishment for the sake of training

And finally the British *Chambers Dictionary*:
1. Instruction, training or mode of life accordance with rules
2. Subjection to control, order, severe training

While the Swedish and Israeli definitions of discipline emphasize the passive, accepting role of discipline (that is, listening and obedience), the U.S. definition lays emphasis on the active imposition of—or subjugation by—discipline. The former perceive discipline as following a code of conduct on a more or less voluntary basis, based on blind trust in authority and on acceptance of authority in general; the latter approach regards acceptance of orders as fundamentally a coercive process, enforcing a specific pattern of behavior.

Already in biblical times, the people of Israel—when accepting the laws on Mount Sinai—responded with: "We shall do and listen" (Exod. 24:7)—We shall accept the order, carry it out without question, and only later will require explanation or motivation. This emphasis on blind obedience in all areas of behavior has also been the theme of the then chief education officer of the Israeli Defense Forces—General Shalev—as expressed in an interview reported in a daily paper (*Ha'aretz*, 14 July 1978): "You receive an order—carry it out. One does not argue, there is no need for explanations or ideology . . . the command decides that the hat will be on the head—on the head will it be . . . it does not require logical explanation." We shall later return to the hat—the symbol of all that lies behind a good soldier, according to General Shalev! Discipline for him is a virtue in itself: It is the end, rather than the means. Apparently, however, even Shalev realized that such blind obedience needs explanation—at least after the order has been fulfilled—for he continues in his interview to say, "The hat embodies elements of appearance, the esthetic aspect and habits of tidiness that one explains [to the soldiers]. Sloppiness is contagious—sloppy in one area,—sloppy in all . . . the hat is the identification of the soldier with his unit." Rules were created to define the framework, and to be obeyed as the words of the Lord. "Their's is not to reason why, their's but to do or die," as Tennyson described it in "The Charge of the Light Brigade" during the Crimean War—and, alas, as the chief education officer implied in 1978. In contrast appears the standard dictionary's definition, which views discipline as training of specific physical or psychological modes of response.

DISCIPLINE—MEANS OR AN END?

I have been referring to formal and functional discipline. The latter is aimed at specific patterns of behavior relevant to specific situations, while the former is aimed at more generalized behavior appropriate to a wide range of situations. Another way to dichotomize discipline is to ask whether it is a means or an end in itself. Functional discipline can be viewed as a means for better performance in a given situation, while formal discipline is an end in itself—an acquisition of a personality trait or ingrained habit, which is expected to prove functional in all situations.

Although such a dichotomy can be drawn on paper, much overlap does occur in practice. Further, it is very common for those who impose formal discipline to view it as functional—a view not necessarily shared by those subjected to the discipline. One can argue that, for discipline to be functional, it must not only be objectively so (that is, really relevant to the task), but must also be so to those subjected to it. For the soldier who cannot see why a particular discipline is imposed on him—regardless of its real usefulness—such discipline will be perceived as formal only. Thus, a further question to be asked is: "functional for whom?" Imposing of discipline might be functional only for the command. They require the discipline in order to cater to their psychological or technical needs; but, so far as the soldier is concerned, this discipline has no function whatsoever.

A critical meeting of all the senior generals took place in the military headquarters in Tel Aviv, after the Yom Kippur War. The commander in chief presided and the main topic on the agenda was labeled: "The Hat."

When the Israeli Defense Forces were established as a regular army in 1948, they were generally modeled on the British Army—in methods, organization, and discipline. Among this inheritance also came their concept of the uniform, including the hat. It was decreed that every soldier must wear a hat at all times. Israeli norms in those days were very much in opposition to all uniforms or any formal dress. Wearing a jacket—not to say a tie—was considered an act of decadence, typical only of the bourgeois who had no feeling for the spirit of the new pioneer country. Wearing a hat (other than the compulsory head covering of the religious Jews or the functional sun protector in the kibbutzs' fields) was considered equally queer. Not surprisingly, the Israeli soldiers did not take to the idea. The result was an excessive preoccupation of the military police with handing out summonses for the grievous offense of being hatless; and of the disciplinary courts, with meting out the appropriate fines. Arguments in favor of wearing the hat were not based on the hat's intrinsic value as sartorial decoration, but primarily on it being a symbol for discipline—or even for the subjugation of the individual to the special code of military behavior. Nonetheless, it failed to produce discipline or respect, but induced tension and alienation between the soldiers and the military establishment.

For years, the "hat conflict" went on, with thousands of soldiers losing a substantial part of their meager pocket money. Eventually, it became obvious to the military command that punishments and threats (as well as lectures and explanations) did not increase the number of covered heads, and were counterproductive both for discipline and morale. After the Six Day War—due both to a change in attitude of the command and to the large number of reserve soldiers who were in active service but refused to wear a hat (or even had none, as part of their uniform)—the hat was relegated to the epaulet. Hats could now be worn under the epaulet, except on more formal occasions such as parades. The income from fines levied by the disciplinary courts was drastically reduced, as was the atmosphere of conflict and tension.

Then came the 1973 war. Whatever the objective military analysis of the final outcomes of that war, from a psychological point of view it was a disaster for Israel. For the first time since 1948, Israel was seriously defeated in battle, had been caught unawares, and lost territory (even if only recently acquired) to the enemy. As always happens when things go wrong, a scapegoat had to be found. In fact, a whole herd was gathered. Generals, senior officers, politicians, and organizations—all were variously blamed, discharged, or vilified. More serious attempts to analyze the cause of the disaster pointed to two major factors: (1) faulty analysis of data and decision making (some of which has been discussed above); and (2) poor discipline, which found its expression in poor maintenance of equipment, disregard for standing orders, and poor reliability of information gathered and transmitted. Lessons were learned; and many weak points, corrected. A massive reorganization of data processing procedures and evaluation occurred, as well as a tightening up of the controls and discipline of equipment maintenance, registration, and storing. For some, the most critical failure appeared to be the failure of discipline, while all other aspects were of secondary importance—or even an outcome of poor discipline.

But even among those who saw the failure of discipline to be the critical factor, there was a differentiation into emphasis on operational or battlefield discipline—on the one hand—and formal discipline—on the other. Discipline in following specific orders concerning equipment maintenance or deployment, and discipline in gathering and transmitting information were viewed as different from formal discipline—that which concerns behavior not directly related to military tasks. Other officers showed no such differentiation. Their basic creed was that a soldier who does not obey all orders and regulations to the letter—who disobeys any order whatsoever—is a poor soldier. Thus, not saluting, not standing at attention, not folding blankets into perfect rectangles—all are predictive of, and associated with, being a poor soldier. Such a general disregard for discipline—claimed some—could explain why Israel had lost the war. "It is clear that we had to lose the war; there was no discipline; just look at the hat" was the cry of some generals (usually in the reserve service); and pressure mounted to return the hat to the head.

So, I was asked to present the case to the General Staff on a sunny day in 1974. I arrived with a film I had borrowed from the university's psychology department, and I proceeded to show it to the assembled officers. The film was entitled *Induction of Experimental Neurosis in Rats*. It showed a rat sitting in a cage with a metal floor wired to deliver a shock to the occupant of the cage. When the shock was given, the rat escaped to a neighboring cage attached to the first. However, when the poor rat arrived at the second cage, another shock was delivered. After several attempts to escape from one cage to the other—without gaining relief—the rat gave up. It sat on its haunches and started grooming itself—licking its back, legs, and head. It became clear that, when the rat found itself in an insoluble predicament, it gave up and occupied itself in neurotic (functionally useless but psychologically helpful) behavior—grooming. The film came to an end, and I made no comment. After a short (but tense) silence came the voice of an irate officer: "Do you mean to say we are like rats?" Luckily, I did not have to answer this question explicitly. The following discussion was rather heated, but its outcome was clear: The hat remained on the shoulder, at least for the next few years.

GENERALIZATION OF DISCIPLINE

The case for formal discipline is based on the principle of generalization: What is learned in one area is applicable to several others. But in practice it appears that insisting on absolute discipline in one area does not imply abrogating the option to ignore it in another. On the other hand, it is likely that one who ignores discipline in general in one area will do so in many others. Arik Sharon justified the vengeful murder of Arabs by the notorious "Indian fighter" of Israel; Meir Har Zion. The same Sharon disregarded direct orders during the 1973 war—and then, as minister of agriculture, refused to comply with the law that required him to sell his ranch so as to avoid a conflict of interests. It is also Sharon who pursued a cynical and partisan settlement policy in the West Bank—disregarding directives and decisions of parliament and the government. As defense minister he disregarded all directives under the Lebanon offensive in 1982, and lied to parliament about his aims. The tendency to disregard discipline may be an individual characteristic—whether learned or innate—that is mirrored in many domains of behavior. But it is only rarely that compliance with discipline in an individual is a general characteristic that he will apply universally and indiscriminately.

General Elazar, the commander in chief during the Yom Kippur War—who kept the hat under the shoulder epaulet—would probably have agreed that discipline can be broken at times. Certainly, he himself broke it on several occasions (Bartov 1978). While a commander on the northern front during the Six Day War, he ignored an order to cease advancing beyond a certain road in the Golan, and misinformed the commander in chief about the state of readiness of a paratrooper division so as not to have an operation called off. But as commander in chief himself, he placed great emphasis on those rules that—he felt—reflected the moral code of military behavior, such as those preventing the misuse of military vehicles and officers' drivers for private use.

An extreme example of the lack of congruence between formal and functional discipline is shown by the behavior of General Gonen. This general—who, as a tank regiment commander in the Six Day War, exhibited most outstanding leadership and courage—is also known for his strict adherence to all forms of formal discipline. He employed methods of bullying, violent punitive tactics, and—at times—frank terror against any infringement of orders. But he is also the same general who—according to the findings of the investigating commission appointed to explain the Yom Kippur War debacle—contributed by his misinformation, deliberate distortion of facts relayed to the commander in chief—as well as by his ineptitude in decision making—to the setbacks of that war. From my personal contacts with him, I have no doubt that his almost fanatic insistence on absolute obedience and order was not a put-on act. This man at least did not generalize the concept of discipline. His real and profound belief in—and, indeed, adherence to—discipline in one area did not guarantee similar behavior in another area or context.

It may be that one can talk of the generalization of discipline in any one domain (such as equipment maintenance or information handling), but it seems doubtful that a group or even an individual would tend to generalize discipline across different aspects or domains.

ENFORCEMENT OF DISCIPLINE

Up to now, I have referred to discipline as a way of behaving—as a code of conduct. But the word is equally often used to describe the reinforcement of the rules, rather than the rules themselves: "He is being disciplined." It has been shown that codes of behavior are often specific to their setting, and not necessarily generalized. Similarly, discipline as a way of imposing rules is not generalizable, and its own norms and standards also vary from context to context.

An investigation (carried out by the military psychology unit) into the nature of punishments administered by the military disciplinary courts revealed that assessment of the nature or gravity of disciplinary breaches is affected by their setting. The investigation compared punishments for similar offenses, meted out to soldiers of equal rank, but of different ethnic origins. The Israeli population—as I have mentioned before—is dichotomized into "Eastern" and "Western" Jews. Their proportion in today's national servicemen is roughly equal, but more Eastern Jews appear in disciplinary courts. This might well reflect the fact that the latter are over-represented in the lower status and lower standard units (such as service and support troops), as well as on the fact that the tendency of the commanding officer is to view breach of discipline by a higher quality soldier (of whatever origin) more leniently. However, comparison was made between soldiers serving in similar units and of equal seniority. A most striking difference was noted: Soldiers of Eastern origin were given a more severe punishment, regardless of the ethnic origin of the commanding officer sitting in judgment. On average, the Eastern soldiers were given detention sentences more often, and these were 2.7 days longer (the maximum allowed in a disciplinary court being 30) than those meted out to the Western soldiers. The latter also received suspended sentences more frequently than the former. It may well be that this is a result of a self-fulfilling prophesy. Bell et al. (1973) have shown that a prophylactic interview with the type of soldiers expected to be a disciplinary risk increased the chances of their becoming a disciplinary problem, as compared with similar soldiers who were not so interviewed. The Eastern soldiers must have been aware of the fact that they are expected to be more problematic—an issue often made public—which might have affected both their behavior and the sensitivity of the command to their behavior.

Such differential punishment was not affected by ethnic origin alone. Another, statistical investigation—carried out in the Israeli Defense Forces in the early 1980s—showed that senior generals granted mitigation of sentence imposed by military courts to 80 percent of appealing officers, but only 9 percent of soldiers received mitigation during the same period. Further, there was a marked tendency not to bring officers to trial for offenses for which other ranks were prosecuted.

While such discrimination does seem to occur, it would also appear that is is often perceived to occur without justification. A careful investigation of alleged discrimination against Blacks in the U.S. Navy (Thomas, Thomas, and Wards 1974) showed that there was no discrimination of those against whom reports were filed (but reports against Blacks were filed more often!). Yet, Blacks clearly perceived discrimination in the punishment meted out. In this context, it is perhaps not surprising to note the report (Beusse 1977) that the same disciplinary action is judged as fair by officers and as too extreme by men.

Norms as to what behavior merits disciplinary actions vary not only with the perceivers of the action, but also with the actors involved. An offense committed by a responsible person—a bank president or a policeman, say—will be treated as more serious than the same offense committed by someone else. It is also known that a group will tolerate more antinormative and deviant behavior of its high-status members than of its rank and file. The higher the status, the less disciplinary measures will be taken against the offender. Neither is it the act that determines the extent of the breach of discipline, but rather the context of that act. Israelis often feel (and probably justly so) that the world forum expects different standards of behavior from them than from other nations in the area. This double standard means that the Israelis are expected to behave in a more tolerant, compassionate way toward the enemy—who is known to behave very differently—and that sanctions and criticisms leveled toward the Israelis for breach of conduct is much more severe than that leveled at their enemies for identical acts.

There are different norms for judging a breach of discipline in behavior toward a class of people classified or perceived as inferior. When a group of people are dehumanized—as the Jews were in the eyes of the Nazis; the Allied prisoners, in the eyes of the Japanese; as some religious Jews view non-Jews; and as some nationalistic Israelis view the Arabs—then the code of behavior that applies to them is different from what applies to "normal people." The wanton killing and terror tactics employed by the PLO against the Israelis contribute greatly to perception of the PLO as "nonpeople" and might well lead to the application of different norms or criteria toward them.

Norms of discipline include not only the regulations that proscribe which behavior leads to sanctions, but also the "tariff" for infractions. Beccaria, the great eighteenth-century reformer who laid down the foundation of the modern criminal code, stated as his first precept on crime and punishment that crimes are more surely prevented by certainty than by severity of punishment. In order to check on this theory, we carried out a survey of the effects of disciplinary punishment and recidivism. Comparison was made between the occurence of repeated disciplinary offenses in units where the CO issued—as a rule—the maximum penalty, with other units in which penalties were varied and unpredictable—the same offense could lead to a warning or imprisonment, following no apparent logical rule. It was very clearly observed that the latter punitive method, in which the soldier was least certain of the penalty he would be given, was the more effective deterrent. Uncertainty creates the more effective deterrent; it is more stressful, and thus affects behavior most. Certainty—even of an objectively less desirable outcome—is less threatening and stressful, and thus affects behavior less.

Obviously, the ideal situation is that in which self-discipline—the rules each person sets for himself—are congruent with the discipline imposed by authority. Such congruence can be achieved either by coercion and imprinting—active imposing of the authority's norms on the individual, so as to shape behavior—or through teaching and explanation, so that the desired modes and norms of behavior will be internalized as values in the individual and will require no external coercion or control to produce and maintain the desired behavior. Whatever the method, its effectiveness can be assessed in terms of obedience.

OBEDIENCE

In spite of "the hat" (and the increase in discipline that was expected to follow its return to the head), Operation Litani—which later became the 1982 Lebanon War, which was the biggest Israeli military operation since the Yom Kippur War, and involved the occupation of southern Lebanon in order to eradicate and control the Palestinian guerilla bases there—was characterized by extreme lack of discipline. Disregard of orders, untrustworthy information, sloppiness, as well as the breach of the acceptable codes of war were brought to public attention. It soon became clear that not only had many of the faults noted in the 1973 war not been corrected, but that new and serious breaches of discipline had occurred. While lack of discipline was no doubt to blame for part of these problems—and appropriate problem-oriented means were deployed for their correction—new "grooming behavior" also manifested itself. The commander in chief now decreed that discipline—and thus the efficacy of the armed forces—would be improved if all ranks were forced to wear standard, uniform khaki underwear. It was only technical difficulties and expense (and possibly public ridicule, as well) that prevented the implementation of this new sartorial device for increasing military efficiency.

General Eitan personally jumped out of his car and chased a soldier through the streets, in order to bring him to justice for not wearing a hat. This same general caused a public outcry for his dismissal—for the first time in the history of Israel—because of his way of administering justice and imposing discipline, involving a most fundamental and critical issue, raised in many armies and many countries—the question of when a person must not accept discipline or obey orders. Furthermore, the question was also raised as to whether discipline and punishment for its breech are the same for all or different according to rank.

A military court had found two officers—a lieutenant colonel and a lieutenant—guilty of murder of Arab prisoners during the Litani campaign. They were both given prison sentences, and the military court of appeal confirmed the sentence of the lieutenant (eight years) and increased that of the colonel to five years. The commander in chief chose to mitigate both these sentences to much shorter periods (2 and 2½ years, respectively). As the facts became known, the military then attempted to suppress them, by censorship as well as other means. Members of parliament tried to bring these matters to public attention, while others did their best to suppress the information and labeled those who wanted the issue made public as traitors. It was only because the facts were leaked to the international press that the Israeli public was allowed to become acquainted with most of the details. It then turned out that not only had the commander in chief mitigated the sentences in opposition to the norms of conduct and the code of arms acceptable to the average Israeli, but that he had deployed different standards of discipline according to rank. Two other soldiers—a more junior officer and a sergeant—who were sentenced at the same time for the same offense also appealed for sentence mitigation—but received none. Further, it became clear that not only did the commander in chief behave in an unacceptable way with regard to this issue, but that he attempted to lie to parliament and the public when the issue was finally taken up.

While General Eitan failed as a leader in this domain, in many battles he had proved to be an outstanding leader of men. By his personal example, calmness, and confidence—without the use of coercive discipline—he had men following him blindly in most courageous assaults. In this capacity, General Eitan was an outstanding example of the "follow me" style of leadership—the style found to be the most optimal in modern warfare (Gabriel and Savage 1978) and most approved by soldiers (Smith 1978). The soldiers ranked leadership by example to be the most effective, followed by that of leadership by management; dominating coercive leadership was judged to be the least effective. Janowitz (1964) described the dominating leader to be the one who expects an order to be filled just because it is an order. The managerial-style leader is one who explains and tries to motivate action. General Eitan vacillated between the styles: leadership by example in the field; dominant leadership in a bureaucratic context. His leadership by example produced trust and blind obedience in his soldiers, and he must have felt that this same attitude would be transferred to his new role and task. But in his role as commander in chief, he had no chance to show personal example; and, since he did not deploy the managerial-style leadership that can develop trust and identification through explanation, his high-handed dominating style produced alienation and conflict. There was no congruence between the perception of his disciplinary demands and norms and the perception of the soldier's (and much of the whole population's) norms. This incongruence must produce "poor confidence," in terms of the basic model previously discussed. When combined with high aggression, poor confidence will result in poor morale—which, indeed, was the case both within and without the Israeli military at the time. The final outcome was that the commander in chief had to retire as a result of his conduct in the Lebanon War.

The defense of the officers accused of murder was based on the fact that they had obeyed the orders of a senior officer. The officers claimed to have understood Eitan to say that the enemy must be killed. The formal battle order for this operation, which was carried out against the Palestinian terrorist bases in Lebanon, was "to kill the enemy"; and the accused officers claimed that this order was understood to mean that no prisoners should be taken. Throughout history, obedience to orders has been the excuse offered for murder and other atrocities. This was the major defense in the Nuremberg trials, as well as in a trial in 1956 held in Israel against soldiers who murdered Arab civilians in Kfar Kassem. It is a defense that has been rejected by most courts, because judges always found that the ultimate responsibility for a person's behavior in relation to an accepted code of conduct lies with the individual—who must differentiate between acts that are right and those that are explicitly wrong. There are acts that must be self-evident as immoral; and a person ordered to carry them out must disobey. As General Laskov—the commander in chief at the time of the trials—wrote in his explanation to the troops:

A soldier must obey orders, even if illegal—as long as they are not potentially and self evidently so illegal that any reasonable person, without doubt, would view them as opposing the basic human, morale or military principles. Such an order awakes opposition in the conscience of whoever receives it, and it requires no investigation to recognise it. . . .

The rule of obedience is paramount, the military code of behavior is seen to override and displace the civilian one e.g. a soldier told to drive at a speed greater than the permitted speed limit must do so—because it was an order. But he must also be able to retain the power of discrimination—to identify that order which oversteps the boundary of the basic morale code. A soldier must give up his right as free member of society, as an integral human being—but in the end it is his humanity which must determine at which point to rebel against a system.[1]

The point at which this rebellion should occur—when the individual "should" rebel—must vary in different societies. What is considered "an action against basic human rights" has no fixed universal criterion. The same action might be viewed by one society as a blatant offense against human rights, while viewed as much less offensive in another society. The actions of an individual can be judged only with reference to the norms of his group. I suggest that it might be considered morally unjust to condemn a person for an action that is in "opposition to the conscience of who ever sees it" in the condemning society, but not so in the society of the condemned.

General Laskov goes on to differentiate between two functions of discipline:

1. It is the tool of the military arm, helping it to fulfill its tasks.
2. It is the means by which military power is prevented from being used against the country's will and laws. It is both the driving and the braking force; it is the

framework and the structure that determines behavior. In order for this to function, mutual trust must exist between the giver of the order—who knows that the response will be according to the order—and the receiver—who knows that the order will not be in conflict with the basic values of his society.

But such trust is built not only by knowing that the orders will not be basically immoral, but also—as previously said—by knowing that they will not be unreasonable (even if perfectly legal). Thus, orders to behave in a ritualistic and apparently meaningless way—causing a breach in trust—will not only lead to a weakening of the power of discipline to lead, but also in its power to restrain. Unreasonable discipline in apparently irrelevant areas will lead to lack of discipline in critical areas.

As Hare (1979) explains it, absolute obedience to authority is normally justified only if we can assume that the authority is completely good or just. The greater our mistrust in authority, the greater is the responsibility that we have to take on ourselves in vetting its orders. Clearly the military system is based on obedience, and one cannot operate in the stressful conditions of war while carrying out discussions and symposia in a democratic way. But obedience is differential: Some areas or conditions demand blind acceptance, while others require explanation and critical evaluation.

Naturally, it is most unfair to blame all the unacceptable and shameful behavior reported during Operation Litani on poor discipline. In Chapter 6, I discussed the problem of who and what the enemy is and how perception affects behavior toward him. The enemy in Operation Litani were the Palestinian guerilla troops based in southern Lebanon. These Palestinians are not perceived in the same way that the regular armies of the Arab countries are perceived. It is probably mostly due to their own tactics—which include terror campaigns and indiscriminate bombing of all citizens of Israel—that contributed greatly to the dehumanizing of them. The enemy is thus not perceived as a soldier; the codes or norms of war do not apply to him (as the guerillas themselves do not apply them toward the Israelis); and thus, the fight against them is not perceived as one aimed at controlling and winning (Ag5)—as is perceived the combat with a regular army—but as a fight aimed at destroying (Ag1). The picture changed during the 1982 Lebanon War. The conflict caused by the perception of the enemy there has led to serious psychological and combat consequences, which will be taken up in Chapter 10. It is worth noting that, under some circumstances, acts of reprisal or protective retribution and acts breaking the laws of war so as to dissuade the enemy from doing so can be considered justified (Taylor 1979). That approach, which was considered unacceptable during the regular wars, became the normative behavior of a greater part of the forces during this campaign. The level of the moral code has not changed; but, in this conflict, a different code—with different aggressive strategies—was deployed.

Rather paradoxically, the military code demanding that a soldier should refuse to shoot civilians seems contrary to the mores of some civilian attitudes. A majority (66 percent) of people in the United States believed that members of the company responsible for the My Lai killing should not have been brought to trial, and that soldiers ordered to shoot civilians should do so (37 percent, compared with 45 percent who state they should refuse) (Harris Survey for Boston *Globe*, 10 January 1970). Mann (1973) reports similar attitudes by Australians, of whom 59 percent advocated that the soldiers should have been let off; while 30 percent reported that they themselves would have shot, if ordered to do so. The question was not an abstract one, but direct and personal; and yet 30 percent were willing to state that they would shoot, if so ordered. This is no justification for such acts. But behavior of an individual must be understood in the context of the norms of his reference group. And as pointed out previously, disciplinary demands that are contrary to a society's general norms are both difficult to impose and likely to cause internal conflicts. Responsibility for behavior appropriate to the normative and moral code of the society concerned lies not only with the individual. As Taylor (1979) shows, development of the military code has placed direct responsibility on the commander, for the behavior of his troops: "He is directly responsible if he has, or should have knowledge . . . of unacceptable behavior."

It can occur that undisciplined or even illegal behavior (as judged by the country's civilian code) is sanctioned by a commanding officer, and that—while he is formally reprehensible—his orders would (according to the social norms) be viewed as highly laudable. One of the best-known expressions in the Israeli military is "supplementation of equipment." This is a euphemism for stealing from others so that one's own unit will have more or better equipment. The unit in this case is usually a squad, platoon, or company, although even brigades and divisions have been known to participate—all depending on the perception of the "supplementing" agent, the level of group integration, and the attitude of the commanding officer. Although such a procedure is not unknown in other armies, in Israel it is rather well developed, for clear historical reasons. Up to the date of the foundation of Israel, its various underground military groups had to rely to a great extent on acquisition of arms and equipment by such supplementation. Everything from bullets to tanks were acquired from unwilling donors. Such acquisitions were heralded; and the acquirer, greatly admired. All these supplementations were for the good of the unit—never for the private benefit of an individual, who would be considered a common thief if he had done so for his own gain.

Even today, although it is clearly known to be against the good order of things and a severe breach of discipline, commanders will be found who directly or indirectly encourage such illegal behavior. To quote General

Adan (1979)—an armored division commander during the 1973 war—who describes the third, most critical day: "A crew under the command of Lt. Col. Rosen repaired 10 tanks on the shore route, but the 'Magen' division 'confiscated' them on the way to us. I learned my lesson and appointed a special escorting officer to the other tanks we were repairing." It would be wrong to describe soldiers who engage in such criminal activity as having poor discipline or morale. On the contrary, they are often viewed as possessing the very highest morale, good fighting spirit, and loyalty to the group, and as directly contributing to the fighting capacity of the unit. Nor is this attitude of approval toward criminal acts of acquisition restricted to the military. When accidentally brought to justice, party leaders such as Asher Yadlin have clearly shown that a special code exists for evaluating a breach of accepted morals when the ends are for the good of the group.

One wonders if, in societies such as Israel, which developed under a colonial or oppressive rule and had to establish norms of breaking the rules in order to survive, the code of acceptable behavior is applied to the ends rather than the means. "All's fair in love and war" is often stated and not often condoned, but it does become the acceptable code. This code appears much more generalizable than that of means-directed discipline. It may be difficult to generalize from sartorial discipline to battle discipline, but it is easy to generalize "all's fair" from stealing to murder—if the aims are considered justified. A military order "to kill the enemy" and a police order to "disperse the crowd" are more likely to lead to unacceptable or undisciplined behavior than an order to capture a stronghold (which might well involve killing the enemy) or to clear a street (which might involve violent methods).

DISCIPLINE AND MORALE

Good discipline—the extent to which soldiers follow the rules and obey orders—has often been used as an index of good morale. The opposite—the number of disciplinary offenses—is often used as an index of poor morale. "Morale" in this context is taken to be the willingness to fight, and to persevere in fighting. Thus, fighting potential is often taken to be directly related to the degree of discipline. A link is sought between the willingness to fight (not the ability to fight), and discipline. It is not because a primarily high degree of discipline is seen as an index of greater technical competence and reliability, but because it is believed that those individuals who are willing to fight are also those who are willing to follow the rules and regulations. According to this viewpoint, it appears that those who submit to the constrictions and directives of authority in one area are also those who are expected to accept the same authority's emotional and ideological directives, which encourage them to fight. Certainly, overt submission and acceptance of the authority's directives will make the soldier go through some of the required motions, at least to an extent sufficient to avoid conflicts. I have often met the poor commanding officer who described as "good soldiers" those who followed all the rules, and did not appear to oppose authority. But, perhaps not surprisingly, these soldiers did not prove to be the best in battle.

Bauer et al. (1974; 1976) analyzed the concept of discipline—using as criteria for its measurement the perceptions of men in service (rather than the punitive measures deployed) in the U.S. military. He arrives at the conclusion that the perception of good discipline depends on three components:

1. Performance. This can be associated with perception of morale, leadership, satisfaction with the military role, quality of living conditions, and recreation. In the case of combat units, the first three factors were the best predictors. In the support units, morale was also most associated with performance, but less so in the combat units. Leadership was the best predictor for the units under training. Thus, good discipline was perceived to occur in those units that performed best; and for them, performance depended on morale or leadership.

2. Appearance. Although found to be associated with discipline, appearance was less predictable for combat and support troops. Morale and leadership predicted best appearance in those troops, but did not do so in the troops under training.

3. Conduct. This was a measure of obedience to the leader. It was most associated with a perception of high morale, and general satisfaction (as well as feelings about racial discrimination). Of these three factors, performance was most linked with discipline, followed by conduct—while appearance predicted it least.

Discipline is an outcome of three behavioral domains: two functional—performance and obedience; and, to a lesser extent, the formal—appearance. Discipline can be used as an assessment of attitudes reflected by morale or evaluation of leadership, but only in those troops to which these aspects were perceived as relevant.

That good morale will lead to discipline, as reflected by obedience to officers—rather than vice versa—was also the finding of a Swedish officer (Förander 1974), who recommended training officers in communication with their men as the means for improving both morale and discipline. This finding is also supported by Crawford and Thomas (1974); they showed that, on U.S. Navy ships in which human resource management was best applied, the least disciplinary measures were necessary.

The use of the criteria of good discipline—conformity and obedience—as a general predictor of a good soldier is not restricted to the military or to the poor commander. The best soldiers and leaders in Israel are assumed (with some justification) to come from the kibbutz movement. These youths, who are highly motivated to serve in the most demanding units—such as pilots, and commando—are much sought after by those units. The kibbutz movement is much involved in the placement of their youths, and tend to have influence on the placement and distribution of their boys among the specialized units. Each kibbutz movement has a central committee that evaluates and assesses each boy before his enlistment, and recommends to the military authorities his general suitability for a demanding service.

While selecting candidates for attack divers—a much-sought-after unit that was notorious for its high rejection rate—I used to receive from the kibbutz military committee their evaluation of the boy who wanted to join. The committee quite often recommended the rejection of some of the candidates, even though they had volunteered. Besides evaluation of skills and cognitive potential, the selection procedure also involved a quite thorough social and sociometric assessment. After a while, I noted a curious pattern: Those boys rejected by the kibbutz committee were also those shown to be nonconformists in our selection procedure. They were also the boys who, after real-life selection (that is, behavior in battle), proved to be the best soldiers. This led me to a disproportionate and alarming rejection of the boys who were ranked best by the kibbutz's defense committee and a high rate of acceptance among those ranked poorest. The problem was eventually settled when, after some heart searching, we realized that assessment of a boy as a potentially "good soldier" was indeed very heavily affected by the aspect of his behavior that indicated a high degree of socialization and conformity in the kibbutz. Those who had difficulty in absolute conformity—in accepting the very strict norms and mores and the demanding informal discipline of kibbutz life—were perceived as potentially poor soldiers. An investigation carried out in Sweden (Shalit 1980, unpublished report) showed a very similar halo effect among Swedish officers. Soldiers who had a simple, "no questions asked" attitude to their national service were ranked as the better soldiers, while those who did not accept the system blindly and who tended to see alternatives to the "school solutions" were ranked as poor soldiers. In Sweden, there has been no opportunity for proving that the latter way of perception would be associated with better fighting capacity; but it has been shown elsewhere (Shalit 1979) that a perceptual style leading to an awareness of many alternatives and to less rigid conformity contributes to coping in other stressful situations.

It makes perfect sense to use discipline or acceptance of the rules of behavior in any one context as predictive of adjustment to that specific context. The critical issue is whether one can generalize from disciplined behavior observed in one situation to potential behavior in another. Investigating the behavior of U.S. soldiers during the Korean War, Little (1964) found that they observed the rules and kept order and discipline for one purpose only—to avoid conflict with higher authorities. Such disciplined behavior was unrelated to morale or fighting capacity and might only be viewed as an index of the fear of punishment for breaking it. It might well be argued that keeping good order and properly looking after equipment—for whatever motivation—are a direct contribution to the ultimate fighting capacity. This may be so; but keeping order for fear of a punitive authority could not have contributed to a willingness to fight, even if it kept the equipment in good shape. The best-kept equipment is useless, if the soldier does not want to deploy it. Discipline that ensures one aspect but does not take care of the other will only detract from the fighting potential; and using it as an index of the willingness to fight will lead to a false assessment.

According to Marshall (1947), discipline is a function and result of high morale, not its precursor. Morale is the way men feel about any aspect of life—and discipline is one of the products. If men feel well about, identify with, and accept the army's or their unit's way of life, then they accept the codes that these impose. There is no point—says Marshall—in imposing discipline that is not perceived as being related to the requirements of the unit. Functional discipline—whether that of maintaining equipment, handing in reports, or keeping to timetables—must be seen as being relevant to the unit's well-being. Uniform, hats, salutes, and other symbols—if seen to be relevant (for example, because they contribute to and reinforce the sense of uniqueness of the unit, and are congruent with the soldier's pride in his unit)—are easily accepted and willingly carried out. But one cannot develop pride in the unit—make the soldier feel it to be special—by imposing coercive, external rules and codes: "Discipline is not a more or less mechanised response to orders, but is derived from the decision of the intellect, based on self interest, to accept the military system."

Twenty years later, (Marshall 1966) he seems to have modified his views somewhat. Discipline is now viewed as a means to an end. Possibly its existence still serves an index of morale, but its application is viewed as a means of establishing morale. Marshall assumes the role of the officer to be most critical for the combat effectiveness and willingness of the soldier. The officer must be viewed as superior and controlling ("must be viewed as a magistrate," says the author), and discipline—obedience, as well as salutes—serves to emphasize his superiority in the rigid hierarchical structure. The function of discipline is thus to structure the situation. As Stouffer et al. (1949) have put it: "Coercive authority played a big role in prescribing concrete actions to be taken in a situation which might be so confused and uncertain that none of the possible actions seems desirable." Discussing these findings, Zentner (1951) points out that officers were trained to command, not lead; thus, they tend to rely on discipline, rather than interpersonal behavior. It was noted that "ability to carry out orders" was rated as most important by 87 percent of officers—but by only 44 percent of privates—when asked to describe the desirable characteristics in an NCO.

This dependence on orders to structure behavior—rather than on leadership to explain behavior—might be related to the low incidence of soldiers' deploying their weapons, which will be discussed below.

Marshall is indeed correct when he states that it is on the basis of self-interest that a soldier accepts the military system. If the discipline is seen to make sense—if, on a cognitive level, it adds structure to potential chaos—it will be welcome. Similarly, one can extend this to the affective level, in terms of the model described previously: When the coping appraisal leads to congruence between both cognitive and affective evaluation of the soldier's self-perception with that of his perception of the military—as well as to congruence between the perception of personal needs and the demands imposed by discipline—the result is a feeling of confidence, as well as a good coping potential. This congruence is a prerequisite for good combat performance.

But discipline that makes no sense will only undermine structure and further increase the chaos—with detrimental effects on the coping capacity. Besides reducing confidence and therefore the combat potential, discipline that the soldier perceives as unreasonable will also make the authority imposing the discipline appear unreasonable—thus destroying the trust a soldier has in his command. Reduction of such trust will naturally further detract from combat efficiency. As Wesbrook (1980b) shows, discipline perceived as meaningless will alienate the soldier from the military—and thus reduce combat effectiveness.

Marshall observed that, during World War II, not more—and often less—than 30 percent of the soldiers fired at the enemy during combat. He concluded that training men to fire and move "as if by instinct" is an unsuitable method for modern warfare. One cannot—through rigid discipline, fixed rules, and codes—train soldiers to react to conditions that, in reality, require initiative and constant adaptation to the unexpected. Nor is such discipline sufficient to overcome the most crippling factor—fear. While the rigid and perfect discipline of the advancing Roman phalanx might have been the most appropriate behavior for carrying out their attack tactics, when applied to the tactics of changing defense entrenchments in World War I—and even more so, in today's wars—it would only lead to destruction. Perfect order, predetermined drills, and attack modes that cannot be rapidly adapted to fit new requirements are destined to lead soldiers to their doom. Rapid changes of response are required, to be coordinated by orders. But a soldier will fire on order only if he has previously learned and accepted that this is functional for his survival and that he can trust the one giving the order to do so appropriately. He will fire when he has a clear understanding of the effect his firing will have on the action, or because he trusts his leader to have such an understanding.

Kranss, Kaplan, and Kranss (1973) investigated the factors that make a soldier fire. They found that students who had no combat experience assumed that the occurrence of enemy fire—"being fired upon"—would be the critical factor in making them fire. However, Vietnam veterans listed "order"—being told to fire, regardless of other circumstances—as the most critical factor. Both groups rated "ambiguity of target" as the second most critical factor. In the confusion of battle (which the veterans experienced), the order to fire makes sense and offers structure. One often has no time to analyze and evaluate events ("Is the enemy firing; and from where?") and one will rely most on any information—or order—that will coherently direct behavior. For an order to be rejected (as must have been the case in World War II, when only a third of the soldiers fired) must indicate such lack of trust in the command that it was even unacceptable in the ambiguous battle situation, where any factor adding structure is welcome. Discipline—orders—must be backed by acceptance of their meaning, not only by virtue of their authority.

Although training to move "as if by instinct" has been shown to be detrimental to overall battle performance, an "instinctive" or well-drilled routine of acting in a specific situation is of great benefit. Olmstead (1968)—discussing "quick kill" training with the use of a rifle—showed that such intensive training contributed to confidence in the weapon and in the military in general. Functional discipline perceived to have a purpose contributes to a general positive attitude toward the system, while rigid discipline in a meaningless area contributes neither to greater confidence in the weapon nor in the military in general.

Many other factors will certainly act as intermediate variables between the acceptance of the need to fire and the actual firing—from courage and fear, to evaluation of the situation. But the basic understanding or acceptance of the need to fire is the first stage in this critical sequence.

The ultimate responsibility to fire or to carry out any action must lie with the individual, regardless of his rank. The more senior the soldier, the more independence is expected from him—while the private is thought to leave decisions to his commander. The relegation of responsibility to higher authority increases the dependence on discipline and, thus, the importance of its acceptance. A highly centralized military organization must have greater dependence on discipline and, thus, must place more emphasis on getting its discipline accepted. A military organization such as the Germans had—especially during World War I—was based on the assumption that communication during battle would be poor. Thus, its lower level command should be independent. In contrast, the British military relied on effective communication, and thus allowed for less local independence. Discipline in the German units was therefore generated and imposed by commanders who were in close contact with their men and the situation—a discipline easily seen as relevant and appropriate. On the other hand, the British often perceived their centrally initiated discipline to be "bullshit."

It may be that such differences can account for the noted differences in morale and combat effectiveness (see Shils and Janowitz 1948).

The most recent developments in electronic data processing, which led to the C^3 (communication, command, and control) system, could well lead to a decrease in combat effectiveness, because of its effect on command autonomy (Savage 1980). This system effectively reduces the lower level of command to a passive communication function—transmitting direct and continuous orders from the higher levels, who have a better and more total coverage of the situation. Obedience must be blind on the part of both officers and soldiers, who lose both initiative and ability to structure the situation—and thus lose effectiveness and reduce morale.

With Marshall's report in mind, I have often sought to find corroboration for his finding that only 30 percent of the men fire at the enemy. Other reports from different wars give much higher figures, around 75-80 percent. My observation—carried out on ordinary infantry units, as well as in select commando units—left me with the impression that nearly 100 percent fired, when told to do so or when circumstances demanded. In fact, my very strong impression (as well as my own experience) is that firing is a very effective method of relieving tension and fear, and is often engaged in even when there is no need for it. As Glass (1953) has also noted, "Firing gives the most relief from combat tension."

Some people do react to danger by freezing; but, if one does react at all, it seems to me that the tendency is to fire excessively, rather than not to fire. A group of naval commandos carried out a raid across the Suez Canal in 1970. It was the first action for this group of highly trained and motivated soldiers—an action that involved overunning an Egyptian post and removing its equipment. The post was guarded by a contingent of guards, which—judging by their appearance and behavior—were not the cream of the enemy's troops. The raid started with the commandos creeping up to the perimeter and then—from a very short distance—opening fire on the guard. The attackers were not detected, and commenced firing when the first shot was fired by their commander. Very little resistance was encountered. The firing that broke out was very intense, and mostly one-sided. The guards hardly had a chance to respond and were quickly destroyed. But before the raiding soldiers were allowed to proceed, the colonel who commanded the joint naval and infantry forces (but was not in direct command of the operational phase, and had stayed a little behind during the previous phase) called a halt to the operation. He went from soldier to soldier, took each one to the guard or guards he had killed, and made him count the bullet holes in the body. "Why," he said, "is it necessary to drill a man with 25 bullets when 2 would do? Was it necessary to expend all your magazine on this poor man? How much ammunition can you carry with you that you can afford to waste it?" The comments of the soldiers at the time are best not reproduced here. But the effect on their subsequent behavior was very noticeable: The calmness and self-control that characterized the second phase of the operation was most striking. The counterattack that shortly followed was dealt with by short bursts of fire. Gone was the long uninterrupted hammering that had characterized the initial raid. It was evident that the soldiers had gained much confidence, self-control, self-discipline, and understanding—all of which led to reduced firing.

Like whistling and yelling in the dark, firing has a calming effect. The drumming and thudding of the weapon serves to cover up the throbbing fear within oneself. One often fires not so much to destory and conquer the enemy, as to overcome and control one's own fear. Such firing is often ineffective, and it requires learning and example by a good leader to control. To me, such firing seems to be a more normal response than to withhold fire. Perhaps, besides their possible attitude to the officer ordering the fire, the soldiers in Marshall's report reasoned that, if they did not fire, they would not be fired on—probably because they would not be detected. If a skirmish was avoidable, it was best to avoid it. The soldiers obeyed their group norms aimed at survival rather than the norms of the organization demanding engagement in battle (see Wesbrook 1980a;b).

I do not believe that a person who is fired on does not fire back, or that a person who sees himself directly threatened by the enemy does not retaliate. The exception to this is the "freezing" response, which has been discussed previously (see Chapter 3) and is a result of the failure of the orientation appraisal phase. However—if such a direct threat is not perceived, but the firing is required from the soldier as part of a group's task, ideology, or obedience to order—then his feelings of responsibility and identification with the group or commanding officer will determine his behavior. When the soldier feels himself to be part of a cohesive group, there will be pressure on him to behave according to the needs of the group. When he sees himself as an individual, his behavior will primarily depend on what he feels to be best for his own survival or his own emotional needs. This may be the cause of collapse of the fighting ability of individuals in a unit after a certain proportion of the unit has been destroyed. Reports vary on what proportion of the group has to be injured or killed before it will affect combat behavior; but it is clear that there comes a point when the group does not function as a group, and its effectiveness is destroyed—although individuals in it could, technically, proceed to fight.

To perceive oneself as a member of a group requires that the individual perceive at least one other as relevant to him and as one he can rely on and interact with. Unless such a channel of communication exists, the individual cannot form a link with the group. The simplest form of group can be described as a chain—a pecking-order structure. At the top stands—for example—the squad leader; and at the bottom, the green private. The latter communicates and relies on the veteran private, and so on. The squad leader must have communication with his platoon chief, but—at the same time—must also rely on his assistant in the squad. In contrast, one can look at a group in which each and every member has lines of communication with each other. This forms a diamond-shape structure. A schematic presentation of these two kinds of groups is given in Figure 8.1.

The loss of an individual in the group will break a line of communication. If this happens in a chain group (type A) the individuals below the lost soldier will be cut off from the group; and, for them, the group will cease to function. Thus the loss of—say—Number 2 may lead to a breakup of the whole group, if Number 1 had no alternative communication with those below. On the other hand, the loss of Number 7, followed by 6, 5, and so forth will not break up the group. Thus, the group could sustain five losses, but the last two individuals will still act as a group or team. By contrast, in the diamond group (type B), no individual's loss will break all channels of dependence and communication; thus, its members will function as a group even after heavy losses.

For an individual, the loss of a line of communication and reliance on the rest of the group means that his actions will now be motivated by his individual needs and drives. No longer will he be subject to the group's norms

Figure 8.1
A Schematic Presentation of Groups with Different Degrees of Cohesion: A—a Chain—each individual has but one link to another dependent; B—a Diamond—multiple links between members

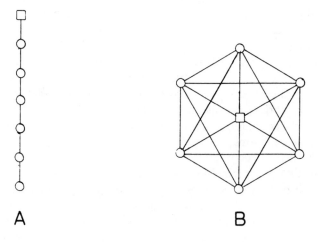

A   B

Source: Author.

and discipline; no longer will he fire for the sake of the others; his actions will be appraised as functional for himself only.

It appears impossible to give a general answer to the question of which proportion of its members a group can lose before it ceases to function as a unit. This must relate to two factors:

1. The cohesiveness of the group. If the group has maximum cohesiveness (diamond), it could function as a unit with just two surviving members.
2. The position of the man lost. In every group other than the totally cohesive type, the position of the break in the chain will determine the effectiveness of the remaining members. Clearly, the optimal group state, which will assure functioning even after heavy losses, is the totally cohesive group. This is the group whose members will retain the norms and discipline of the total group, appraise the situation according to their collective needs, and not revert to individual appraisal and egocentric behavior.

A cohesive group is one in which all members share and identify its norms and set of appraisals. This communality of appraisal leads to cohesiveness. Cohesiveness is a symptom, not a cause. The similarity in the process of appraisal among its members—having the same valence and coping appraisal—is what creates the sense of coherence. Success in action, in survival, and in fulfilling tasks leads to common appraisal—thus, cohesion. Effectiveness in action is the cause of cohesion, not the result of it. By deploying functional discipline toward tasks that show the group it is effective, cohesion is attained. This cohesion will then sustain the group under new conditions, because their appraisal of their coping capacity has been strongly developed.

In modern warfare, direct contact with the enemy soldier is much reduced. More often than not, "firing" involves control and guidance of weapons by mechanical and electronic means, rather than direct face-to-face actions. Impulsive firing as a means of acting out and for attaining relief from stress becomes less relevant. Firing under the new conditions requires much more sense of responsibility to the group, understanding of the overall situation, and obedience to the leader than is required when facing the enemy directly. Today, it is much more those engaged in paramilitary actions—such as police actions—who are involved in face-to-face battle conditions. In those situations, discipline is more often required to curb the policeman's action than encourage it.

Another interesting point that Marshall makes (in 1947) is that one cannot use the level of prebattle discipline to predict battle discipline: There is no guarantee that the troops that behave best—behave in the most orderly and disciplined way during training—will also be the ones who will fight best. To behave in a very disciplined way during training may be the most functional behavior for dealing with and surviving the threats posed by the authorities, and for coping with the stresses of training. But unless these are also perceived as the best ways to handle the very different threats and stresses of battle, other behaviors will be adopted. The soldier has to accept both intellectually and emotionally that the behavior required from him—whether firing or maintenance routines—are indeed the optimal responses for survival of his group and himself. If he himself has not acquired the necessary discipline for handling the situation, his only remaining guideline for response is to follow others—optimally, his commanding officer. This must depend on trust and acceptance, not on regulations.

Good fighting ability—morale B (resilience)—has also been discussed (in Chapter 3) as combining aggressive disposition with congruence of appraisal—an example being the conflict between disciplined behavior and initiative. How strong this conflict can be is shown by Luckham's (1971) analysis of a rebellion in the Nigerian military: "Rebellion rose out of a central paradox of authority in an organisation of a military type, *that of the need to reconcile initiative and discipline,* heroism and hierarchy" (my italics). "Discipline" is defined by Luckham as "Unconditional obedience to persons in defined status in the hierarchy, subject only to obligations to give priority only to the orders of persons even higher in the system, less adherence to known rules." Discipline and initiative can be reconciled when discipline follows the guidelines laid out by the superior, but not when it involves following rigid rules predetermining all responses.

Analyzing the Israeli military system, Perlmutter (1969) concluded that its fostering of initiative at all levels (down to the platoon *niveau*) is the critical factor in its military success. Morale, courage, and combat effectiveness all depend on the individual's ability to adjust, show initiative, and adapt to unexpected situations. In his opinion, display of rigid, "perfect" discipline not only cannot be viewed as an index of morale—but is very likely to be a predictor of poor fighting ability and morale.

According to Fiedler et al. (1979), a demanding and stressful commanding officer inhibits intelligent behavior, but supports routine and previously structured—experienced-based—behavior. Leadership leading to initiative and adaptability must be noncoercive. This has caused the development of the military system from domination-based leadership to manipulation-type leadership (Janowitz and Little 1974). Just such a development had been observed earlier by the same authors (Janowitz and Little 1969); they showed that participating in a modern officer's course caused a decrease in authoritarianism because of its emphasis on group function, rather than on the rigid and disciplinary commander. This type of discipline proves to be the most functional for handling the demands of modern warfare, modern equipment, and today's social climate. All the same, Gabriel and Savage (1978) claim that the personal-example style of leadership is even more effective—possibly because personal example is but a more dramatic form of manipulation or management leadership, in which the leader by his actions "explains" and "persuades" in deeds rather than words. The effect of actions on the process of coping appraisal is louder than words.

STRUCTURE AND DISCIPLINE

Luckham (1971) states: "The only way for combat effectiveness is if military commanders, down to the tactical level, are able to *control a wide area of uncertainty* for subordinates, if they are not too encumbered with formal rules which may circumscribe their authority and hinder effectiveness" (my italics).

Probably the most stressful element in most battles is what is described as "battle fog"—the condition in which nothing makes sense; it's all an avalanche of sounds, smells, and sights from a monstrous orchestration that the individual cannot analyze in any meaningful way. Even when suddenly faced with a small attack—a single firing incident—a certain time must elapse before the nature and location of the threat is determined, and some appropriate response formulated. When faced with massive attacks such as caused by air or artillery attacks, the initial phase feels most like being caught in the onslaught of breakers on the seashore. One is tossed about and tumbled head over heels—one minute, scraping the sand with one's head; and the next, grappling with the slipping grain in a vain attempt to get a steady hold with the hands. Now, there is a glimpse of light, which soon vanishes; and then, only the roar of water in the ears and pressure on the head; until, at last, the feet find firm ground, and the eyes gradually begin to receive a coherent picture of the sea and of the shore lying ahead. To quote Keegan (1976): "In a modern warfare a soldier is coerced by powers of unchallengeable forces to which he must ultimately submit and towards which he cannot strike directly back." Only when the situation becomes clearer, can one begin to sort out the real events and the elements involved, and evaluate their relative importance.

Under such chaotic conditions, anything that makes for a quicker analysis and understanding of the situation is a direct contribution to successful coping. Our most pressing need in any unstructured situation—and the fog of battle, particularly—is to make sense as soon as possible. This makes us clutch at straws and seek any anchoring point or possible explanation, around which we can build our understanding and determine our mode of response. Discipline—knowing which predetermined, unquestioned responses one should make, is most effective in reducing the primary stress of the fog of battle. Confusion is effectively reduced; reaction time, decreased; and feelings of disorientation, best controlled. The "instinctive" response of the veteran and the well-drilled soldier to throw themselves to the ground when fired on must have saved many lives. The difference between the veteran and the nonexperienced—but well-drilled—soldier is that the former will also know when this routine response will not be optimal, and he will then be able to modify his response. The more confusing the situation, the greater our dependence on predetermined patterns of behavior. However, the greater our dependence on prelearned and unquestionably accepted routines, the greater the danger that we will be unable to adapt to unexpected conditions that do not fit our routines. What is gained in terms of coherence of perception may be lost in terms of incongruence of response.

Combat veterans quickly learn to accept orders and discipline as integral parts of their battle roles, rather than as impositions (Cockerham 1978). It appears that their battle experience leads them to accept the army's way of doing things, rather than rely on their own ability to interpret the situation. Their acceptance of functional discipline increases as they learn of its direct value for their survival. However, they do not generalize from the *formal* discipline required by the military system to the *functional* discipline of the battlefield; on the contrary, they tend to generalize from the specific functional discipline they have learned to accept, to the acceptance of the more general military way of doing things. It was also found that veterans—more so than nonveterans—rejected the right of a soldier to disobey any military order, even if patently immoral.

It is not only the demand for blind obedience that leads people to behave in ways contrary to accepted norms and without exercise of their own moral judgment. Cognitive learning, growing dependence on the authorities' ways of doing things, and unquestioning trust in the authorities' wisdom could also lead an individual to an unquestioning acceptance of orders. Obviously, in order to counteract such a development, individuals have to be taught to question all orders. Equally obviously, the military's effectiveness and the individual's chances for survival will be much reduced if such persistent questioning were to take place. Maintenance of the individual's critical faculties—while accepting discipline—is the cardinal problem. This is a tightrope that cannot be walked without the assistance of a good leader, who can maintain balance by serving as an intermediary between the tendency of the individual to regress in the service of attaining coherence; his need for disciplined, drilled actions; and the demand for maintaining a critical, questioning faculty. To fulfill this role, a leader should be able to create a sufficiently large zone of elasticity—maintaining freedom of choice and independence of evaluation—and yet fit within the required functional framework.

An argument for the importance of discipline's "making sense" is presented by Baynes (1967). According to this author, soldiers often prefer the heavy hand: This way, they know where they stand. Clear demands and rules—harsh discipline—"allow for the freedom of the soul even if not of the body. . . . Harsh, even spiteful discipline, has been more acceptable to the soldiers than tolerance—though not likely to be admitted." Discipline is perceived by Baynes to offer a strong frame of reference that defines for the soldier how to react and behave, and removes the stress of having to make a decision (thus "freedom of the soul"). It is rather odd to view "freedom" as the absence of the stress of decision—the constriction of choice. It is certainly easier to follow orders, to abrogate responsibility, to delegate the right to decide one's fate to superior powers—whether that of the commanding officer or God—but this does not seem to me to be freedom. Freedom seems to me to be the ability to make free choice—however stressful this may be. It is this ability that distinguishes us from lower forms of life; and to give this up—for whatever gain—is to give up an important part of our humanity. "It is not for us to reason why . . . " is the explicit target for the discipline advocated by Baynes. The purpose of his discipline is that the soldier should carry on—even under great stress—"according to orders, even at the cost of his life," so as "to leave no doubt where his duty lies." Discipline is used as a coercive instrument to force behavior in accordance with the aims of the powers that be. It is not primarily conceived as an aid to the individual to handle problems, but for the ruler to handle the individual. The freedom of soul that the soldier gains is like Fromm's (1942) "freedom from"—absolving of responsibility at the price of the loss of self—rather than the "freedom to"—by which man expresses his uniqueness.

This dichotomy of approaches is often expressed in the basic training camp setting. Traditionally, the "breaking in" of the new recruit was the formal target of most basic training; and, although there is a marked tendency to change this aim, it still persists on some levels. The basic training camp was designed to undermine all the past concepts and beliefs of the new recruit, to undermine his civilian values, to change his self-concept—subjugating him entirely to the military system. An extreme analysis of such military aims is offered by Hippler (1971): "Armies maintain their internal discipline by evoking and reenlisting unconscious oedipal and preoedipal anxieties and solving them repressively." This is to be followed by creating a new "military man," who will blindly reflect and accept the norms and values of the system. Discipline explicitly serves the purpose of the command and not of the soldier. Today's approach tends to view the basic training course as a phase in which the soldier acquires functional discipline, related to his future tasks. This change much reduced the stress on the individual soldier, as is most evident from the reduced rate of attrition; but, at least in some cases, it increased the stress on the officers.

In response to this new line, Baynes (1967) comments that the imposed discipline of the past is replaced by self-discipline, which includes loyalty and group pressure. For him, even the concept of self-discipline includes strong coercive pressure, such as is imposed by group pressure and dependence on the group. Self-discipline—he states—is nearly synonymous with high morale, which is in turn described as behavior aimed at attaining group approval or avoiding group censure and contempt. It is true—as Katzev et al. (1978) have shown—that individuals will be more helpful to their group after receiving a reprimand, and in proportion to the severity of the reprimand: Group pressure and coercion lead to cooperation. But does such a change in behavior reflect self-discipline, or is it the adjustment of the individual to external coercive forces? The structure and nature of the military organization allows a coercive system to easily develop. Already in 1927, Bartlett described morale as obedience under external circumstances that impose great strain—the source of authority being within the man, or the group.

However, Bartlett goes on to state that morale—discipline—will break down when punishment is reduced or the framework collapses. According to Bartlett, morale is acquired stagewise:

1. By shaping behavior with the aid of punitive rules
2. By codifying these rules to generalize from the specific to the general
3. By hero worship, developed through observing the desired—or absence of the undesired (for example, cowardice)—behavior in the leader
4. By the risk of the game, and communal sharing of the goal and behavior specific for the group
5. By generalizing from the specific group or situation, thus forming a general code of conduct.

Although the final stage is an internalized goal—a stage in which the abnegation of the individual occurs in the service of the group—it still requires a punitive framework to maintain it. One needs a system that will shape the individual's perception and behavior in a way different from—and possibly repugnant to—the rest of society and even the individual himself. Two kinds of pressure can contribute to this result:

1. Punishments that follow antinormative (from the military point of view) behavior—in the form of direct punishments, loss of status, or constriction of rights
2. Support and reinforcement gained when behaving in the normative way—in the form of approval and rewards, as well as by being able to make sense and coherently structure one's interaction with the military environment.

One might suppose that such a structure—with the pressures it can exert—would indeed lead to deindividualization of those who are in it. Some authors—for example Eisenhart (1975)—see combat training as producing in the individual: (1) acceptance of psychological control; (2) equation of masculine (that is, self) identity with military performance; and (3) equation of the entire military mission with raw aggression. An individual is produced who has been molded into a particular form of behavior and perception—apparently suitable for battle, but incapable of functioning in other conditions. Defending the military system, Petersen (1974) shows that, although military training/experience tends to increase the perception of aggression as a means of coping and responding, it also increases the sense of social responsibility—thus, presumably, allowing for discriminate control of the aggressive behavior. He further shows that those who remained within the military (presumably, those who identified with the system) are also those who gave the most support to the moral codes of society in general.

From my personal—and, no doubt, biased—experience, I am convinced that those serving in the military (at least in Israel) are not characterized by deindividualization and loss of personal identity. Greenbaum (1979)—having also had direct experience with the military in Israel—comes to the same conclusion. He states that the image of the individual as deindividualized by the army is given no confirmation. Living under the military system does not increase—and might even decrease—authoritative behavior. That is, not only does one not tend to become more submissive and blindly obedient; neither does one tend to impose such discipline on others, as a result of functioning within the military system. (This is essentially similar to the observation made by Janowitz and Little 1974; see above.) Part of this possibly surprising finding may not be so much a reflection of the more liberal personalities and values involved, but rather an artifact of the authoritarian structure itself. The pecking order within the military is the most explicit of all social orders. One has only to count stripes, stars, or pips glitteringly displayed on shoulders and sleeves to tell which position a man occupies in the hierarchy. Informal power, knowledge, or ability notwithstanding, it is these very explicit labels that determine the pyramid of power. In any discussion, debate, and even clash of opinions, the threat to the senior person is much reduced by virtue of the safety of his rank. In fact, he can afford to listen to those below: Even if they oppose him, they are still guaranteed to stay below. In most civilian organizations, there is a much stronger threat that the boss might be replaced and surpassed by a bright new star; this will not happen within the military, with very few exceptions. Thus, the military organization offers a certain rigidity and security that (in spite of its inherent disadvantages) allows for a greater freedom of discussion and expression of opinion—hence, also, less authoritarianism.

Of course, I have met—as many others must have—the type of officer for whom "might is right" and brains are measured by the weight of brass. It is this type of officer who would not discuss with me (a junior lieutenant, at the time) any problems in his command, because he could not admit that a lower ranking officer—even if professionally competent—might have insights that he himself lacked. We field psychologists learned to best deal with his type by wearing civilian clothes: So disguised (although he well knew our military standing), we could be perceived as professionals, not just as lower ranking officers. However, this type of officer does not seem to survive the demands of a combat unit, and is soon relegated to minor or even major administrative roles—where his rigidity and authoritarianism is not so totally incompatible with the demands of combat, and might even be compatible with administrative tasks.

Schild (1973), who has also experienced military service in Israel, concludes that resourcefulness is a trait valued in soldiers more than orderliness and obedience. Sticking to the goal—rather than the plan—is important. (Again, is this emphasis on the ends, rather than the means?) And finally, the officer is perceived as a leader, rather than manager. A manager follows rules; a leader creates rules and patterns. Control—states Ashley's law (1956)—can only be attained when the variety of strategies used by the controller are at least as great as those of the controlled. In other words, the commanding officer will be successful if he increases his variety of responses, not if he reduces that of his soldiers, by the use of repressive discipline.

RULES FOR THE APPLICATION OF DISCIPLINE

Functional discipline can be described as a set of rules that shape behavior and determine the response to be made under specific conditions. These rules must be perceived to be relevant. Some basic thumb rules can be specified:

1. The demands imposed by the discipline must be clearly codified, structured, and so specified that adherence or deviance from them are clearly observable and assessable. They must be made public.

2. Discipline must be perceived as being functional toward attaining a clearly acceptable and understandable target. Expected behavior should not be described in general terms such as "dependability" or "diligence"; ambiguity must be avoided. Expected behavior must be set out in functional terms or described by critical incidents, and not left open to individual interpretations and varying norms that change with groups or occasions.

3. The codes of discipline must be congruent with the general norms of the population to which they are applied. This does not imply that they must be identical, but the behavior that they demand cannot lie in opposition to existing norms. It may be necessary to introduce a stagewise progression from existing norms, by imposing at each stage a new code that is only somewhat divergent—and never opposed—to the existing norms of behavior.

4. The code of discipline and expected behavior must be presented in a language understood by the relevant population. Verbal concepts must be understood in a similar way; and nonverbal behaviors—such as body signals—must be appropriate to the culture or subculture concerned.

5. When disciplinary sanctions are specified and applied, their type and severity must be seen to be justified by the expected gains or outcomes.

The concept of equity, loosely defined as the *feeling of equality of returns obtained in relation to the effort made*, is also relevant to the perception of the "fairness" of disciplinary sanctions. In fact, this is another way of expressing the importance of congruence between the expected (in this case, accepted as fair) punishment in relation to the accepted or perceived breach of the code. Even if they are not accepted with pleasure, punishments that are perceived as appropriate to a specific breach of discipline will not arouse resentment. It is the punishment perceived as too severe—or too mild when given to others, compared with what we ourselves received—that will cause resentment. The ratio of discipline demanded (D) relative to punishment given for its breach (P), to behavior expected (B) relative to possible misbehavior (M) as perceived by the soldier when applied to himself (s) must be equal to that ratio as perceived when applied to others (o):

$$\frac{Ds/Ps}{Bs/Ms} = \frac{Do/Po}{Bo/Mo}$$

Thus, for discipline (in the punitive sense) to be effective, congruence must be perceived in four aspects:

1. Punishment must be congruent with the initial discipline demanded. For example, one should not have severe punishment when only loose discipline is demanded.

2. What is labeled as breach of discipline must be in proportion to the expected behavior. For example, a slight sloppiness in uniform can be accepted as misbehavior only when there is a generally very strict norm of tidiness; and again, failing to carry out an order to the letter can only be perceived as misbehavior when absolute obedience is the standard expected to such orders.

3. The discipline and its sanctions must be perceived to be in proportion to the behavior and its breach. For example, not wearing the hat should be seen as sufficiently severe to merit imprisonment; or the murdering of prisoners, sufficiently severe to always demand long imprisonment.

4. These ratios of discipline to punishment and behavior to its possible breach—being accepted as appropriate for one soldier or group—must be seen as equally relevant to other soldiers or groups.

NOTE

1. Personal communication with General Haim Laskov, 1977.

9

Assessment of the Coping and Combat Potential

MAPPING ATTITUDES BY QUESTIONNAIRE

Most morale assessments and measurements of fighting potential are based on questions that reflect the soldiers' attitudes and perceptions of their environment, command, peers, weapons, enemy, and so forth. These are usually summarized by some index, along dimensions such as poor–good or little–much. The questions asked usually relate to dimensions that the investigator considered relevant and often lack a weight factor indicating their relative importance in the eye of the beholder.

During the Yom Kippur War, a morale questionnaire was administered to a substantial part of the front-line units. This included general attitude questions, as well as "criteria" questions aimed at measuring actual psychological combat potential by mapping the soldiers' perception of their ability to withstand stress, as based on five questions:

1. During battle, did it occur that you felt you could not go on? (four-point scale: often–never). Please give details.

2. How many more days did you feel you could go on? (not one; 1; 2–3 days; a week; 2 weeks; unlimited)

3. In your unit, did you have officers who did not function as they should have, because of fear? (none; 1; 2–3; most)

4. To what extent were you frightened by the following enemy weapons? (five-point scale: very much–very little)
- light hand weapons
- antitank weapons
- air attack
- artillery

- tank warfare
- chemical weapons

5. In your unit, did you have peers who did not behave as they ought to, during battle? (none; 1–2; quite a few; most)

A related and critical area was that of the evaluation of officers, with questions such as:

1. Are you willing to go to battle with:
- the group leader (tank commander)
- platoon chief (battery officer)
- company commander (battery commander)
- battalion commander
- brigade commander (if you had one)
2. Under whose direct command would you like to be in the next battle? (from battalion commander to platoon sergeant)
3. Which of the following do you feel to be your commander? (from battalion commander to platoon sergeant)

The questionnaire was used to give continuous information to both the direct CO and the General Staff on the psychological combat readiness of the troops. However, the analysis was not only made in order to know how many of the respondents have which attitude or belief, but also in order to establish the structural relationship between the different elements covered by the questionnaire. The analysis was made by means of the SSA program, which displays structural relationships in a form of a map. The result is presented in Figure 9.1.

The analysis was based on a sample of 4,723 soldiers, representing (proportionally) all branches and categories of the armed forces (except the navy and air force) that actively partook in combat during the 1973 war. Each point on the map represents a separate question or questions that deal with specific attitudes or evaluations by the soldier of different aspects of his military environment. Those points or questions that lie nearer to each other were found to have a closer association or correlation, while those that lie farther apart have less correlation with each other. By looking at the questions' distribution, it is possible to mark zones or areas on the map according to the questions' content. When such a delineation can be made in a coherent way (questions on different domains falling into different areas, and those on similar domains falling in the same zone), a structural relationship between the domains and the questions in them is revealed.

In Figure 9.1 four clear domains and a core area can be marked:

1. *Attitude to peers.* The top right area contains all questions relating to peers—their evaluation, as well as trust in them. In this area also falls the

Figure 9.1
SSA Analysis of the IDF Troop Morale Questionnaire Response

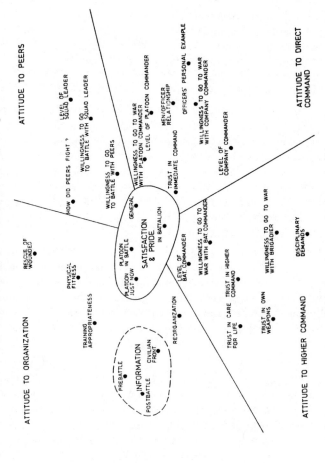

ATTITUDE TO PEERS

ATTITUDE TO ORGANIZATION

ATTITUDE TO DIRECT COMMAND

ATTITUDE TO HIGHER COMMAND

RESCUE OF WOUNDED?

LEVEL OF SQUAD LEADER

HOW DID PEERS FIGHT?

WILLINGNESS TO GO, TO BATTLE WITH SQUAD LEADER

PHYSICAL FITNESS

WILLINGNESS TO GO TO BATTLE WITH PEERS

WILLINGNESS TO GO TO WAR WITH PLATOON COMMANDER

LEVEL OF PLATOON COMMANDER

TRAINING APPROPRIATENESS

GENERAL

MEN/OFFICER RELATIONSHIP

OFFICERS' PERSONAL EXAMPLE

PLATOON IN BATTLE

TRUST IN IMMEDIATE COMMAND

WILLINGNESS TO GO TO WAR WITH COMPANY COMMANDER

PLATOON JUST NOW

SATISFACTION & PRIDE IN BATTALION

LEVEL OF COMPANY COMMANDER

LEVEL OF BAT. COMMANDER

PREBATTLE

INFORMATION

CIVILIAN FRONT

REORGANIZATION

WILLINGNESS TO GO TO WAR WITH BAT. COMMANDER

WILLINGNESS TO GO TO WAR WITH BRIGADIER

DISCIPLINARY DEMANDS

POSTBATTLE

TRUST IN CARE FOR LIFE

TRUST IN HIGHER COMMAND

TRUST IN OWN WEAPONS

Source: IDF, Unit of Military Psychology, unpublished report, 1974.

156

question assessing the squad leader. This shows that he is seen more as a peer than as a commander.

2. *Attitude to direct command* (bottom right). The questions in this area pertain to the attitude, evaluation, and trust toward the company commander. (In the case of company commander's evaluation, this domain would probably relate to attitudes toward the battalion commander.) In this area also falls the importance of the officer's personal example. It would seem that it is the company commander's or possibly the platoon leader's example—rather than that of the battalion commander—that affects the soldiers' attitude or combat effectiveness. The professional level of both the platoon and company commander is equally important (as well as that of the battalion commander, which falls in the next domain). Trust—the emotional, rather than cognitive, assessment of the command—is primarily focused on the immediate command (the platoon commander). The questions pertaining to the platoon leader lie nearer to the peer domain, while those pertaining to the company commander lie nearer to the next domain—that of the higher command.

3. *Attitude to higher command* (bottom left). The questions relevant to the battalion commander lie nearer to the core or center. On the periphery of that area lie the more distant or abstract attitudes: attitude toward the brigadier, trust in weapons, and trust in the authorities' attempt to protect the soldiers from as much danger as possible. Even farther out lies the attitude toward disciplinary demands.

4. *Attitude to organization* (top left). This is a somewhat less specific domain, which contains those questions that do not directly relate to a person but to more abstract or technical aspects. Nearest to the core lies the question pertaining to the perceived ability of the military to reorganize—to recover and adjust to setbacks or new demands. Then come the attitudes toward training—both the general training of military skills (that is, how appropriate they seemed to have been) and the physical fitness of the soldier. In a sense, these questions relate to attitudes of the soldier toward himself. His skills and ability as well as his confidence in his place in the organization. It is therefore not surprising that all questions pertaining to the information a soldier has about the battle—before and after—as well as about the home front fall in this domain. There are the cognitive, affective, and instrumental aspects of the person's perception of himself and his relationship to the environment—rather than his assessment of the environment, which was covered by the other domains.

A very unexpected finding was that the question concerning the attitude toward the rescue of the wounded proved to be so marginal. The Israeli military has always placed immense importance on not leaving the wounded or even the dead behind. This has often led to dangerous and very costly rescue operations in which more lives were lost in order to recover some wounded. It was always argued that this is a very critical factor in determining the morale of the soldiers. I cannot explain this surprising finding other than by resorting to Moskos' (1975) argumentation. According to him it is not the unit's spirit that is of primary importance as a motivator for combat, but rather the perceived operational reasoning and its effects on the self-interests of the soldier.

Hence, while dependence on peers and on the direct command is seen as important and relevant to self-interest, removal of the injured is not so—provided the
soldier does not feel it likely that he will be injured. Although logically we all
know that it is quite possible to be injured in war, for many, the possibility is
emotionally rejected—even if cognitively acknowledged. This is a type of defensive appraisal, as previously discussed.

5. *The core—satisfaction and pride.* In the center of the map—covering all four domains—lie the questions that deal with satisfaction and pride in the platoon and
battalion, but not in the company. It would appear that the platoon is seen as the
primary group; while the battalion, as the greater group to which one belongs.
The company is probably seen just as a functional group—its efficiency is important (hence, the importance of the evaluation of the company commander), but
has little emotional significance. The result of all the different evaluations in the
different domains is distilled into attitudes of pride and satisfaction.

Within the domain of "attitude to organization" we can see a cluster of
questions relating to information. Those are seen to belong to the organizational domain, it is the institution—rather than the direct commander—who is seen to be responsible for orienting the individual in his environment. It is possible that the transmission of information is one of the
most critical and effective ways of attaining identification with the institution—identification essential for combat effectiveness (see Wesbook 1980a).
While identification with the CO occurs by personal communication, formal information is necessary for identification with the organization. In this
connection, I should mention that one of the most predictive morale questions that one can ask in the field is "How much do you know?". This is a
direct measure of the structure appraisal!

Many questions that appear in the questionnaire are not present on the
map. This shows them to be unrelated to other questions. Noteworthy for
their absence are questions pertaining to ideology. Belief in the country,
historical reasons for war, rightness of the government, and so forth—all
were irrelevant. George (1971) argues that ideology is important in helping
to create a primary group. And it is on the strength and cohesion of this
primary group that combat effectiveness lies. However, as was the case in
Israel in 1973, if primary groups can be effectively formed without
ideological basis, the importance of ideology disappears. However—as seen
during the Lebanon War and reported in the next chapter—when the
ideology clashes with the demands of war, it negatively affects combat performance.

Primary groups can be formed by appropriate military and organizational practices. This was shown by Janowitz and Little (1974) in their
analysis of the high Nazi morale, which they explained by basing group
structure on technical rather than ideological means. Wesbook (1980) also
points out that high primary-unit cohesiveness—as well as higher unit

(for example, battalion) cohesiveness—can exist, even though there is not national cohesiveness.

What creates the groups in Israel (perhaps indeed—as Herzl, the Father of Zionism, argued—what creates Israel) is the common enemy. The Arabs have repeatedly stated that their aim is the total annihilation of Israel. Under such circumstances, all members of the threatened society tend to form a tight and cohesive group. "The common enemy" is the strongest basis for ideology, and has always been a most powerful cohesive force. As the perceived outside threat decreases, the need for an alternative ideological or organizational backing increases. It is not unknown for some societies lacking ideological argumentation to try increasing the perceived threat from outside—to create enemies—so as to keep the society together.

Motowildo and Borman (1977) developed behaviorally anchored indexes of morale: They asked soldiers to state which behaviors are indicative of their own and their unit's high morale. The correlations between the different behaviors and morale are presented in Table 9.1. Pride in unit, army, and country is the one outstanding index—which corroborates our findings. Pride in army is probably equivalent to pride in brigade; pride in country, to our "general" pride category—while the unit in both cases is the platoon. Officer–men relationship was assessed to be critical by the soldiers for their own morale, but less so for unit's morale. While actual performance was perceived to be relevant to the unit's morale, it was less so to the individual

Table 9.1
Correlations between Enlisted Personnel Self-Report Indexes and Behavioral Ratings of Platoon Morale

Scale	Own Morale	Unit Morale
Community relations	.23	.25
Teamwork-cooperation on the job	.19	.23
Reactions to adversity	.13	.21
Superior–subordinate relations	.29*	.28
Performance and effort on the job	.24	.29*
Bearing, appearance, and military discipline	.16	.20
Pride in unit, army, and country	.40**	.47**
Use of time during off-duty hours	.21	.19
Overall morale	.33*	.28

Note: $N = 47$ platoons; *p • .05 (two-tailed); **p • .01 (two-tailed).

Source: Motowildo and Borman (1977).

morale. This data is gathered from a peacetime army, and the criteria for self-assessment must be different from an army at war. Yet the core in both is similar—pride.

The critical issue from the point of view of the psychologist or the commanding officer interested in increasing combat effectiveness is to establish what makes for pride. And the critical issue for the psychologist or commanding officer who wants to assess combat effectiveness is to assess pride. Thus, the most critical questions extracted from the questionnaire—the ones that gave a rough-and-ready, but reliable, guide to morale or combat effectiveness—were those in the core, along with a few others relating to trust and willingness to go to battle with the commanding officer and peers. At the same time, the psychologist was seeking to identify the critical behaviors that indicate the existence of pride.

Questions pertaining to pride were phased as "Are you proud of . . . ?"; for the most part, they were questions of attitude, or affective appraisal. In terms of the model for combat behavior, a positive answer to these questions indicates confidence—a result of positive appraisal of different aspects of self and one's own reference group, compared with that of the enemy. This—rather than cognitive appraisal (reflected in questions about "willingness to follow a leader" or "trust in weapons")—is the nucleus of the perceptual map of battle.

Wesbrook (1980) investigated the relationship between military effectiveness and morale. He showed that alienation—lack of trust in command, organization, and society as a whole—were strongly related to ineffectiveness. The author concludes that the core of all military effectiveness is identification and trust: When they are absent, leadership and training can have but a marginal effect on combat performance. A similar conclusion is drawn from the SSA analysis, the map of which graphically illustrates the point. This would also be expected in terms of SAM, since training—the third (instrumental) phase—cannot be effective if failure occurred during the second (affective) phase.

As a check and supplementation to the morale questionnaire, a sample of soldiers was asked (during a break in battle, or shortly after it) to answer the following directive: "Think of the situation in which you were most scared and describe it shortly." Description was requested of the soldier's task; the availability of ammunition, equipment, and so forth; the nature of the enemy's attack; and the physical setting. The soldier was asked to assess his own fears, trusts, and certainties; his dependence on peers, and on different levels of command ("Who did you feel to be responsible for your life at that moment?"). These questions allowed us to obtain the completely subjective map of an event about which we had at least some objective data (such as rate of casualties, duration of action, and its success). The basic findings reinforced those obtained from the structured questionnaire—showing the same critical aspects determining combat effectiveness. But one additional factor was also very obvious: The more concise and clear the picture the soldier presented of the situation—*regardless* of whether it was experienced as very positive or very negative—the less stressful he found the situation to be.

By whatever definition used, morale reflects the fighting spirit or an at least semipermanent potential for action. Questions like "How do you feel about . . . ?" are likely to reflect a very transient, momentary state of mood, rather than morale. Moods are subject to rapid swings; they are the result of status appraisal and are thus not predictive of real combat effectiveness. Morale assessment instruments must focus on the three perceptual phases.

It is also interesting to look at what contributes to the formation of a coherent structure. The coherence of the structure of the organization—the clarity of the functions of the different levels of leadership, the chains of command, and so forth—are essential for combat effectiveness. The different commanding officers in Israel are referred to most often by their function—platoon chief, company commander, and so on—rather than by their rank. The perception of the organization is based on its functional structure, rather than its formal structure. Such perception is clearly more resilient and powerful, offers a better basis for appraisal, and might lead to (as well as be a result of) higher combat effectiveness.

This may also account for the finding that different task units have a different perception of who is "them." Soldiers always experience some estrangement (if not alienation) toward a level of command—"them"—who are perceived to be the ones who give orders without being in touch with the situation. A small investigation into this perceived level showed that, for the infantry soldier, the battalion commander was "them." In the artillery, the company commander was the outsider; while in the armored forces, it was the brigade commander who was so perceived. It would appear that what determines the alienation from the command is based on a perception of the function of that command level. The infantry soldier can feel the role of the company commander as contributing to his performance and well-being—as the tank crew feels toward their brigade commander—but these soldiers cannot feel the direct relevance of the higher levels of command.

The question "Who is your commanding officer?" quickly reveals the perceived psychological—hence, functional—structure of the organization. The question "What characterizes the battle for you?" reveals the critical factors that the soldier has to successfully cope with in order to attain combat effectiveness. The next section of this chapter describes an instrument designed for mapping these critical aspects of perception.

ASSESSING THE APPRAISAL PROCESS

The morale questionnaires described above showed the importance of assessing different aspects of the appraisal process. Their limitation from that point of view is that the aspects were not explicitly assessed.

Description of the Instrument

A new instrument—"the Wheel" Questionnaire (WQ)—was specifically developed to map perceptions of any situation and be able to analyze this perception in terms of the appraisal process—thus obtaining a measurement of the effectiveness of the appraisal of the structure, valence, and coping. At the same time, a mapping of the relative importance of the different perceived domains can be made. The questionnaire consists of one page and is presented in Figure 9.2.

Administration

This is an open-ended questionnaire. It can be administered individually or in groups. The subjects are asked to "write down those factors that are characteristic or most typical of the situation [the war, the military service, or whatever]." The subjects are allowd to write as many factors (maximum 12) as they wish—one factor in each of the Wheel's segments. There is no time limit.

Next, the subjects are asked to "rank the factors in order of importance for you." The ranking is entered for each factor in the inner circle. It is early explained that ties are allowed: The same rank can be given to two or more factors. When this is done, the subjects are asked to evaluate "which of these factors you consider to be negative; and which, positive—or which do you feel can contribute to you, and which might harm you." These assessments are marked on a five-point scale (from + + to − −) at the appropriate place on the Wheel's outer rim. Lastly, the subjects are asked to assess "how much control you feel you can (or could) exercise, or how much influence you feel you have (or had) over each factor." This was entered on a three-point scale (much, little, none) in the appropriate section on the circle's rim. WQ scoring can be based on both the form of the answers and on their content.

Scoring the Form of the Answers

The following information is noted:

		range
• The number of factors filled in	d	(1–12)
• The rank assigned to each factor	r	(1–12)

Figure 9.2
The Wheel Questionnaire (WQ)

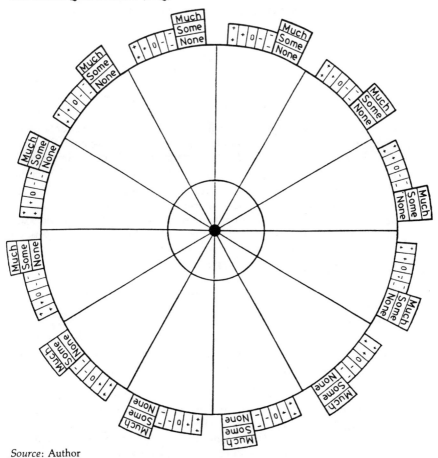

Source: Author

- The least rank assigned   r′ (1–12)
- The loading (positive, zero
  negative) given to each factor   L (from ′—′ = −2 to ′++′ = 2)
- The degree of control attributed
  over each factor   (from ′none′ = −1 to ′much′ = 1)

Based on the above, four indexes of appraisal can be calculated:

1. Structure (R)—the level of the structure of cognitive appraisal, or the level of
   ambiguity. Structure is viewed as the effectiveness of differentiation—the

degree to which the perceived elements are distinct and unique, at least in terms of their relative importance. This index is based on the maximum number of ranks assigned, divided by the total numbers of factors.

$$R = \frac{r' - 1}{d}$$

The range is from 0.92 (12 factors and 12 ranks) to 0.0 (1 rank, regardless of how many factors). Thus, the higher the R value, the less ambiguous and more differentiated is the appraisal of the universe mapped by the WQ.

2. Motivation (M)—the degree of emotional investment in the situation, positive or negative. M is based on the absolute sum of + and − responses (L). Thus, two plusses (+ +) and one minus (−) give M = 3. M ranges from 0 to 24.

3. Emotional balance (E)—the net direction of emotional involvement; the sum of the positive and negative evaluations. In other words, is the final picture perceived as attractive, noxious, or benign? This index is calculated by algebraically summing up the total number of positive and negative signs and then standardizing them (dividing by the number of factors given). Thus, the intensity of the direction of involvement is shown by the net valence value associated with the extent of perception.

$$E = \Sigma L/d$$

The range of possible responses is from −2 to +2 (−24/12, 24/12).

4. Coping (CI)—the extent to which the individual feels that he or she can control the factors in the mapped universe, in relation to their perceived importance. The index is calculated in two stages:

1. Each factor's valence or loading (2, 1, 0, −1, −2) is noted, based on the number of positive, neutral or negative signs assigned to it. Then, the loading (L) for the factor is divided by its rank r. Thus, for example, a factor with two plusses (+ +) ranked first will have more weight than a similar factor ranked seventh (2/1, 2/7, respectively).
   This ratio is called i (intensity).

$$i = L/r$$

2. To each i for each factor is added a weight according to the perceived control (c). "Much" control is given the value of + 1; "some" control, 0; while "none," − 1 (for example, 2/1 + 1, 2/7 + 0, and so on). The rationale is that even a negatively perceived factor has a less negative effect if possible control over it is perceived, and vice versa: A positive factor that is perceived as a chance factor—with no ability to control it—has a less positive value in the final appraisal.

$$CI = \Sigma (i + c)$$

alternatively

$$CI = \Sigma c + \Sigma i$$

The possible range of this index is -36 to $+36$.

Thus the four indexes reflect three levels on an appraisal process: the structure (cognitive), the emotional involvement and concern (affective), and the feeling of control (instrumental).

Scoring the Content

The analysis is based on two dimensions:

1. The focus of the answer—whether the response dealt with:

   1. The individual himself
   2. A specified frame of reference—such as family, the organization, the equipment, or the enemy
   3. A diffuse nonspecific reference—such as general feelings, mistrust, knowledge, people in general, or the nation

2. The aspect of the answer—whether the response dealt with:

   1. Knowledge, understanding (cognitive)
   2. Feelings, emotions, attitudes (affective)
   3. Functions, actions, equipment application (instrumental)

Thus, a 3 × 3 matrix is generated. Each response was categorized in one of nine possible categories. The rank, loading (positive or negative), and control associated with each response was noted. The average rank, load ($+$ or $-$), and control index for each category—across subjects—is calculated.

The above is a general code for content analysis. However, it may be desirable to have content analysis that is specific for a situation. For example, when analyzing the question "What characterizes war for you?" the content would be categorized into physical, social, and psychological factors relating to self, the enemy, and so forth.

Whatever method of categorization of domain is used, this can be summarized as follows:

1. The frequency of occurrence of each domain, and its percentage of all domains = PDOM

2. The mean rank given to each domain = RDOM
3. The relative weight of each domain = PDOM/RDOM
4. The mean valence of each domain = the Load (L) associated with it
5. The mean control over each domain = the Control (C) associated with it

Thus, our perceptual map includes four indexes of the effectiveness of the appraisal of any specified situation—as well as a mapping of the domains involved in its perception, and their relative weight.

APPLICATION OF THE WHEEL

The Wheel has been used to predict coping effectiveness in military situations, as well as in other threat situations. The structure index (R) has predicted individual soldiers' evaluation by their CO (Shalit 1981). The better the structure the soldier had of his military service, the higher his rating. The coping index (CI) has been shown to be positively correlated to military groups' effectiveness, as assessed by both the NCOs' evaluations and sick-absenteeism (Shalit 1982).

Peri (1986) has shown the R and CI indexes to differentiate between national servicemen who adjusted or failed to adjust to their service in the Italian Navy. The clarity of perception of the expected service situation predicted adjustment to it. The indexes were also used to assess the different levels of psychological combat potential among troops involved in an action against a border infringement by a Soviet submarine and frogmen in the Swedish archipelago in 1984 (Shalit and Carlstedt 1984). Populations of civilians, new recruits, and commando troops could be differentiated by their structure, motivation, and coping indexes—as well as by the content of their perception of the situation.

A similar result was obtained when investigating the perception of the population of a town exposed by an industrial accident to a noxious gas (Shalit 1986). In this investigation, the different Wheel indexes were related to the reported behavior of persons living in an area exposed to the gas, compared to a nearby control area. The findings showed that behavior disturbance could be related to the index quality. The most severe disturbances—such as sleeplessness and disorientation—were associated with poor structure. Low emotional index values were associated with feelings of anxiety, mistrust, anger, and conflicts within the family. Low coping index values were associated with flight and dissatisfaction with one's own ability to cope.

The Wheel is also used to map the perception that soldiers have of war (Shalit 1982a). In Sweden, this is a completely theoretical concept after approximately 190 years of peace. Nevertheless if war comes, it is this expected perception that will determine the initial effectiveness in coping with it. The better the appraisal, the more effective the coping and adjustment to the unexpected. Combat potential is determined by the appraisal one has of the expected situation. Units are differentiated by this means and by a morale index that predicts their psychological coping potential, which then has to be combined with other indexes of their skills, physical status, and so forth.

Morale in its different levels (mood and resilience)—as well as confidence in one's coping ability—are reflected by the indexes. The areas of concern for the soldiers—what they are most afraid of—can be obtained by a content analysis. Such information is used to design the soldiers' training and instruction (see Shalit 1982), so as to deal with areas that the soldiers perceive as most stressful and relevant.

From the indexes one can also learn whether the factors reducing combat effectiveness are structural (such as information and role clarity), emotional (such as identification and committal), or instrumental (such as confidence in ability and trust in equipment). As the SAM model specifies, these aspects must be treated in order. There is no point in motivating soldiers unless a clear structure underlies their perception of—for example—who the enemy is, or what the purpose behind a given task is. This is a problem in Sweden, where—for neutrality's sake—one is not allowed to mention the enemy. This was not a problem in Israel up to 1982, but became a problem in Lebanon—where the nature of the enemy was rather diffuse at times. A further possible use is the mapping of the level of perceived stress in any given situation and its subsequent reduction of training (von Schéle 1986).

SUMMARY

The basic idea offered in this book is that the effectiveness of the perception process sets the limit to coping with any stress in general and combat situations in particular. The perceptual process—a sequential process—involves three modalities: cognitive, affective, and instrumental. Assessment or prediction of coping potential must include a mapping of the perception of the expected situation in these three modalities.

Conventional questionnaire techniques can be used for such mapping; but, to achieve maximal value, one should define the items in terms of the perceptual modalities they relate to. An example of such an analysis is the application of the SSA technique, as used on the Israeli Defense Force morale questionnaire administered during the 1973 war. An alternative instrument—the Wheel—is offered. Its advantages are twofold:

1. The perceptual process and stages are explicitly mapped.
2. The domains of concern—the areas perceived as most salient to the individual—are determined by him, rather than by the investigator's biases and expectations.

Morale—as a concept predicting long-term resilience and coping potential, rather than a fluctuating mood—must be assessed by relatively stable
attitude and disposition parameters. A critical part of these parameters is
the perceptual process that interprets the impact of the environment into a
meaningful stimulus to be acted on and—if needed—coped with.

10

Lebanon—The Face of Battle

LEBANON—ISRAEL'S VIETNAM?

Milgram and Hobfoll (1986) discuss and compare the Vietnam War and Israel's 1982 Lebanon War on 11 points, in terms of psychological stress. These points are:

1. The wars were *unconventional*. Neither the ideological reasons for the war nor the target population were those associated with previous wars. In SAM terms, this would be described as Structure problems.

2. *Blurring* of the identity of the enemy. The authors state that, while this was of serious consequence in Vietnam, no such blurring occurred in Lebanon. However, blurring of "who is the enemy" cannot be analyzed only in terms of what social or ethnic group the enemy belongs to. Blurring can also occur as to the actual category of the protagonist. For the first time, the Israeli soldier faced an enemy who was not a soldier. He was not even necessarily an adult male. The enemy could be a sexy teenage girl who blows up herself and her car beside a convoy of military vehicles. The enemy could be a 12-year-old boy throwing a grenade or an old woman discharging an RPG. This is a blurring of all concepts and expectations—a breakdown of structure, which must affect the ability to cope with the situation. The reported number of Combat Stress Reaction (CSR) cases was higher during the first phases of the Lebanon War than in later stages (see below). One possible explanation is that, for the new arrivals—especially the national servicemen who had not served previously—this type of enemy was not so unexpected as for soldiers who had been involved in previous wars. The newcomers had heard and read about this new enemy, and thus had less problems in structuring their appraisal.

3. Vietnam was *a dirty war* in which the civilian population was often mistreated. According to the authors, Israel's war was less so. However, the comparison should not be made in absolute terms. As discussed in Chapter 6, the perceived psychological distance from the enemy determines the alienation toward him and the

degree of aggression that one will deploy. The psychological distance between the Israelis and the Lebanese is not so great as that between the Americans and the Asians. Thus, the perception of the mistreatment of the Lebanese—even if the actual mistreatment were not so cruel—might have had a similar psychological impact. The possible negative psychological impact of a ''dirty war'' is not because of the acts themselves, but because of the self-evaluation or emotional impact of the acts. When and if such behaviors lead to negative self-perception, they reduce the coping capacity—and hence increase the likelihood of CSR.

Comparison of the wars is also made with regard to the circumstances and technical aspects:

4. *Tours of duty.* The tour of duty in Vietnam was based on the individual soldier's rotation. This led to a serious breakdown in group cohesion. The Israeli model is based on unit rotation, thus greatly increasing the potential for group cohesion and decreasing the likelihood of CSR. However, the Israeli military rely heavily on the reserves, who are supposed to be called up for a specified and limited time. This scheme did not always work out. As a result the reservists had difficulty in structuring their normal life—which, in turn, increased the stress of duty. Nor—because of the disinformation issued by Sharon—did they have a chance to form realistic expectations as to the course and duration of the war. ''Realistic'' in this connection is not to be equated with accurate. It means a coherent appraisal, even if incorrect. This could not be attained because of the continuously changing information on what the war's aims and targets were.

5. *Ratio of combat to support troops.* In Israel, as in all armies, the combat troops have strong sentiments against the ''others''—the support contingents. However, because of the wide involvement of a large part of the population (both men and women) in the armed forces, this conflict is less serious in Israel than in the United States.

6. *Drug problems.* This problem is generally much less serious in Israeli society, and thus also affected the soldiers less. However, access to drugs in Lebanon was extremely easy; and as the war and the occupation continued, more and more were involved—both as users and dealers. This aspect probably did not affect combat effectiveness during the actual war; but, without a doubt, it has had negative effects since.

7. *Level of psychiatric treatment.* Milgram and Hobfoll state that the level of psychiatric treatment in Israel was much better and led to less postcombat stress reaction. The Israeli treatment model emphasizes in situ treatment. The affected soldier is most likely to recover if given the right support by his peers and CO or by competent professionals (psychologists, psychiatrists, or psychiatric social workers) at—or as near as possible to—the front line or in an environment as similar to it as possible (Noy, Nardi, and Salomon 1986). In fact, Milgram and Hobfoll's use of the term ''psychiatric treatment'' is inconsistent with the concept of Combat Stress Reaction, which treats the disorders as a coping problem rather than a clinical issue. The essence of the treatment is to allow the soldier to reform his appraisal of the situation. The support he receives helps him to restructure, reevaluate the dangers, as well as reappraise his ability to cope with the situation. That such support at the

front greatly reduces the number of psychological casualties evacuated to conventional psychiatric institutions is evident. However, when reporting the extent of CSR, one should include all soldiers who—because of nonphysical factors—had reduced combat capacity. Such statistics are rarely available. This might account for the discrepancies that occurred in the reporting of CSR rates as discussed below.

8. *Extent of antiwar protests.* According to the authors, this was less in Israel than in the United States. However, it seems to me that, even if the antiwar manifestations in Israel were less violent, their psychological impact was no less. The party in power was not thrown out, but many of its senior members were. Israelis may not have fled the country to avoid service; but, for the first time in Israel, soldiers went to prison rather than serve in Lebanon. A brigade commander asked to resign, rather than follow the order to attack Beirut—an action that highlighted the serious nationwide conflict tearing through the Israeli population.

Milgram and Hobfoll also compare three points concerning factors after discharge:

9. *Transition from military to civilian life.* This was obviously much easier in Israel, where the soldiers were much less isolated—both geographically and mentally—from home.

10. *Biases in antiwar protests.* These were much more vitriolic and one-sided in the United States. However, if one were to listen to some of the authorities, one would be led to believe that the Israeli mass media was not less one sided.

11. *Conspiracy of silence* in discussing the war and its morale issues. In Israel, no such conspiracy exists.

These last three factors must certainly help in the adjustment of soldiers, regulars, and reservists to the postwar situation, but can hardly be relevant to acute CSR. In fact, it may still be too early to assess these effects.

COMBAT STRESS RESPONSE

During the International Conference on Stress during War and Peace, which was held in Israel in 1983, Colonel L. Levy—at the time, commander of the behavioral science unit of the Israeli Defense Forces (IDF)—presented an analysis of the background factors for 2,600 CSR casualities. Yet, Milgram and Hobfoll (1986)—summarizing several other reports from the mental health unit—consider the rate of CSR to be very low. The percentage they refer to is about 5 percent. If we assume 2,600 cases to be 5 percent of the total injuries, one would expect the total number of injuries to be in the order of 52,000! This is incongruent with the published data, which are of a much lower order. On the basis of the available data, one can assume that the CSR cases referred to by Levy account for about 25 percent of the total casualties.

It is not within the scope of this book to discuss the different forms of treatment and categorization of CSR. However, it is clear that this concept can have a different definition depending on time and place (see Baron et al.

1986), and will vary with the nearness (time and place) to the actual battle. One cannot generalize from one war to another: A high CSR during the Lebanon War does not imply low postcombat casualties, while the reverse might be true after Vietnam.

The better the units, the higher the degree of awareness on the part of leaders regarding the psychological factors that lead to CSR, and the better their ability to deal with them, the less will be the recorded number of CSR cases. Should soldiers, unwillingness to fire against the enemy (see Marshall 1947: In the best units, only about 25 percent fired at the enemy) be considered as a CSR? Should fear and tiredness be (at least at times) treated as a CSR? A much-reduced fighting capacity (beyond that imposed by physical parameters) could well be so classified, although it would not appear as such in the records.

There are no published "morale" indexes from the Lebanon War. As seen above, the information available is unclear. Its interpretation—as presented, for example, by Milgram and Hobfoll (1986)—is debatable. One is thus forced to use observations and public records when trying to obtain some information as to the psychological issues and stresses imposed on soldiers during the Lebanon War. Using the media, radio, TV, and—especially—extensive reports from the outstanding Israeli daily newspaper *Ha'aretz*, I have summarized some of the relevant issues in the more or less journalistic-style sketch below.[1]

THE LEBANON WAR IN THE EYES OF THE ISRAELI

"Little Head"

A brigade of regular soldiers met again at its base in the center of Israel, after having been split up during their long service in Lebanon. In a meeting at the camp—one in which they could relax for the first time after many months; one in which there was no need to carry weapons and have guards on the alert—all ranks from sergeant on upwards were present. Their experience in Lebanon was varied. Some saw their comrades killed and injured by terrorist activities (I shall use the terms as perceived by the Israelis: "Terrorist activities" are those initiated by the various Arab factions—whether Amal Shiite Muslims, PLO, or one of the other groups); others experienced the devastating feeling of their own failures, and the worst feeling of all—helplessness and the inability to fullfill their mission, as well as the experience of "little head." "Little head" is the term used by the Israeli soldier to describe the phenomenon of "holding a low profile"—avoiding responsibility, decision making, and initiative. "Little head" is a symptom of the failure of identification and of command—the collapse of leadership. All present had experienced the problems of the moral issues of that war—especially those caused by the tough policy instigated against the Sheite villages, and other confrontations with the civilian population.

The soldiers were gathered in their units. They heard talks and discussions by military and civilian lecturers and were encouraged to ventilate their feelings, questions, doubts, and criticims about all issues: from the failure of military action and planning, to the unnecessary sacrifice of life and the feeling of total failure. Not all were willing to talk; it would appear that the lower the rank, the less willing they were to talk. In contrast, similar gatherings of reserve brigades showed that rank had little effect on their willingness to talk, question, or criticize. In the past history of Israel, criticism and questioning of military actions was kept in-house. Loyalty generally prevented public expressions of doubts. After the Lebanon War and during its later phases, no holds were barred: The holiest cows were slaughtered, and the very basic concept of the rightness and moral code of the IDF was no longer a clear, unquestioned tenet.

The meetings gave one the impression that everyone would like to have heard that the IDF did not lose the war, the IDF acted correctly, the Lebanese are at fault, and the mass media is to blame for distorting the picture. The regular soldiers—even if doubting—were not willing to accept outsiders' overt criticism. They refused to accept criticism against the government's decision to send them to Lebanon. Their loyalty and their image of the regular soldier still prevents them from political criticism. It is only the reservists who were willing to engage in political criticism, and even form active movements for political actions. A very strong need to criticize the political system among the regular soldiers found its vicarious release through the reservists. If this were not available, I suspect that the symptoms of stress, psychological injuries, and even desertion among the regulars would have been much more extensive.

"We entered Lebanon as a proud military machine, and look at how we leave it," says one battalion commander. "We were told to use chess pieces on a backgammon board. We had to fight in a crazy and cruel world and those at home demanded that we shall stick to the old chess rules."

The soldiers showed their hate for all the Lebanese, in fact for all Arabs. (In contrast, during the 1967 and 1973 wars, in which the very existence of Israel was threatened, there was very little hate toward the attacking Arabs; see Chapter 6). Some soldiers even ridiculed the concept of the "purity of arms." This is one of the most important tenets of Israel's military, a term coined many years before the foundation of the state. "Purity of arms" means that weapons are to be used only within a strict moral code quite similar to the spirit of the Geneva Convention. This code limits violence to the need of combat and self-defense. Instead, some coined a new term: "purity of the finger"—that is, to drive through a Sheite village and never relax the finger pressing the trigger; never to stop firing: "This is the only safe way. If one detains a Sheite and gives him to the SLA [South Lebanon Army] they kill him anyway—so what is the difference?"

Some officers were asked if they would act similarly in the occupied West Bank. "Why only the West Bank?" said one, "Even in an Arab village within Israel, if they have an RPG we shall go in and spray them all; so have we learned." In another group, the officers prepared the following list of problems caused by the Lebanon war:

1. The degeneration of the moral code ("the pure finger")
2. No motivation for command, shirking of responsibility ("little head")
3. Lack of courage and daring
4. Political polarization to the right and left; the splitting of the soldiers into hostile political factions
5. The deterioration of conventional military skills, because of the need to adapt to guerilla warfare
6. The deterioration of the personal moral code; lack of mutual caring
7. The tendency to generalize from the Lebanon Arab to all Arabs
8. The feeling of desertion ("The military do not have the home-front backing")
9. Avoidance of responsibility ("passing the buck")
10. Loss of proportion in action; massive power, massive firing; false feeling of security and dependence on massive artillery and air support
11. Problems with the handling of prisoners; looting

This is the second time the IDF has returned from war with shame. It required some time after the Yom Kippur War to assess that war's effects on the Israeli population and the IDF's own image. The war was a military victory, but clearly perceived as a loss. It was followed by a period of self-chastisement ("mea culpa"), and then much soul-searching. In 1985, there was little self-chastisement. The whole Isreali society—including its soldiers—tried to return the war equipment to its lockers and forget the whole issue. The memory of the convoy of lorries traversing Lebanon—death traps, offering a target for continuous terrorist attacks—is a memorial to failure. The best one could hope for was to get out of Lebanon—to complete one's tour of duty without incident; to lie low and never take any initiative that might lead to action; to avoid confrontation, rather than (as in previous campaigns) to seek it; to have as "little head" as possible.

Listen to these comments by a military journalist: "In the 1970th when we returned from raids in Lebanon we were met by the population of north Israel with cheers, flowers and much coffee; when we returned from Lebanon now no one even looked at us as our convoy crossed the border."

This war led to a feeling of betrayal on two fronts. IDF betrayed the civilian population because it did not bring about the promised victory and security. The home front betrayed IDF because it did not give the needed backing and support. Gone were the spontaneous acts of volunteer help to soldiers—knitting of hats, food and drink on the way to the front, and so on. But—even more serious—there was an obvious decrease in overt concern for the dead and wounded. While, during previous wars and half-wars, any loss of life had been mirrored in the atmosphere in the street, in decrease in attendance at public entertainment, and so on, the involvement with this war on the simplest overt emotional level was less. I do not think that this was due to real disinterest, but rather to a defense—an inability to tackle the issues of an unjustified war. But the effect of the feeling of alienation ("At home, they don't care") was nonetheless very strong, and led to the feeling of betrayal. After the 1967 war and up to the 1973 war, many songs had been written praising the IDF. Special songs were written for special units—like the parachutists, special services, or the medical orderlies. No hero songs followed the Lebanon soldiers—only bitter jokes and—on the whole—just ignominy and silence. Even in the commercial world, gone were the ads depicting the brave soldiers for whom one should open a savings account or buy beer, and gone were the volunteer shows by artists for the units at the front.

Newspaper headlines used to say: "Our Forces Were Fired Upon," and "No Losses to Our Forces." IDF was always the symbol of "us"—the tribe; the society. Today, the papers write more on the individual level. The collective experience and identification with IDF has decreased enormously. Its military spirit no longer embodies the spirit of the land. Not that the land was previously more militaristic; but the military encompassed all the unity, the values, and the moral code that the nation stood for. Today's descriptions of the military—and even the songs about the military—show the troops' focus on "I want" and "I need [love, songs, or peace]," rather then "we will" and "we shall." There have even been songs protesting against the service in Lebanon, "which can end up in the graveyard". This line is met with storming hand claps. For many soldiers, the ideal service is in a military band or support services, not in the fighting units.

The number of volunteers to the special units has decreased, but not drastically so. However, the number of those willing to take command—to go to an officers' course—has markedly decreased. Even more telling, the number of those who avoid service has greatly increased. For the first time in Israel's history, there is a measurable number of soldiers who use self-mutilation to avoid military service. The number of desertions (not in battle) has also increased.

Self-respect

An investigation carried out in 1969 showed that service in the IDF had second place in the status rank of occupations. In 1976, another investigation showed the position of a colonel in the IDF to occupy the 15th rank—lower then jobs such as biologist, dentist, lawyer, or economist. A major was ranked in the 38th position—after journalist, high school teacher, and pharmacist. Clearly, deterioration set in after the Yom Kippur War. Although no more recent parallel survey is available, it seems more than likely that a further deterioration has occurred. A recent military survey asked soldiers and officers what they thought to be the status with which society perceives them. Only 15 percent of the soldiers and 30 percent of the senior officers answered "high status" or "very high status." In the past, officers used to go about in their uniforms even after duty. They felt that their uniform earned them respect and even assisted in receiving certain services in government offices, shops, and so forth. Today, many of them avoid wearing uniforms even on informal occasions, such as weddings. Some also report that, at times, they are exposed to hostile comments and remarks thrown at them by passersby in the street.

Estrangement

Discussions with infantry, armored, and ranger soldiers show apathy, near depression, sadness, and lack of spirit. Gone are the enthusiasm and pride in being a front-line soldier; it is no longer shameful to be in a service or support job. It is permitted to openly discuss ways and means to avoid difficult service. "At times one is viewed as a 'frier' [a word meaning one who takes no responsibility, or is unreliable], because one is in Lebanon; previously we called those who avoided combat service a 'frier.' Once a ranger beret was an important card with the girls, today they would rather that you come home every weekend." Soldiers hitchhiking never used to have to wait for a lift. "If you had a helmet everybody knew you came from the front and stopped directly; today you can wait for a long time."

The same experience that the ordinary soldier has in the street, the generals have in their contacts with politicians. A senior officer states that the highest political level now shows much less concern and respect for the senior officer. As an outstanding example, one of them relates an episode in which, when the chief of military intelligence gave his report to the cabinet, one of the ministers who had no military background at all commented that this was a "fairy story." Reciprocally, there is a crisis of trust on the part of the military toward the politicians. The latter are perceived to have demanded a result, but had not given the military the means to attain it. "They have no idea what this is about," says a general. A clear result of this conflict is the marked decrease in financial resources that the military receive, a lessening of their priorities, and a very skeptic approach to all their demands.

General Ivri—one-time chief of the air force is reported to have said (*Koteret Roshit*):

There is one area in which the attitude of society to the IDF has changed. After the Yom Kippur War a process occurred which led to the rejection of all that was holy. We killed many sacred cows, but at the same time many other sacred things that were not cows. The result is that there is too much involvement of the mass media and the public in the uninformed immature stages of decision making in the defense domain. There is an inability to reach relevant decisions because of irrelevant pressures—especially in the infantry in which there is a greater involvement of reservists and social exposure. One does not look effectively at the relevant issues, one pays attention to "what others will say." It did not used to be this way, decisions were more isolated from involvement. Possibly that had a price—which we paid for during the Yom Kippur War—but now we exaggerate the other way. I am for criticism, but at the right time and place. . . . What happens is that journalists who are aware only of part of the problem, bring about pressures and thus an unbalance during decision making. We went from a state in which the army was too sacred to one where it is too exposed. I remember how during the period before Lebanon we were exposed to criticism that we have no defense against the Soviet ground-to-air missiles. How can one answer this? One works 24 hours a day to find a solution. You cannot reveal it even if you have a solution; besides you are never sure it will work until you have used it operationally.

Fear

Soldiers were afraid in all wars; and in all wars, there were cases of CSR—of psychological injuries. In both 1967 and 1973, the percentage of psychological injuries out of the total injuries was in the range of 5–8 percent. As discussed above, the CSR ratio appears much higher in Lebanon. In the beginning of the war, it was still considered wrong (as in previous wars) to openly discuss fears. However, as the war continued, those fears became legitimate. They were taken up by the mass media, openly discussed, and reported on TV and radio. A sociologist who is against the Lebanon War comments: "When I see all these exposures on TV of fears and anxieties I feel that this is not constructive for Israel." Similar comments are made by officers, who fear the damage to morale.

A group of boys in their last school year (mainly from the more established part of the population) talk, just before call up, about the association between the "demoralizing effects of the mass media who show only the bad in the IDF" and their own fears and desire to avoid combat duty. "Fear," says an army commander, "is natural; we all feel it. But as soldiers we must repress it and conquer it. The mass media damaged the IDF; it gave legitimation to the soldier who grins from ear to ear in front of the TV camera and with his whole heart says that he is afraid.''

These youths made a list of the positive aspects of the coming service: ''independence, advancement, meet new people, physical fitness, and moral fiber. To know yourself, challenges, discipline and coping with stress.'' The list of negative aspects was: ''degradation, depression, bad place, meaninglessness, waste of time, the army restricts the ability to think, poor food, one could die.''

Fear of death is often expressed. This is in contrast to previous findings (see Chapter 4) showing this fear to be not a very high priority in the range of fears associated with war. The biggest concern in previous wars had been ''not to let the side down''—the concern for peers or, among the officers, for the men they led. One of the most sad results of the Lebanon experience is the decrease in concern for others—the focus on survival of the individual, rather than on the welfare of the group. Group cohesion, which is one of the primary morale and combat effectiveness factors, has markedly decreased; and many feel it to be directly reflected in combat effectiveness.

Many of the schoolboys described above felt that their parents are more keen for them to serve, generally—and to serve in combat units, specifically—than they themselves are (this, in a group that was mainly kibbutz based. I would expect to find less of this kind of parental attitude in the rest of the population). ''The officers came and told us long stories about the need to serve, the historical Israel. But we do not want to get killed.'' The feeling was that they are expected to get killed. The kibbutz pupils felt the demands placed on them by the ideology of the society. Town pupils from a technical school saw the army as a job—a place to learn a profession and earn money. The contrast between the two groups used to be very great. The kibbutz population used to detest the town's norms; but now they look at town thinking as sensible and acceptable, and feel that they themselves are indeed the stupid ones. Although about 80 percent of the boys from the kibbutzim do volunteer to special combat units, they do not talk about it. It is the minority who identify with the norms of easy life and ''getting away with it'' who are the vocal ones, and who have no hesitation in expressing their ''shameful'' attitude. One cannot but wonder how those who are driven to combat units by social pressure and ideological norms can be expected to adjust to the demands of war, especially to sustain morale in a long-drawn-out conflict.

Apathy among the youth is marked. One cannot really provoke them by nationalistic or antinationalistic statements. A teacher in the kibbutz movement says, ''What interests these youths is the 'I.' In the movement we educate for and demand that they shall have a 'meaningful' service in the IDF, but when they ask us what we mean we can only stammer and do not know what to answer. I think they feel that our demands on them are somewhat false. I myself do not know what to answer. They go on volunteering for special units but this is only out of habit, it cannot go on for long." A lieutenant colonel says, "Today's youth do not go through the naive enthusiasm stage we went through. Call it realism or cynicism. They have a different style. The danger is that their attitude will affect the next generation."

Says General Ivri: "There is a psychological tiredness in the land. I and my generation had the illusion that if we fight, our children will not have to fight. But we failed in that; it is probably impossible to succeed in it. This is what leads to tiredness, the knowledge that one will have to go on like this for many years without reaching a solution."

The Officer

During August 1983, it became clear to Shoni that he and his company—as well as the whole IDF—are in the wrong place. It was also time to decide whether he—the company commander—should renew his contract, which was about to expire. He decided to stay on:

It was precisely then, when I realized that our presence in Lebanon is unjustified, and when I realized that we shall remain there for a long time to come, that it became important not to leave the army. I did not want my soldiers to feel that given the chance I shall desert them.

This is a typical description of the attitude of many officers; it is an approach based on "in spite of"—a picture characterized by doubts and conflicts and guided by the need to change and to create something new, instead of the present. They are determined to not give up, but to keep fighting from within the system. They are sustained by basic loyalty to past ideals and norms.

When interviewed in *Ha'aretz*, Shoni—a law student—was 24. When the war in Lebanon started, he was second in command of an armored company. Three months later, he became the company commander.

Before the war we had many preparations for it. It was clear that we shall go into Lebanon on some sort of operation. We waited for it and when the war started there was a great relief of tension. I remember that I wanted to experience war. This is the natural sequel to training, running, fire tests, and giving orders. To some extent I wanted to apply all that I have learned and to test myself to see how good I am at the real thing. The military setting builds up these primitive feelings, even if the soldiers, on a realistic level, do not want war. I personally in my political ideology am against war.

Shoni's circle of friends and his ideological reference group were those who—from the very first days of the war—had protested, demonstrated, and agitated against it. Even in 1984, Shoni still felt that the protest was unnecessary:

After the first 6 days of the war we felt very patriotic [having removed the direct threat to northern Israel's population] and suddenly came a flood of doubts from the home front. We had the feeling that the civilians have no business to interfere. Most of us identified with the then stated aim of the war: the destruction of the PLO bases. We were certain that the war will not take more than a few weeks. Remember that as soldiers we experienced a very unpleasant war, and suddenly we found ourselves without backing. Even today I am angry at that. During those days one should have shown some sense of national responsibility, believe that Israel functions under the rule of law, and that the military must fulfill orders as best it can.

He believed that his "coming to his senses" was inevitable and that he came to it independent of the home-front reactions, which he considers unnecessary:

When we went to the war it was to protect the civilians at home. Even before anything became clear and while friends were being killed beside me, doubts were voiced. A pity. I feel that this war would have been justified if we had left Lebanon after 2 weeks, after destroying the PLO bases. It is when we started building our own bases there that naturally the questions arose: "What are we doing here?" Slowly, from the events, we understood that we are here to stay. Not because of the need to defend the Galil, but because the politicians needed justification for their actions. I feel that IDF entered Beirut because the order was given, but there was no identification with the action. It was an unnecessary operation which risked many soldiers' lives.

New Concepts

In his position of command Shoni was forced to act against his good judgment. He could only affect what happened within the company: the operational performance, the relationship of the soldiers to the Arab population, and their self-image as IDF's soldiers. He says,

To a certain extent I guided my soldiers but I did not dare to convince them that the war is justified. However, I did convince them that one must keep to the moral code, to the "purity of arms." This is a term which now one can place in apostrophes. It is difficult to talk about the purity of arms when fighting in the middle of a population center. This term, by the very circumstances, changed from the absolute to the relative. I personally tried to even avoid driving my tanks over planted and ploughed fields—for me this is also included in the concept of "purity of arms."

The circumstances in Lebanon had to affect the soldiers—the shift in values from the clear absolute to the relative.

In the first two weeks the soldiers met completely unknown conditions: fighting in built up areas full of civilians, and civilians who met them with rice and bread. I remember that I was frightened by the first bag of welcoming cherries thrown towards me as if it were a bomb. The real problems started after the first few weeks. Then we had to learn the new concept of the IDF. IDF as a policeman, of keeping order. At the same time IDF as an occupation force. We the soldiers faced many moral issues; each of us had much time to consider the real problems of this war. There was terrible tension. Because each civilian in the street could have been the enemy. We set out to fight against the terrorists and we found ourselves fighting against the Syrian army and against civilians. But the most difficult of all was that we were not sure of the rightness of our actions.

A serious problem in Lebanon was the feeling of power; one feels so mighty in relation to the civilians. Each soldier has the potential of a dictator, one that can do whatever he wants. This went on up to the point when clear orders were issued as to how to relate to the civilian population; previously there were too many behaviors which felt like misuse of power. Soldiers who started serving in Lebanon who had never experienced the other IDF, had an even more serious problem. Because of them, because of a new company that I was in charge of before my discharge, I am glad I stayed on. I could make them fully aware of the moral issues in Lebanon and of problems in their own perception and in that of the Lebanese.

Relationships with the Lebanese civilians were a problem both because each of them offered a potential threat and because we were continuously suspicious of them. From the first day the Lebanese were continuously present in the fields of action. Some of them shooting in all directions, some clapping hands, some trying to ingratiate themselves with us. The same people could be friends one moment and throw a bomb at us at the next. A boy could be a playing child or be the figure behind an RPG. The conditions in Lebanon were such that they forced the soldiers to have a light trigger finger. They needed to have very fast responses which increased the chances of hitting the innocent.

From other officers' remarks, one forms a more acute picture. The new IDF norms were called "Levantinization." Values became more fluid and adaptable; reactions toward previously unacceptable behaviors, less harsh and more forgiving. Soldiers who were in an NCO course were given the task of covering another platoon on patrol. Instead, they engaged in looting. Some were removed from the course, but not punished; and a few even later returned to the same course. There were cases where soldiers who had been ordered to search houses wantonly destroyed property, just for revenge. The officer in charge described how, on a previous day's search, they had not thoroughly investigated a house because a woman was crying loudly, until an expert assured them that this meant there were arms hidden—and, indeed, a big ammunition dump was discovered. "The whole time, I thought about this woman," said a soldier. "She was like my mother; how could I behave like this towards her—and then I saw that the expert was right." Another soldier who was there said that after they found a radio control for exploding mines hidden in a bed, they started shooting at all the furniture in the house.

The developing of racist and even Nazi movements has caused a great deal of concern in Israel. But the IDF was the first to actively organize the fight against this. Its education branch spent a great deal of effort in educating soldiers to have a more tolerant attitude. At the same time, it is from among the soldiers that the extreme right-wing movements received disproportionately more votes in the 1984 elections.

Cohesion

A basic schism within the Israeli society lies between the Sefardim—Jews originating from Muslim countries—and the Ashcenazim—Jews originating from Western countries. The number of Ashcenazi officers has always been out of all proportion to their part of the population. This situation has become better over the years, but the gap is still large. Similarly, the proportion of volunteers to the elite units out of the Ashcenazi (and especially the kibbutz population) is very much higher than their percent in the population. Although the Sefardi population more frequently and vocally supports the IDF and approves the deployment of harsher methods, in reality they do not equally share the needs of the IDF. Although very vocal with criticism, the kibbutz population actively supports the IDF and is its backbone. But even in that, the situation has changed to the worse. Although 90 percent of the kibbutz population is of an officer potential, only 20 percent—compared with 40 percent a few years age—volunteer to become officers. A high proportion of those who recently became officers do not renew their initial contract. This process of "natural selection" has led to the spread of mediocracy. In the past, IDF could boast that it included the best in the land—a claim that is no longer valid. This is often assumed to be a result of the loss of status and the loss of any feeling of meaningfulness of service in the IDF—a situation caused primarily by the alienation between the people and the armed forces. The unity of the first 25 years of Israel's existence—in which "all the nation is the army"—has eroded. The collapse of the myth of invincibility of the IDF—which started in 1973—has been accelerated by the Lebanon War in which, besides the military failure to cope with unexpected forms of battle, moral and political chaos undermined the basic structure of the nation's frame of reference.

ANALYSIS

The technical, geographical, and social circumstances of the Lebanon War are unique for Israel; but the psychological parameters involved are relevant to many wars, regardless of the setting. Any conflict in which a whole country is involved—especially if, due to reserve forces, a large part of the population is involved—could be affected in a similar way. The main levels of impact and dissonance are summarized below:

1. The individual. Fear became an overt and guiding factor. Soldiers are naturally afraid of war, but this fear is often controlled. In Lebanon, as the war went on, the degree of perceived control and the wish to control decreased. This also affected behavior—concern for oneself became more important than for the group. Soldiers often used ways that would never have been used previously—for example, self-mutilation—to avoid battle. The number of psychological malfunctions was 3–4 times higher than in previous wars. Tiredness and apathy were prevalent.

2. The group. The better groups increased cohesion, because—feeling betrayed by the home front and their political leaders—they united. Others deteriorated and lost the sense of responsibility for each other and other groups. The commanding officer was a critical factor in determining the group's cohesion. The conflict of loyalty and identification between the regular IDF forces and the home (as well as IDF) reservists place strain on the group's cohesion. Often, the feeling was that the country expected the IDF to pay for its mistakes.

3. The military. The military had to adapt to a completely new form of warfare. Not only were new tactics required, but also new moral codes and evaluations. The concept of "purity of arms" was no longer applicable in its original form. At the same time, much sharper and tighter control of all military actions—and criticism by civilians, especially mass media—undermined the myth of the great officer and supreme leader.

In order to adequately cope with any stress situation, three elements must exist in its perception:

1. One must have a clear picture or *structure* of what is involved—what the rules of the game are—and which priorities one should place on all aspects concerned.
2. One must be *concerned and involved*. One must want to commit oneself to a course of action.
3. One must feel "up to it" in order to *cope*—to be able to do something about the situation.

The previous description clearly shows how the attainment of these three elements on the three levels was problematic in the Lebanon situation:

1. The purpose of the war was not clear to many. The nature of the enemy and rules of war were very diffuse.
2. Moral issues prevented many from identifying with the war; and conflict with home-front perceptions further reduced the potential for committal.
3. Loss of trust in the military skills and ability to handle the new situation, loss of status of the leaders, and the inability to protest—all led to a decreased feeling of adequacy and control.

These are the prerequisites for psychological combat potential—indeed, the coping potential for any conflict situation. Any training for war must assure the adequacy of the perceptual process. Since the actual war scenario can only be predicted in a very diffuse way, training must be focused on the ability to perceive—how to structure, evaluate, and have confidence in one's ability to cope.

To be able to "think the unthinkable," to imagine emotional stresses (for example, how it will feel when comrades are blown up beside you, or when you have to order others into very dangerous situations), and to think through the actions one must take—all these are mental preparations for coping. These steps are essential, and in the order given. There is no point in preparing for the stressful emotions before one has structured the possible scenarios. There is no point in teaching skills and tactics before one has dealt with the emotional problems involved in their application.

NOTE

1. Some of the main newspaper articles used are: *Ha'aretz*—Maroz, T. (16/3/84), Shif, Z. (20/2/85, 2/8/85, 7/2/86), Tal-Shir, R. (7/6/85), Erlich, E. (16/5/86); and *Koteret Roshit*: Shavit, A. (15/5/85, 22/5/85).

11

Conclusion

Adjustment is always based on the perception that an individual (or a group) has of his resources, compared with the perceived demands on him. This perceptual process has been described as a nine-stage sequential process. One can predict adjustment and coping in general and combat performance in particular by following this process of effectiveness, stage by stage. A total failure to clear any one stage will result in total inability to cope or fight, while a decrease in efficacy in one stage or more will lead—cumulatively—to a reduction in the combat potential. Thus, a prerequisite for any successful coping is adequate perception of the structure of the situation, of its significance, and of an ability to handle it.

One feels that a book such as this should end with some general remarks—possibly justifying its very existence and the message it carries (if any). This book is devoted to the issues of conflict and combat. Obviously, it is supposed to be used to enhance the combat effectiveness of military (and possibly other paramilitary or semimilitary) groups. It is a book that could be claimed to serve the ends of war and destruction; and, in this day and age, such a book needs some justification. Basically, there may be no justification for war (although all wars have been justified by some of their participants); therefore, I have the feeling that I have to explain why this book, which appears to be aimed at enhancing combat capacity, may in fact contribute to reduction of conflicts.

This is a book about violence and aggression. It contains facts, anecdotes, and much speculation about what leads all men and women to engage in conflicts of different kinds and levels. No one will argue that thinking about these problems should not be done; and yet, as Whyte (1950) states: "Thought is [a] form of failure. Only when action fails to satisfy human needs is there ground for thought. To devote attention to any problem is to confess a lack of adjustment [to it] which we must stop to consider." The problem exists; we must indeed think about it and discuss it. Bettelheim (1980) argues that the root of our failure to deal with violence lies in our refusal to face up to it. We deny our predilection for aggression; we condemn violence and repress its appearance—rather than try to handle it, accept and modify it, and incorporate it in a less virulent form in our very existence.

It is not sufficient to study the roots of violence; one has to understand the role it has in human experience. It has been suggested (see Chapter 4) that activities such as competitive sports could substitute for social violence. This has failed because those activities proved to be no substitute. However, it may still be possible to substitute socially acceptable forms of aggressive and conflict behavior for the unacceptable expressions of these needs. In any case, the needs themselves cannot and must not be denied, nor ignored. Such a substitution can only be successful if the replacement fulfills the psychological needs that were the genesis of these behaviors in the first place. By mapping the impact of perception and the appraisal process on the interaction between a person (or a group) and environment—the interaction among needs, experience, abilities, demands, and impositions—one might understand the patterns of conflict and aggression.

Such an understanding can certainly be used (or misused) to increase combat effectiveness in "unjustified" wars; but such an understanding is also essential if we are to reduce the danger of holocausts of wars, and it can form the basis for successful channelization of aggressive behavior. Much as prophylactic immunization to disease is based on the administration of a less virulent form of the very disease we seek to combat, so must the reduction of aggression be based on its very application in a mitigated and controlled form.

Bibliography

Adan, A. 1979. *On the Banks of the Suez* (in Hebrew). Jersusalem: Edanim.

Ardrey, R. 1966. *The Territorial Imperative.* New York: Atheneum.

_____ . 1970a. *The Social Conscience.* New York: Atheneum.

_____ . 1970b. *The Social Contract.* London: William Collins.

Aristotle. 1953. *De Anima.* The Loeb Classical Library, London: Heinemann.

Ashley, W.R. 1956. *Introduction to Cybernetics.* London: Chapman and Hall.

Babad, E.Y., and Salomon, G. 1978. "Professional Dilemmas of the Psychologist in an Organizational Emergency." *American Psychologist* (September): 840-46.

Bandura, A. 1973. *Aggression: A Social Learning Analysis.* Englewood Cliffs, N.J.: Prentice-Hall.

_____ . 1977. *A Social Learning Theory.* Englewood Cliffs, N.J.: Prentice-Hall.

Bar Kochba, B. 1980. *The Macabean War. The Days of Judah Macabee* (in Hebrew). Tel-Aviv: Ben Zvi.

Baron, R.A. 1977. *Human Aggression.* New York: Plenum.

Baron, R., Salomon, Z., Noy, S., and Nardi, C. 1986. "The Clinical Picture of Combat Stress Reactions in the 1982 War in Lebanon: Cross War Comparisons." In Milgram, N.A. (ed.), *Stress and Coping in Times of War.* New York: Brunner/Mazel Publishers.

Bartlett, F.C. 1927. *Psychology and the Soldier.* London: Cambridge University Press.

Bartov, H. 1978. *Dado 48 Years and 30 More Days* (in Hebrew). Tel-Aviv: Ma'ariv Books.

Bauer, R.G., and Stout, R.L. 1974. *Research on the Social-Psychological Factors Underlaying the Idea of Discipline,* Volume 1 of *Conceptual and Predictive Models of the Army Unit Discipline.* Final Report May 74, Benedix Corporation Department of Applied Science and Technology, Ann Arbor, Mich.

Bauer, R.G., Stout, R.L., and Holtz, R.F. 1976. *Developing a Conceptual and Predictive Model of Discipline in the U.S. Army.* Army Research Institute for the Behavioral and Social Sciences, Problem Rev. 76/5.

Baynes, J. 1967. *Morale.* London: Cassel.

Beaumont, R.A., and Snyder, W.P. 1980. "Combat Effectiveness: Paradigm and Paradoxes." In Sarkesian, S.C. (ed.), *Combat Effectiveness.* Beverly Hills: Sage.

Bell, D.B., Bulin, S.F., Houston, T.J., and Kristiansen, D.M. 1973. "Prediction and Self-Fulfilling Prophecies of Army Discipline," *Proceedings of the Annual Convention of the American Psychological Association* 8: 747-748.

Ben Shushan Dictionary. 1972. Kiryat Sefer, Jerusalem.

Berkowitz, L. 1964. "Aggressive Cues in Aggressive Behavior and Hostility Catharsis," *Psychological Review* 71:104-22.

———. 1974. "Some Determinants of Impulsive Aggression: Role of Mediated Associations with Reinforcements for Aggression," *Psychological Reports* 84:165-76.

Berkowitz, L., and Le Page, A. 1967. "Weapons as Aggression-Eliciting Stimuli," *Journal of Personality and Social Psychology* 2:202-07.

Berkowitz, L., and Turner, C.W. 1974. "Perceived Anger Level, Investigating Agent, and Aggression." In London, H., and Nisbett, R.E. (eds.), *Cognitive Alteration of Feeling States*. Chicago: Aldine.

Berlyne, D.E. 1960. *Conflict, Arousal and Curiosity*. New York: McGraw-Hill.

———. 1971. *Esthetics and Psychobiology:* New York: Appleton-Century-Croft.

Bettelheim, B. 1960. *The Informed Heart*. New York: The Free Press.

———. 1980. *Survival and Other Essays*. New York: Vintage Books.

Beusse, W.E. 1977. *Factors Related to the Incidence of Disciplinary Actions amongst Enlisted Personnel*. Air Force Human Resources Laboratory, Brooks AFB Texas, Report No. AFHRL-TR-75-21.

Blake, J.A. 1973. "The Congressional Medal of Honor in Three Wars," *Pacific Sociological Review* 16:166-76.

———. 1978. "Death by Handgrenade: Altruistic Suicide in Combat," *Suicide and Life-Threatening Behavior* 8:45-59.

Blake, J.A., and Butler, S. 1976. "The Medal of Honor, Combat Orientations and Latent Role Structure in the United States Military," *The Sociological Quarterly* 17:561-67.

Bourne, P.G. 1969. "Urinary 17 OHCS Levels in Two Combat Situations." In Bourne, P.G. (ed.), *The Psychology and Physiology of Stress*, New York: Academic Press.

Bourne, P.G., and Coli, W.E. 1968. "Affect Levels of Special Forces Soldiers under Threat of Attack," *Psychological Reports* 22:363-66.

Bowman, D.C. 1973. "Combat Stress," *Infantry* 63:40-47.

Bramson, L., and Goethals, G.W. (eds.) 1964. *War*. New York: Basic Books.

Broadbent, D.E. 1971. *Decision and Stress*. New York: Academic Press.

Browne, A.T.A. 1976. "A Study of the Anatomy of Fear and Courage," *Army Quarterly and Defence Journal* (July):297-303.

Buss, A. 1961. *The Psychology of Aggression*. New York: Wiley.

Chambers Twentieth Century Dictionary. 1959. London: W.K. Chambers.

Cockerham, W.C. 1978. "Attitudes toward Combat among U.S. Army Paratroopers," *Journal of Political and Military Sociology* 6:1-15.

Crawford, K.S., and Thomas, E.D. 1974. *Human Resources Management and Non-Judicial Punishment Rates on Navy Ships*. Navy Personnel Research and Development Center, San Diego, Report No. NPRDC-TR-76-5.

———. 1977. "Organizational Climate and Disciplinary Rate on Naval Ships," *Armed Forces and Society* 3:165-82.

Cummings, T.G., and Cooper, C.L. 1979. "A Cybernetic Framework for Studying Occupational Stress," *Human Relations* 32:395-418.

Deci, E.L. 1975. *Intrinsic Motivation*. New York: Plenum.

Dengerink, H.A., Schnedler, R.W., and Covery, M.K. 1978. "Role of Avoidance in Aggressive Responses to Attack and No Attack," *Journal of Personality and Social Psychology* 36:1044-53.

Diener, E., Dineen, J., and Endersen, K. 1975. "Effects of Altered Responsibility, Cognitive Set, and Modeling on Physical Aggression and Deindividuation," *Journal of Personality and Social Psychology* 31:328-37.

Dollard, J.B., Doob, L., Miller, N., Mowrer, O.H., and Sears, R.R. 1939. *Frustration and Aggression*. New Haven, Conn.: Yale University Press.

Du Picq, T.N. 1959. *Battle Studies*. London: Stackpole.

Durbin, E.F.M., and Bowley, J. 1938. *War and Democracy*, Part 1. London: Kegan Paul, Tench, Trunber.

Durkheim, E. (1897), trans. Spaulding, J.A., and Simon, G. 1951. *Suicide*. New York: Free Press.

Eisenhart, R.W. 1975. You Can't Hack It Little Girl: A Discussion of the Covert Psychological Agenda of Modern Combat Training. *Journal of Social Issues* 31:13-23.

Feshbach, S. 1956. "The Catharsis Hypothesis and Some Consequences of Interaction with Aggressive and Neutral Play Objects," *Journal of Personality* 24:449-62.

———. 1970. "Aggression." In Mussen, P.H. (ed.), *Charmicael Annual of Child Psychology*, Vol 11. New York: Wiley and Son.

———. 1978. "The Environment of Personality," *American Psychologist* (May): 447-55.

Fiedler, F.E., Potter, E.H. III, Zais, M.M., and Knowlton, W.A. Jr. 1979. "Organizational Stress and the Use and Misuse of Managerial Intelligence and Experience," *Journal of Applied Psychology* 64:635-37.

Finan, B.G., Borus, J.F., and Stanton, M.D. 1975. "Black and White American-Vietnamese Relations amongst Soldiers in Vietnam," *The Journal of Social Issues* 31:39-48.

Fisher, S., and Cleveland, S.E. 1968. *Body Image and Personality*. New York: Dover Publications.

Folkman, S. 1984. "Personal Control and Stress and Coping Process; A Theoretical Analysis," *Journal of Personality and Social Psychology* 46:839-52.

Folkman, S., and Lazarus, R.S. 1980. "An Analysis of Coping in Middle Aged Community People," *Journal of Health and Social Behavior* 21:219-39.

Folkman, S., Schaefer, C., and Lazarus, R.S. 1979. "Cognitive Processes as Mediators of Stress and Coping." In Hamilton, V., and Warburtin, D.M. (eds.), *Human Stress and Cognition*. Chichester: Wiley and Sons.

Förander, N. 1974. *Morale and Discipline in the Forces*. Militärpsykologiska institutet, rapport B 101. Stockholm.

Fox, R.P. 1974. "Narcissistic Rage and the Problem of Combat Aggression," *Archives of General Psychiatry* 31:807-11.

Fraczek, A. 1977. "Functions and Emotional and Cognitive Mechanisms in Regulation of Aggressive Behavior," *Polish Psychological Bulletin* 8:195-200.

Freedman, J.L., Levy, A.S., Buchanan, R.V., and Price, J. 1972. "Crowding and Human Aggressiveness," *Journal of Experimental Social Psychology* 8:528-48.

Freud, A. 1937. *The Ego and the Mechanisms of Defence*. New York: Hogarth Press.

Freud, S. 1933. *New Introductory Lectures on Psychoanalysis*. New York: Norton.

Friedman, M., and Rosenman, R.H. 1974. *Type A Behavior and Your Heart*. Greenwich, Conn.: Fawcett.

Fromm, E. 1942. *Fear of Freedom*. London: Kegan Paul, Trench, Trubner.

――――― . 1955. *The Sane Society*. New York: Rinehart.

Gabriel, R. A., and Savage, R. L. 1978. *Crisis in Command*. New York: Hill and Wang.

Gal, R. 1981. "Characteristics of Heroism." In Breznitz, S. (ed.), *Stress in Israel*. New York: Van Nostrand Reinhold.

Gal, R., and Lazarus, R.S. 1975. "The Role of Activity in Anticipating and Confronting Stressful Situations," *Journal of Human Stress* 1:4-20.

Gault, W.B. 1971. "Some Remarks on Slaughter," *American Journal of Psychiatry* 128:450-54.

George, A.L. 1971. "Primary Group, Organisation and Military Performance." In Little, R.W. (ed.), *Handbook of Military Institutions*. Beverly Hills: Sage.

Gillooly, D.H., and Bond, T.C. 1976. "Assaults with Explosive Devices on Superiors," *Military Medicine* 141:700-702.

Glass, A.L. 1953. *"The Problems of Stress in Combat Zones,"* Symposium on Stress, Army Medical Service Graduate School, Washington, D.C.

Green, R.G., and Berkowitz, L. 1967. "Some Conditions Facilitating the Occurrence of Aggression after Observation of Violence," *Journal of Personality* 35:666-76.

Greenbaum, C.W. 1979. "The Small Group under the Gun—Uses of Small Groups in Battle Conditions," *Journal of Applied Behavioral Science* 15:392-405.

Greenbaum, C.W., Rogogsky, I., and Shalit, B. 1977. "The Military Psychologist during War Time: A Model Based on Action Research and Crisis Intervention," *Journal of Applied Behavioral Science* 13:7-22.

Grinker, R.E., and Spiegel, J.P. 1945. *Men under Stress*. Philadelphia: Blatiston.

Hare, R.M. 1979. "Can I Be Blamed for Obeying Orders?" In Wakin, M.M., *War Morality and the Military Profession*. Boulder: Westview Press.

Harris, M.B. 1973. "Field Studies of Modeled Aggression," *The Journal of Social Psychology* 89:131-39.

――――― . 1974. "Mediators between Frustration and Aggression in a Field Experiment," *Journal of Experimental Social Psychology* 10:561-76.

Harris, M.B., and Samerotte, G. 1975. "The Effects of Aggressive and Altruistic Modeling on Subsequent Behavior," *The Journal of Social Psychology* 95:173-82.

Hauser, W.L. 1980. "The Will to Fight." In Sarkasian, S.L. (ed.), *Combat Effectiveness*. Beverly Hills: Sage.

Himmelstein, P., and Blaskovics, T.L. 1960. "Prediction of an Intermediate Criterion of Combat Effectiveness with a Biographical Inventory," *Journal of Applied Psychology* 44:166-68.

Hippler, A.E. 1971. "Some Psychosocial Aspects of Army Life," *Journal of Human Relations* 19:97-114.

Hogarth, R. 1980. *Judgement and Choice*. New York: Wiley and Sons.

Howard, M. 1978. *War and Liberal Conscience*. London: Temple Smith.

Ingraham, L.H. 1984. *The Boys in the Barracks: Observations on American Military Life*. Philadelphia: Institute for the Study of Human Issues.

Ingraham, L.H., and Manning, F.J. 1980. "Cohesion in the Army: Who Needs It, What Is It Anyway, and How Do We Get It to Them?" Paper delivered at the Twentieth Interuniversity Seminar on Armed Forces and Society, Chicago.

Janis, I.C., and Mann, L. 1977. *Decision Making: A Psychological Analysis of Conflict, Choice and Commitment*. New York: The Free Press.

Janowitz, M. (ed.) 1964. *The New Military—Changing Patterns of Organization*. New York: Russel Sage Foundation.

Janowitz, M., and Little, R. 1969. *Sociology and the American Military Establishment*. California: Sage.

Janowitz, M., and Little, R.W. 1974. *Sociology and the Military Establishment*. London: Sage.

Jung, C.G., ed. by de Lazlo, V. 1959. *The Basic Writings of C. G. Jung*. New York: Random House.

Karsten, P. 1978. *Law, Soldiers and Combat*. London: Greenwood Press.

Katzev, R., Edelsack, L., Steinmetz, G., Walker, T., and Wright, R. 1978. Person the Effects of Reprimanding Transgressions on Subsequent Field Behavior. *Personality and Social Psychological Bulletin* 4:113-200.

Keegan, J. 1976. *The Face of Battle*. London: Jonathan Cape.

Keinan, G. 1986. "Confidence Expectancy as Predictor of Military Performance under Stress." In Milgram, N.A. (ed.), *Stress and Coping in Times of War*. New York: Brunner/Mazel Publishers.

Kilham, W., and Mann, L. 1974. "Levels of Destructive Obedience as a Function of Transmitter and Executant Roles in Milgram Obedience Paradigm," *Journal of Personality and Social Psychology* 35:272-78.

Kloskowska, A. 1970. "Heroism and Personal Symbols of Cultural Value," *Dialectics and Humanism* 1:47-58.

Koestler, A. 1964. *The Act of Creation*. London: Hutchinson.

———. 1978. *Janus—A Summing Up*. London: Hutchinson.

Kranss, B.J., Kaplan, R.D., and Kranss, H.H. 1973. "Factors Effecting Veterans' Decision to Fire Weapons in Combat Situation," *International Journal of Group Tensions* 3:105-11.

Kroll, J. 1976. "Racial Patterns of Military Crimes in Vietnam," *Psychiatry* 39:51-64.

Kruuk, H. 1972. "The Urge to Kill," *New Scientist* 29:735-37.

Langer, W.L. 1969. Discussion of the article. In Mack, J.E., and Lawrence, T.E.: A Study of Heroism and Conflict. *American Journal of Psychology* 125:1083-92.

Larsen, K.S., and Giles, H. 1976. "Survival or Courage as Human Motivation: Development of an Attitude Scale," *Psychological Reports* 39:299-302.

Lazarus, R.S. 1966. *Psychological Stress and the Coping Process*. New York: McGraw-Hill.

_____ . 1976. *Patterns of Adjustment*. New York: McGraw-Hill.

_____ . 1983. "The Costs and Benefits of Denial." In Breznitz, S. (ed.), *The Denial of Stress*. New York: The Free Press.

Lazarus, R.S., Averill, J.R., and Option, E.M. Jr. 1974. "The Psychology of Coping: Issues of Research and Assessment." in Coelho, C.V., and Hamburg, D.A.A. (eds.), *Coping and Adaption*. New York: Basic Books.

Lazarus, R.S., and Cohen, J.B. 1977. Environmental Stress. In Altman, I. and Wohlwill, J.F. (eds.): *Human Behavior and the Environment: Current Theory and Research*, pp. 89-127. New York: Plenum.

Lazarus, R.S., and Folkman, S. 1984. *Stress, Appraisal, and Coping*. New York: Springfield.

Lazarus, R.S., and Launier, R. 1978. "Stress Related Transactions between Person and Environment." in Pervin, L.A., and Lewis, M. (eds.), *Perspectives in Interactional Psychology*. New York: Plenum.

Levav, H., Greenfeld, H., and Baruch, E. 1979. "Psychiatric Combat Reactions during the Yom Kippur War," *American Journal of Psychiatry* 136:637-41.

Levy, R. 1983. *"Forward Treatment of Combat Reactions."* Address delivered to the Third International Conference on Psychological Stress and Adjustment in Times of War and Peace, January, Tel-Aviv.

Leyens, J.P., Camino, L., Parke, R.D., and Berkowitz, L. 1975. "Effects of Movie Violence on Aggression in a Field Setting as a Function of Group Dominance and Cohesion," *Journal of Personality and Social Psychology* 32:346-60.

Little, R.E. 1964. "Buddy Relations and Combat Performance." In Janowitz, M. (ed.), *The New Military*. New York: Russel Sage Foundation.

Lorenz, K. 1966. *On Aggression*. New York: Harcourt, Brace, and World.

Lowe, R., and McGrath, J. 1971. *Stress Arousal and Performance: Some Findings Calling for a New Theory*. Air Force Office of Social Research, Project Report AF 1161-1167.

Luckham, A.R. 1971. "Institutional Transfer and Break Down in a New Nation. The Nigerian Military," *Administrative Science Quarterly* 16:387-405.

Mack, J.E. 1969. "T.E. Lawrence: A Study of Heroism and Conflict," *American Journal of Psychiatry* 125:1083-92.

Magnusson, D. 1981. *Towards a Psychology of Situations: An Interactional Perspective*. London: Lawrence Erlbaum Associates.

Magnusson, D., and Ekehammar, B. 1976. "Perception and Reactions to Stressful Situations." In Endler, N.S., and Magnusson, D. (eds.), *Interactional Psychology and Personality*. Washington, D.C.: Hemisphere.

Mann, L. 1973. "Attitudes towards My Lai and Obedience to Order: An Australian Survey," *Australian Journal of Psychology* 25:11-21.

Markowitz, I. 1972. "The Military Mind," *Psychiatric Quarterly* 45:440-48.

Marshall, S.L.A. 1947. *Men against Fire*. New York: William Morrow.

_____ . 1966. *The Officer as a Leader*. Harrisburg, Penn.: Stockpole Books.

Milburn, M.A. 1980. "Theories of Aggression: A Critique and Possible Reformulation," *Human Relations* 33:353-68.

Milgram, N.A. (ed.) 1986. *Stress and Coping in Times of War*. New York: Brunner/ Mazel Publishers.

Milgram, N.A., and Hobfoll, S. 1986. "Generalization. From Theory to Practice in War-related Stress." In Milgram, N.A. (ed.), *Stress and Coping in Times of War*. New York: Brunner/Mazel Publishers.

Milgram, S. 1963. "Behavioral Study of Obedience," *Journal of Abnormal and Social Psychology* 67:371-78.

———. 1974. *Obedience and Authority*. New York: Harper and Row.

Miller, N.E. 1948. "Theory and Experiment Relating Psychoanalytic Displacement to Stimulus Response Generalization," *Journal of Abnormal and Social Psychology* 43:155-78.

Miron, M.S., and Goldstein, A.P. 1979. *Hostage*. New York: Pergamon Press.

Montagu, A. 1976. *The Nature of Human Aggression*. New York: Oxford University Press.

Moran, L. 1945. *The Anatomy of Courage*. London: Constable.

Morris, D. 1969. *the Human Zoo*. London: Jonathan Cape.

———. 1978. *Manwatching*. St. Albans, England: Triad Panther.

Moskos, C.C. Jr. 1975. "The American Combat Soldier in Vietnam," *The Journal of Social Issues* 31/1:25-37.

Motowildo, S.J., and Borman, W.C. 1977. "Behaviorally Anchored Scales for Measuring Morale in Military Units," *Journal of Applied Psychology* 62:177-83.

———. 1978. "Relationships between Military Morale, Motivation, Satisfaction, and Unit Effectiveness," *Journal of Applied Psychology* 63:47-52.

Napoleon, I.B. 1815. *Memorial de St Hélène*. Las Cases.

Newman, A.S. 1967. "Who Gets the Combat Decorations?" *Army* (January): 30-31.

Noy, S., Nardi, C., and Salomon, Z. 1986. "Battle and Military Unit Characteristics and the Prevalence of Psychiatric Casualties." In Milgram, N.A. (ed.), *Stress and Coping in Times of War*. New York: Brunner/Mazel Publishers.

Olley, R., and Kranss, H.H. 1974. "Variables Which May Influence the Decision to Fire in Combat," *The Journal of Social Psychology* 92:151-52.

Olmstead, J.A. 1968. "The Effects of 'Kill Quick' upon Trainee Confidence and Attitudes," Human Resources Research Office Technical Report 68, 15. USA.

Olweus, D. 1979. "Stability of Reaction Patterns in Males: A Review," *Psychological Bulletin* 86:852-75.

Peri, A. 1986. "Cognitive Aspects in Compulsory Service Perception Amongst Conscripts." Paper delivered at the International Congress of Military Medicine, Rome.

Perlmutter, A. 1969. *Military and Politics in Israel 1948-1967*. London: Frank Cass.

Petersen, A.B. 1974. *Against the Tide. An Argument in Favor of the American Soldier*. New York: New Rochelle.

Priestland, G. 1974. *The Future of Violence*. London: Hamish Hamilton.

Rank, O. 1909. *Der Mythus von der Geburt des Helden*. New Edition 1970. Liechtenstein: Kraus-Thomson.

Rappaport, A. 1964. *Strategy and Conscience*. New York: Schocken.

Richardson, F.M. 1978. *Fighting Spirit*. London: Leo Cooper.

Robinson, B.W. 1971. In Elefhteriou, B.E., and Scott, J.R. (eds.), *The Psychology of Aggression and Defeat*. New York: Plenum.

Rothenberg, G.E. 1979. *The Anatomy of the Israeli Army*. London: Batsford.

Rousseau, J.J. 1962. *Political Writing of J.J. Rousseau*, Volume 1, London: Oxford University Press.

Russell, E.W. 1972. "Factors of Human Aggression: A Cross-Cultural Factor Analysis of Characteristics Related to Warfare and Crime," *Behavioral Science Research* 4:275-312.

Sarkesian, S.C. (ed.) 1980. *Combat Effectiveness*. Beverly Hills: Sage.

Savage, P.L. 1980. Comments delivered at the Twentieth Interuniversity Seminar on Armed Forces and Society, Chicago.

Savage, P.L., Gabriel, R.A., and Richard, A. 1976. "Cohesion and Distintegration in the American Army: An Alternative Perspective," *Armed Forces and Society* 2:240-76.

Schelling, T.C. 1962. "A Special Surveillance Force." In Wright, Q., Evan, W.E., and Deutsch, M. (eds.), *Preventing World War III*. New York: Simon and Schuster.

Schild, E.D. 1973. The Meaning of the Israeli Military Service. In Curtis, M. and Chextoff, M.S. (eds.): *Israel Social Structure and Changes*. New Brunswich: Transalten Books.

Scott, J.P. 1971. In Eleftheriou, B.E., and Scott, J.P. (eds.), *The Psychology of Aggression and Defeat*. New York: Plenum.

Shalit, B. 1970. "Environment Hostility and Hostility in Fantasy," *Journal of Personality and Social Psychology* 15:171-74.

_____. 1977. "Structural Ambiguity and Limits to Coping," *The Journal of Human Stress* 3:32-46.

_____. 1979. *Shalit Perceptual Organisation and Reduction Questionnaire (Validity)*. National Defence Research Institute Report C 55036-H6, Stockholm.

_____. 1981. "Perceived Perceptual Organisation and Coping with Military Demands." In Spielberger, C.D., Sarasson, I.G., and Milgram, N.A. (eds.), *Stress and Anxiety*, Volume 8. New York: Hemisphere.

_____. 1982a. *The Perception of War by Swedish National Servicemen*. National Defence Research Institute Report C 55055-H3, Stockholm.

_____. 1982b. *The Prediction of Military Group Effectiveness by the Coherence of Their Appraisal*. National Defence Research Institute Report C 55053-H3, Stockholm.

_____. 1986. *The Perception of Threat by a Noxious Gas Accident and the Reported Coping Style*. National Defence Research Institute Report C 50036-H3, Stockholm.

Shalit, B., and Carlstedt, L. 1984. *The Perception of Enemy Threat—A Method for Assessing the Coping Potential*. National Defence Research Institute Report C 55063-H3, Stockholm.

Shalit, B., Carlstedt, L., Ståhlberg Carlstedt, B., Täljedal Shalit, I-L. 1986. "Coherence of Cognitive Appraisal and Coping in a Stressful Military Task: Parachute Jumping." In Milgram, N.A. (ed.), *Stress and Coping in Times of War*. New York: Brunner/Mazel Publishers.

Shils, E.A., and Janowitz, M. 1948. "Cohesion and Disintegration in the Wehrmacht in World War II," *Public Opinion Quarterly* 12:280-315.

Shirom, A. 1976. "On Some Correlates of Combat Performance," *Administrative Science Quarterly* 24:419-32.

Siegel, A.I., Pfeiffer, M.C., Kopstein, F.F., Wilson, L.G., and Ozkaptan, H. 1979. *Human Performance in Continuous Operations*, Volume 1. Alexandria, Va.: Army Research Institute.

Smith, S.A. 1978. "The Influence of Military and Combat Experience on Personality and Attitudes," dissertation in *Abstracts International* 38: 4483.

Stanger, R. 1977. "Egocentrism, Ethnocentrism, and Altrocentrism: Factors in Individual and Intergroup Violence," *International Journal of Intercultural Relations* 1:9-29.

Storr, A. 1968. *Human Aggression*. London: Allen Lane.

Stouffer, S.A., Lumsdaine, A.A., Lumsdaine, M.M., Williams, R.M. Jr., Brewster Smith, M., Janis, I.L., Star, S.A., and Cottrell, L.S.Jr. 1949. *The American Soldier, Combat and Its Aftermath*. Princeton, N.J.: Princeton University Press.

Taggert, P., Carruthers, M., and Somerville, V. 1978. "Emotions, Catecholamines, and the Electrocardiogram." In Yu, P.N., and Goodwin, J.E. (eds.), *Progress in Cardiology*, Volume 7. Philadelphia: Lea and Febiger.

Taylor, T. 1979. "Superior Orders and Reprisals." In Watkin, M.M. (ed.), *War Morality and the Military Profession*. Boulder: Westview Press.

Taylor, S.P., and Epstein, S. 1967. "Aggression as a Function of the Interaction of the Sex of the Aggressor and the Sex of the Victim," *Journal of Personality* 35: 474-86.

Tedeschi, J.T., Smith, R.B. III, and Brown, R.C. Jr. 1974. "A Re-Interpretation of Research on Aggression," *Psychological Bulletin* 81:540-62.

The Standard Dictionary of the English Language. 1964. New York: Funk and Wagnall Co.

Thomas, P.G., Thomas, E.D., and Wards, S.W. 1974. *Perception of Discrimination in Non-Judicial Punishment*. San Diego Naval Personnel and Training Research Laboratory, Technical Report No. 22.

Triandis, H.C., and Draguns, J.G. (eds.) 1980. *Handbook of Cross-Cultural Psychology*. Boston: Allyn and Balon.

Trites, O.K., and Sells, S.B. 1957. "Combat Performance: Measurement and Prediction," *Journal of Applied Psychology* 41:121-30.

Tversky, A., and Kahneman, D. 1974. "Judgement under Uncertainty," *Science* 185:1124-30.

Von Schéle, B. 1986. "Assessment of a Multifaceted Treatment of Negative Stress: A Cognitive and Cardiovascular Approach." Doctor's Dissertation, Uppsala University, Uppsala.

Watson, P. 1978. *War on the Mind*. London: Hutchison.

Wayne, R. 1975. "You Can't Hack It, Little Girl: A Discussion of the Covert Psychological Agenda of Modern Combat Training," *The Journal of Social Issues* 31:13-23.

Wesbrook, S.D. 1980a. "The Potential for Military Disintegration." In Sarkesian, S.C. (ed.), *Combat Effectiveness*. Beverly Hills: Sage.

———. 1980b. "Socio-Political Alienation and Military Efficiency," *Armed Forces and Society* 2:170-89.

Wheeler, L., and Gaggiula, A.R. 1966. "The Contagion of Aggression," *Journal of Experimental Social Psychology* 2:1-10.

Whyte, L.L. 1950. *The Next Development in Man*. New York: New American Library.

Wicklund, R.A. 1979. "The Influence of Self-Awareness on Human Behavior," *American Scientist* (March/April): 187-93.

Witkin, H.A., Dyk, R.B., Faterson, H.F., Goodenough, D.R., and Karp, S.A. 1962. *Psychological Differentiation*. New York: Wiley and Sons.

Witkin, H.A., Goodenough, D.R., and Oltman, P.K. 1979. "Psychological Differentiation Current State," *Journal of Personality and Social Psychology* 37:1127-45.

Yager, J. 1975. "Personal Violence in Infantry Combat," *Archives of General Psychiatry* 32:257-61.

Zentner, H. 1951. "Morale: Certain Theoretical Implications of Data in the American Soldier," *American Sociological Review* 16:297-307.

Zillman, P. 1979. *Hostility and Aggression*. Hillsdale, N.J.: Lawrence Erlbaum Associates.

Zimbardo, P.G. 1969. "The Human Choice: Individuation, Reason, and Order versus De-Individuation." In Arnold, W., and Levine, D. (eds.), *Nebraska Symposium on Motivation*. Lincoln.

Index

About the Author

BEN SHALIT is a graduate of Edinburgh University and received his Ph.D. at the Hebrew University, Jerusalem. He was the Chief Psychologist of the Israeli Navy during the Six Day War in 1967 and the Chief Psychologist of the Israeli Defense Forces during the Yom Kippur War in 1973. He has been a Visiting Professor at the Karolinska Stress Research Laboratory in Stockholm, a consultant to the Singapore Ministry of Defense, and is currently an Associate Professor at the National Defense Research Institute in Sweden.